I0759469

BLACK ACES

Essential Stories from Hockey's Black Trailblazers

Julian McKenzie

TRIUMPH
BOOKS

Library of Congress Cataloging-in-Publication Data available upon request.

This book is available in quantity at special discounts for your group or organization. For further information, contact:

Triumph Books LLC
814 North Franklin Street
Chicago, Illinois 60610
(312) 337-0747
www.triumphbooks.com

Printed in U.S.A.
ISBN: 978-1-63727-862-8
Design by Patricia Frey

Contents

FOREWORD *by Jarome Iginla* v

INTRODUCTION vii

CHAPTER 1: Willie O'Ree 1

CHAPTER 2: Herb Carnegie 19

CHAPTER 3: Jarome Iginla. 45

CHAPTER 4: Grant Fuhr 73

CHAPTER 5: P.K. Subban. 99

CHAPTER 6: Anson Carter 125

CHAPTER 7: Fred Brathwaite. 143

CHAPTER 8: Georges Laraque. 159

CHAPTER 9: Quinton Byfield 173

CHAPTER 10: Sarah Nurse 187

CHAPTER 11: Angela James 205

CHAPTER 12: Blake Bolden 221

CHAPTER 13: Kevin Weekes. 237

CHAPTER 14: Duante' Abercrombie 249

CHAPTER 15: Kelsey Koelzer 259

CHAPTER 16: Tony McKegney. 269

ACKNOWLEDGMENTS. 279

SOURCES 281

Foreword

Black Aces made me think back to when I was younger and what it meant for me to follow other Black players into the NHL. Just to be able to see the guys who were in the NHL and trying to follow their stories and what it meant for me to follow my dream and to know that it is possible.

I remember being excited when I saw Dale Craigwell playing for Team Canada at the World Juniors and to be able to follow him. Or Claude Vilgrain in the NHL. Grant Fuhr in the NHL All-Star Game, one of the best goalies in the world. And there's Tony McKegney, who could score 40 goals. I was excited when I looked up Tony and saw that he was a Black hockey player and a goal scorer.

For young kids who may be dreaming or love the sport, I think there are some great stories. From goalies to enforcers, to scorers, to defensemen; I remember looking and trying to find these types of stories when I was younger. So, it's really cool to be part of them now.

I got asked a lot about the chances of playing in the NHL. It's already hard, and there were few Black players in the NHL at the time. It really helped me to not have to say, "Oh, yeah, you're right." It helped me a lot to see that it was possible. It meant a lot to know that it was possible and to have something to say when I was asked that question.

There continues to be more Black players in all different styles of roles. Julian's book will highlight some of those different players who continue that history. Whether it's a stay-at-home defenseman, an offensive defenseman, a tough guy, a goalie, a scorer. I think there's all these different stories out there for young players to look up to.

Jarome Iginla is a Hockey Hall of Famer and a two-time Olympic gold medalist for Team Canada. Iginla's victory with the 2002 senior men's team made him the first Black male athlete to win a gold medal at the Winter Olympics. Iginla is also a former NHLer who played more than 1,500 games for five franchises: the Calgary Flames, Pittsburgh Penguins, Boston Bruins, Los Angeles Kings, and Colorado Avalanche. Iginla is a two-time winner of the Maurice "Rocket" Richard Trophy, as well as the recipient of the Art Ross Trophy and the Lester B. Pearson Award (now the Ted Lindsay Award). Iginla has also won an IIHF World Championship, the World Cup of Hockey, and an IIHF World Junior Championship.

Introduction

It was an August morning in Lethbridge, Alberta, and Bill Peters was moments away from meeting the media at the local ENMAX Centre. Media, Western Hockey League staffers, and local fans awaited a man who hadn't coached junior hockey in 15 years yet was still given a second chance.

Peters' final year coaching in the WHL ended with a league championship in 2008. The very next season, he became head coach of the American Hockey League's Rockford IceHogs. One player he coached during his three-season tenure in Rockford was Akim Aliu, a Nigerian-born, Black hockey player who grew up in Ukraine. Chicago selected Aliu in the second round of the 2007 NHL Entry Draft.

One morning, before a pregame skate, Peters voiced his displeasure for his players' choice of locker room music and repeatedly used the word "nigger" toward Aliu. The coach went unpunished. Aliu said in a May 2020 Players'Tribune article that Peters wrote a letter to the team's GM and says it led to him being demoted to the ECHL. Aliu would soon become a minor league journeyman after the incident, only playing seven career NHL games. Peters, meanwhile, worked his way up to NHL coaching gigs in Carolina and Calgary.

Aliu made the story public after a social media rant, leading to an investigation and eventually Peters' resignation from the Calgary

Flames head coach position in 2019. Peters later resurfaced in Russia, coaching Yekaterinburg Automobilist of the Kontinental Hockey League for two seasons. Then, in the summer of 2023, Peters accepted an opportunity with the WHL's Lethbridge Hurricanes. He used his introductory press conference as a way to apologize to Aliu for his actions.

Minutes before the presser, Aliu claimed via social media that a "current" NHL head coach reached out to him to apologize on Peters' behalf. Aliu says that the coach was Peter DeBoer. When Peters was asked after his opening remarks if he had any intention of apologizing to Aliu personally, he said he was looking forward to the day when he would.

Peters, along with fellow Hurricanes front office members and then-WHL commissioner Ron Robison, were asked about the coach's rehabilitation process. Peters took courses on anti-racism and equity through a consulting firm called Shades of Humanity. But it was clear that his relationships with those in power in Lethbridge and the WHL helped him get the job.

After two seasons, Peters left the Hurricanes following the 2024–25 campaign and became head coach of the Augsburger Panther of the Deutsche Eishockey Liga in Germany. Aliu says he still hasn't received an apology directly from Peters.

This is just one of many hockey stories that sometimes make people of color feel like they don't belong or that their actions carry no real impact in the sport.

There are stories like Jalen Smereck, who was subjected to a racial taunt from an opposing player while in Ukraine. Wayne Simmonds spoke up in Smereck's defense in an interview with Sportsnet's Luke Fox, a decade after a fan threw a banana at Simmonds during his shootout attempt in a preseason game between the Philadelphia Flyers and Detroit Red Wings.

"If I had it up to me, you got two choices: You're gonna either face off against us [and] we're gonna kick the crap out of you or you're banned for life," Simmonds told Fox in a September 2021 interview.

"It's come to a point where it's sickening, it's disgusting. The way that guy did what he did, without any hesitancy, makes me sick to my stomach."

P.K. Subban and Joel Ward were both victims of online racial abuse after playing against the Boston Bruins in the Stanley Cup playoffs. Devante Smith-Pelly had racial taunts delivered toward him while sitting in the penalty box during a 2018 game against Chicago.

"It's sad that in 2018 we're still talking about the same thing over and over," Smith-Pelly told the Associated Press after the incident.

It happens at the youth level as well, with hockey children and parents living with the pain of racial abuse while participating in a sport that claims to be for everyone.

One recent example comes from the Gatineau-based newspaper *Le Droit*, which reported on a story of a young Black Quebecois hockey player named Anthony Allain-Samaké who yelled "I can't breathe" after a youth hockey teammate kneeled on his neck sometime during the 2021–22 season. The gesture mirrored the death of George Floyd, a Black man killed by Minnesota police in May 2020. Allain-Samaké has since been drafted by the Pittsburgh Penguins in the sixth round of the 2025 NHL Entry Draft. Floyd's death prompted protests and reactions around the world, but the NHL was infamously late with its tributes compared to the rest of the sporting world.

Those stories, even for the individuals mentioned above, only scratch the surface.

Groups like the Hockey Diversity Alliance, cofounded by Aliu and other NHLers, and the NHL Player Inclusion Coalition are working to make the sport more diverse and friendly to players of color, including Black players. While each entity is distinct, their ultimate vision is similar. There is also the Black Girl Hockey Club, which offers scholarships, mentorship, summer camps, and community events for young Black female aspiring hockey players. Despite their efforts, some feel that the sport—particularly the NHL—doesn't' do enough to support its Black players.

"Are we standing up for them? Once they are there? Are we making sure that they are being treated properly?" said Omar White, a journalist and podcaster based in Toronto—known in social media circles as TicTacTOmar.

"When things take place, are we sure that the league is doing enough to let them know that you belong in this game? Are they doing enough to change the standard of what that quote-unquote hockey player looks like?"

When we're not focusing on racism regarding hockey, members of the hockey world groan at its inability to market itself to newer audiences—especially those of color.

"Why are the TV rights so low?" Laraque, who is part of the NHL Player Inclusion Coalition, said. "Why isn't everybody watching it? Why are the best hockey players in the NHL not advertised all over the States? Because hockey is not popular enough. Because it's not diverse enough. As long as hockey's going to be known as a white sport, it's not going to be big enough."

Laraque isn't wrong. According to Kurt Badenhausen of Sportico, the NHL ranked fourth in revenue in 2024, trailing MLB, the NFL, and the NBA and only beating Major League Soccer by $4.8 billion. The NHL's largest revenue generator is ticket sales, seating, and suites. Forty-four percent of its revenue through the 2022–23 season came from that category, the largest share compared to the four other North American–based sports leagues. And its growth remains smaller compared to other sports.

"Hockey has already reached maximum growth with its current customer, and it's been at maximum for decades," Cabral "Cabbie" Richards said.

Hockey's accessibility remains an issue for young kids who want to enter the sport, especially those from low-income backgrounds and people of color who don't often see enough people who look like them on the ice.

"Canada's changing," Hockey Canada chief executive Tom Renney told The Athletic in November 2020. "The demographic is changing. So we have to appeal to new Canadians, and we have to make sure that we understand they're not going to come and tap on our door and say, 'Can we play hockey?'"

That year, Hockey Canada reported a total number of 605,963 players who signed up to play. According to writer Sean Fitz-Gerald, it was the governing body's lowest number of signees since 2010–11. Hockey Canada's 2022–23 annual report listed 550,137 total registered participants. That number grew to 589,012 in the 2024 report but was still below the 2020 figure.

Hockey Canada is still working on addressing its culture through events like Beyond the Boards that serve to address various issues like toxic masculinity and gender-sexuality discrimination. According to Hockey Canada, racism and accessibility will one day be topics of discussion at their annual summits.

"We want to reach out to those people and make sure that they feel at home in a hockey rink," Hockey Canada board chair Jonathan Goldbloom said in November 2024, as mentioned in The Athletic. "Which means figuring out ways of rolling out the red carpet so that if you've grown up on a soccer field, you feel that much more at home at one of our hockey rinks."

NHL commissioner Gary Bettman said it's a "priority" to grow the sport toward more diverse communities and that the league needs to do, and has done, more in that regard.

"We want this game to be inclusive, to be welcoming, and grassroots programs that support that will remain a priority," Bettman said.

"We spent a lot of money, a lot of time, a lot of assets, a lot of people involved at all levels, not just at the league level, but at the clubs. Clubs have been very engaged, and we think that's important. The Player Inclusion Coalition is an important element of that, and we're grateful for the players current and former who participate."

But those socioeconomic hurdles still persist for young people of color, in particular Black people, who are taking up hockey.

"There's too many barriers to enter into hockey. It's way too expensive," Aliu said to me in a February 2024 interview with The Athletic. "And even once you get into it, as things that myself and other HDA members dealt with, you feel like an outsider. A lot of times, you're the only person of color.

"You look different, you talk different, you feel different, you abide by different religious norms, all those things. We're showing that it's not a lack of interest to play the game; it's a lack of accessibility that the game and these institutions don't want to open up to everybody."

Those stories won't be ignored in *Black Aces*. There will be stories of racism and economic barriers that threatened many of our subjects' hockey dreams. But the book will also detail some iconic Black hockey moments, players, and people while reminding readers—particularly Black readers—why we fell in love with the sport in the first place.

Every hockey fan can think of the moment that drew them into the sport. A player, a team, an in-person experience, a Saturday night in front of the television watching *Hockey Night in Canada*. Despite the sport being predominantly white throughout its history, hockey has long endeared itself to Black people. Those experiences turned them into hockey players, coaches, media, agents, and fans.

You could be like Jarome Iginla, who played floor hockey at the age of five before attempting to skate for the first time at six. Akim Aliu bought a $10 pair of skates at the age of nine and skated at Trinity Bellwoods Park in Toronto. Cabbie Richards collected hockey stickers and played ball hockey in a neighborhood cul-de-sac in Cambridge, Ontario. Avry Lewis-McDougall got into the game watching the "gritty, hard-working" Edmonton Oilers teams of the 1990s.

"There's just something about hockey that just hit different," said White. "The things these people were able to do on skates. Full speed. The decision-making. The skill. The hits. The defensive commitment. Hockey was one of the first sports where I could watch it and know the difference between what was well coached and wasn't."

And most of their desires of entering the sport were propelled by seeing people who looked like them.

"Where I think the NHL misses the boat a little bit is understanding that for a minority watching sports, it is so important to have representation," hockey reporter Tarik El-Bashir said. "When you see a player like Grant Fuhr, for my kid it was Joel Ward, you see someone who looks like you on the screen playing at the highest level. You can then start dreaming big, right?"

Between the NHL and PWHL, there are numerous examples for young Black players to follow if they want to dream big.

Twenty Black players began the 2023–24 season on an NHL roster, according to the league's internal numbers. NHLers like Anthony Duclair, Darnell Nurse, K'Andre Miller, Quinton Byfield, Seth Jones, Evander Kane, and Ryan Reaves are among the most prominent Black male players today. According to NHL.com's William Douglas, four Black players—Sarah Nurse, Sophie Jaques, Mikyla Grant-Mentis, and Nikki Nightengale—began the 2024 PWHL season on rosters.

Those numbers have grown in both leagues.

Three Black players, Cayden Lindstrom, E.J. Emery, and Tij Iginla—son of Jarome—were taken in the first round of the 2024 NHL Entry Draft. Tij, selected sixth overall by Utah, can say he was drafted higher than his dad, selected 11th overall in the 1995 NHL Draft by Dallas.

"There's a little bit of bragging rights," the younger Iginla said. "But he had a good career. So, I guess I got to build up my résumé a little bit more before I can brag too much."

Two Black players were drafted in the first round of the 2025 NHL Entry Draft in Los Angeles. Kashawn Aitcheson was drafted 17th overall by the New York Islanders, while Bill Zonnon was selected 22nd overall by the Pittsburgh Penguins. Twenty players of Black, Indigenous, Asian, or Latin descent—a league record—were chosen in that year's draft.

Even Black player agents like Eustace King and John Osei-Tutu have a place in the NHL's ecosystem, handling dozens of clients. Brett Peterson was once a player agent before joining the Florida Panthers as an assistant general manager, winning Stanley Cups in 2024 and 2025.

Speaking of general managers, the San Jose Sharks hired longtime NHLer Mike Grier on July 5, 2022, making him the first Black NHL general manager. Grier comes from a family of front office management personnel. His brother, Chris, became the general manager of the NFL's Miami Dolphins in 2016. Their father, Bobby, had various front office and scouting jobs with the New England Patriots and Houston Texans before becoming a consultant with the Dolphins in 2017.

"It's something I'm extremely proud of," Grier said after being hired, according to ESPN. "I realized there was a responsibility that comes with the territory, but I'm up for it [with] how I carry myself and how the organization carries themselves.

"For me, my job is to do the best I can for the San Jose Sharks organization, and if I do that, hopefully it opens the door to give other opportunities to other minorities to get in front-office positions and maybe lead a team down the road as well."

As GM, Grier has worked to accumulate high draft picks to build the Sharks into a contending team, including drafting No. 1 overall pick Macklin Celebrini in 2024.

"You had a feeling that it was it was a matter of time," former teammate Daniel Brière said. "I was excited when I heard the news that he was he was going to be GM in San Jose. Excited for him and his family, and also for the organization. They're getting such a genuine, nice guy. Even though they had to take a step back, I think he's doing it the right way.

"His team is going to be a force down the road. Led by [Will] Smith and Celebrini coming up. In five, six years from now, they're going to be a tough opponent to watch with the centermen they have coming."

If you're watching *Hockey Night in Canada* on a Saturday night, or any other night of the week, you can see David Amber hosting alongside other prominent NHL analysts and personalities. P.K. Subban, Jamal Mayers, Anthony Stewart, Anson Carter, Kevin Weekes, and Saroya Tinker are faces who have established themselves as analysts and personalities around the game nationally. You can add names like Jean-Luc Grand-Pierre, Georges Laraque, J.T. Brown, and Devante Smith-Pelly. They have all embedded themselves on local platforms to talk hockey.

"The NHL is a game that's given back to me and my family so much," Subban said. "So, to be able to step out of the game and instantly be put in a position to help grow the game, celebrate the players and the product on the ice, that's the most important thing."

The Seattle Kraken hired Everett Fitzhugh as their radio play-by-play man in August 2020, and he became the NHL's first full-time Black play-by-play announcer. When Fitzhugh and Brown worked a Kraken game against the Winnipeg Jets together in February 2022, they became the first all-Black broadcast team in NHL history. Fitzhugh worked his way up from the ECHL, all the while serving as the only Black play-by-play hockey broadcaster for a professional team in North America.

The list of accomplishments doesn't stop there.

Tennessee State University, a historically Black university, will debut a hockey program in Fall 2026 with Duante' Abercrombie as their head coach. Kelsey Koelzer has already made strides as head coach of Arcadia University's women's hockey team, becoming the first female Black head coach of an NCAA ice hockey program.

Laila Edwards, a collegiate star at the University of Wisconsin, made history during the Spring of 2024 as the first Black woman to suit up for Team U.S.A at the IIHF Women's World Championship. Jordan Greenway made history in 2018 as the first Black player to suit up for Team USA's senior men's national team during that year's Olympic Games in Pyeongchang.

There is also Blake Bolden, who became the first Black player to play professional women's hockey and eventually become the NHL's first Black pro female scout when she joined the Los Angeles Kings' front office in February 2020. The Stewart brothers, Chris and Anthony, made history as the first pair of Black brothers to each be drafted in the first round of the NHL draft. Chris was drafted by the Colorado Avalanche in 2006; Anthony, by the Florida Panthers in 2003. Of course, there are players like Fuhr, Smith-Pelly, Johnny Oduya, Dustin Byfuglien, Trevor Daley, Kyle Okposo, and more who have played instrumental roles in their teams winning Stanley Cups. Seth Jones helped the Florida Panthers repeat as Cup champions in 2025 with nine points in 23 Stanley Cup playoff games that spring.

Hockey's reach has also extended into Caribbean and African nations. Kenya joined the International Ice Hockey Federation as an associate member in October 2024, becoming the fifth African nation to do so. Jamaica joined the IIHF as an associate member in 2011 and, as of April 2025, is working to build an ice rink in Montego Bay. Chris Stewart is an ambassador and co-coach for Team Jamaica.

An incomplete, yet growing list of firsts, iconic moments, and heroes throughout Black hockey history.

The sport has made significant strides since Willie O'Ree became the NHL's first Black player in 1958. A big reason for that is the characters, personalities, and moments that will live on in hockey lore forever. Even if Black people are in the minority among hockey players, they are an integral part of the sport's fabric.

In *Black Aces*, you'll learn about some of these players and personalities woven into that fabric thanks to their essential and legendary contributions to the sport on and off the ice.

1

Willie O'Ree

When Anson Carter was offered the chance to emcee an event in honor of the legendary Willie O'Ree at the JW Marriott Hotel in Edmonton's Ice District—around the corner from the Edmonton Oilers' home rink, Rogers Place—he didn't think twice. Carter wasn't skipping an event celebrating one of hockey's most important trailblazers. Even if it meant flying in October from his warm Atlanta home to a cold, gray Edmonton downtown core—a place he called home for almost three full seasons of his 10-year NHL career.

"The first thing I did was check the weather here in Edmonton and I was like, 'Oh my goodness, it's freezing,'" said Carter, who yearned for the 75-degree weather back in Atlanta. "But I still never hesitated. All I did was pack my long johns and pack more layers."

Canada Post commissioned a stamp featuring O'Ree ahead of that weekend's Heritage Classic outdoor game between the Edmonton Oilers and Calgary Flames. The stamp features a black-and-white portrait of a smiling O'Ree wearing a hat, shown prominently next to a photo of a younger O'Ree from his playing days as a Boston Bruin. The black, white, gray, and yellow color scheme was a clear homage to the only NHL team O'Ree ever played for. The design drew rave reviews from all attendees that morning.

"More importantly, Willie deserves it," NHL legend Grant Fuhr said. "That's the beauty of it."

What made the moment even more special was seeing the faces on hand to unveil the stamp. Evander Kane and Nazem Kadri were designated player representatives from the Oilers and Flames, respectively. But they were also flanked by former Oilers fan favorites Carter, Fuhr, and Georges Laraque. Sarah Nurse, one of hockey's most prominent stars regardless of gender, was also present.

"I think that it's such a special and unique opportunity," Nurse said. "It's not every day that somebody gets on a stamp."

It was a perfect way to show that O'Ree's actions of breaking the Black color barrier had a ripple effect on future generations.

"Without Willie O'Ree, there's no Georges Laraque, there's no Anson Carter, none of us are playing in the NHL," Laraque told me in an interview for The Athletic. "Somebody had to break the barrier. Breaking the barrier in football, soccer, baseball, is one thing. In hockey, you can still see that today it's still a huge obstacle to be a Black guy and play hockey."

"You kind of look back at the history to see what was going on," Fuhr said. "But at the same time, playing [in Edmonton], pretty fortunate. They didn't worry about color. It was all about whether you could play or not. So, I get kind of lucky in that sense.

"All the stuff that Willie went through, guys like Val James. They all did the hard labor. I get the benefit of it."

Having O'Ree in the flesh would have made the moment even sweeter. But an illness kept him from making the trip. However, he addressed those in attendance through a video message.

"It is a treasured Canadian institution and being a Canadian stamp is a tremendous honor," O'Ree said. "Being a part of hockey and the NHL for over 60 years has been a dream come true. Diversity and inclusion are important to both the game of hockey and in life.

"With this said, I encourage everyone to use the stamp as a reminder to continue to break down barriers and follow your dreams both on and off the ice."

Black people continue to break down barriers in hockey. They might not have gotten that chance without O'Ree's history-making NHL debut.

THERE IS NO WAY this book, the stories and the people inside it, and even the sport itself, can go on without telling Willie O'Ree's story. This includes necessary distinctions that get confused and excluded when telling his story.

O'Ree is the first Black NHLer in league history and has been called hockey's answer to fellow pioneer and baseball icon Jackie Robinson. O'Ree even met Robinson as a 14-year-old during a visit to New York with his local baseball team. Baseball and hockey were the two sports O'Ree played primarily during his youth. When O'Ree met Robinson, he mentioned his hockey attributes and accomplishments to the trailblazing baseball hero.

"I didn't know there were any Black kids who played hockey," Robinson told O'Ree, as the latter recounted in an article he wrote for the Canada Post website in October 2023.

Despite O'Ree's achievement and commonality with Robinson, O'Ree is not the first person to break the NHL's color barrier. That distinction goes to Larry Kwong, an Asian-born forward from Vernon, British Columbia, who made his NHL debut on March 13, 1948, as a member of the New York Rangers. Kwong played a brief but history-making shift against the Montreal Canadiens at the Forum.

"I was quite disappointed because I was only used for about a minute in the last period," Kwong told the *New York Times*, according to a 2013 story. "I didn't get a real chance to show what I can do."

And while O'Ree is the first player to break the NHL's Black color barrier, he is not the first Black player to sign an NHL contract.

Nova Scotia native Art Dorrington signed a minor league contract with the New York Rangers in 1950. Dorrington never played for the Rangers, spending most of his professional career in the Eastern Hockey League.

Five years after Dorrington signed with the Rangers, Edmonton native John Utendale signed a contract with the Detroit Red Wings and participated in training camps with the team but primarily played with the Wings' minor-league affiliate, the Edmonton Flyers. Utendale even played with O'Ree on the Quebec Aces, forming an all-Black line with Stan Maxwell.

O'Ree was still a teenager when Kwong made his NHL debut, growing up in his hometown of Fredericton, New Brunswick, in one of the city's two Black families. Born on October 15, 1935, he is the son and 13th child of Harry and Rosebud O'Ree. According to O'Ree's autobiography, *Willie: The Game-Changing Story of the NHL's First Black Player*, he was one of nine children to have survived upon birth.

The former Bruin is also the great-great-grandson of Paris O'Ree, who fled the United States to Canada through what his family believes is an "early version" of the Underground Railroad, a network of routes used by Black slaves in the 19th century to escape captivity while in the United States.

"I can see him in my mind's eye, this man who was stolen from his homeland, given a new name and as payment to another man," O'Ree wrote in his autobiography. "I can imagine Paris O'Ree spotting his chance and taking it. I am proud of him. For without his taking that risk, putting his life on the line to find freedom, I wouldn't be here now. And there's more than a little bit of him in me."

O'Ree first learned to skate at the age of three in his home backyard before moving to local frozen rivers and ponds. His first pair of skates, according to his autobiography, were "two blocks of wood with two metal blades on the bottom of each, like training wheels on a bike."

"Attached to each block were two leather straps that my father would loop over my shoes and then tighten up," O'Ree wrote.

More than a decade after wearing those skates for the first time, O'Ree decided to pursue a hockey career instead of playing baseball.

"When I was 14, I set two goals for myself," O'Ree told Joshua Clipperton of the Canadian Press in November 2020. "Playing pro hockey and hopefully playing in the National Hockey League."

At 15, O'Ree played for the Fredericton Falcons of the New Brunswick Amateur Hockey Association. He worked his way up his city's local hockey pyramid before joining the Quebec Junior Hockey League's Quebec Frontenacs at 19 and, later, the Kitchener Canucks of the Ontario Hockey Association.

O'Ree's hockey journey should have ended in Kitchener. At least under doctor's orders.

During a game for the Canucks on November 22, 1955, O'Ree brought the puck into the offensive zone while on a power play. After passing the puck to his teammate along the blue line, Kent Douglas, O'Ree parked himself in front of the net.

"Maybe I'd get the tip of my stick on the puck and deflect it into the net," O'Ree remembered in his autobiography.

O'Ree says he was cross-checked by an opposing defender as Douglas fired his shot from the point. The puck then deflected off a stick before hitting O'Ree's face, causing a broken nose, a "crushed" cheekbone, and a shattered retina in his right eye which led to permanent blindness. O'Ree dropped to the ice surface and was immediately rushed to the hospital.

O'Ree recounted what his surgeon told him in the recovery room in an interview with Anna Maria Tremonti of the CBC in 2019.

"I remember being in the recovery room and he came in and said, 'Mr. O'Ree, I'm sorry to inform you.... The impact of the puck completely shattered the retina in your right eye.' And he says, 'You're going to be blind and you'll never play hockey again.'"

But O'Ree refused to accept that his NHL dream was over. O'Ree spent four days in hospital and eventually returned to the ice after five weeks of recovery.

"The only difference I felt about myself was I just couldn't see out of my right eye," he told Tremonti.

As O'Ree fought to keep his blinded eye a secret, he continued his playing career with the Quebec Aces of the Quebec Hockey League in 1956. The Aces were led by future Toronto Maple Leafs legend Punch Imlach, who then was the team's head coach, general manager, and owner.

In his first season with the Aces, O'Ree scored 22 goals and 34 points in 68 games played as the team finished top of the league. For his trouble, O'Ree received $600 in bonuses: $300 for his season and another $300 for making the playoffs. With inflation, that bonus would probably be closer to $6,700 in the present day.

The Aces won the Quebec Hockey League championship that season and earned the right to play for the Edinburgh Trophy against the Brandon Regals, the best team from the Western Hockey League that year.

Almost two years after his devastating eye injury, O'Ree became a key contributor on a championship team. Meanwhile, his teammates and coaches were in the dark about his injury.

O'Ree was never subjected to eye exams throughout his career, and he continued to keep his condition a secret out of fear that an NHL team wouldn't take a chance on him.

"Back then, they were more concerned with your physical condition, and I always kept myself in good shape," O'Ree told Sportsnet's Luke Fox in 2012. "I worked out in the gym and played some baseball. And by the time I was ready to return to training camp I was two pounds away from my playing weight. I kept my fingers crossed all those years hoping that nobody would find out. I just played and eventually forgot about it."

To this day, O'Ree wears a prosthetic eye in place of a real one. He was given the choice to be injected with a "solution" to help deal with the pain or to have his eye removed. He chose the latter.

WHEN O'REE DECIDED AS a teenager to play hockey full-time instead of baseball, he told his eldest brother, Richard. He warned Willie of the unfortunate prejudice and racism that would come his way as a Black player. Richard told him he had to work harder than white players to be given a chance—something many Black people have been told before in other contexts, not just sports.

"That fuelled me to work even harder and stay laser-focused on my goals. I give a lot of credit to Richard for helping to instill in me the confidence to pursue a predominantly white sport like hockey," O'Ree wrote on the Canada Post website in 2023.

The sport had already shown resistance toward players of color trying to make the jump to the National Hockey League before O'Ree was given the chance. And it wasn't just with Kwong's near-minute-long cameo.

In 1951, Herb Carnegie—whom some consider to be greatest Black player to never have played in the NHL—played for the Quebec Aces in a mentorship role for future Montreal Canadiens legend Jean Béliveau.

Carnegie spent years in the Quebec hockey circuit, even making history as part of the first all-Black line in professional hockey alongside brother Ossie Carnegie and Manny McIntyre. During his time in the Quebec Provincial League, he won three MVP awards and a scoring title in 1948 with 48 goals and 127 points. But he never set foot on NHL ice despite his success. Carnegie's teammate, Beliveau, would become an NHL legend and Hall of Famer with more than 500 goals and 1,200 points, as well as 10 Stanley Cups, to his name.

"But the difference between those two giants is that the white one made the NHL and the black one didn't," O'Ree wrote in *Willie*. "How could a guy who'd won not one but three MVP awards not be in the NHL?"

O'Ree himself had faced racism since his preteen days. He remembers being called "nigger" by two boys at school from as early as age 12. During his playing days in Quebec, O'Ree remembered receiving racist taunts from fans in Chicoutimi when the team would travel to play the Saguenéens. Fans yelled "maudit negre"—French for "damn negro"—in addition to spitting and throwing drinks at him during games.

Two years before his NHL debut, O'Ree toyed with the idea of playing baseball one more time when he was given a chance to try out for the Milwaukee Braves baseball team's minor league affiliate in Georgia. The state, along with many other parts of the Southern United States, still had Jim Crow laws in effect which enforced racial segregation in public venues like restaurants, hotels, and even bathrooms. When O'Ree arrived to camp, he was placed in a dormitory with "six or seven other players of color." He even received racist remarks from white teammates. O'Ree's stay in Georgia lasted only a few days before he was cut and sent back to Fredericton.

"I talked to my parents, and my parents didn't want me to go," O'Ree said in the 2019 documentary *Willie*. "They probably thought that I would get killed because of the way Blacks were treated in the South."

But O'Ree pushed through unfair criticism and racism, mostly through the way he played. In addition to the offense he provided, he fought opposing players and showcased his toughness. His play caught the eye of the Boston Bruins, who invited O'Ree to their training camp ahead of the 1957–58 season.

O'Ree and another Black teammate, Stan Maxwell, were invited to Bruins camp that fall. While neither made the team out of camp, O'Ree was given motivation for his NHL dream.

O'Ree began the 1957–58 season with the Aces again before getting called up to the American Hockey League to play for the Springfield Indians in October 1957, becoming their first Black player in franchise history. O'Ree was around the team for six games but only played in one of them.

While O'Ree doesn't think too fondly of his first AHL stint with Springfield, led by head coach and Bruins legend Eddie Shore—O'Ree referred to the team as "Shore's Springfield Lunatic Asylum"—they go down in history as the team where O'Ree made his first professional appearance.

The night of January 18, 1958, however, is when O'Ree's dream came true.

The Bruins needed an extra forward ahead of a two-game set against the Montreal Canadiens. Bruins forward Leo Labine came down with the flu and was unavailable for both games, prompting the team to call up O'Ree from the Aces. O'Ree took a train from Quebec City to Montreal, meeting the Bruins at a local hotel ahead of the game. O'Ree's parents and his brother, Richard, made the trek to Montreal from New Brunswick to see him play.

When O'Ree was growing up, he listened to *Hockey Night in Canada* on the radio, spending his Saturday nights listening to the familiar voice of Foster Hewitt recounting the exploits of his childhood hero, Maurice "Rocket" Richard. Televisions weren't widely commercially available in the 1930s. But it didn't stop O'Ree from envisioning legends like Richard skating circles around opposing players.

And now, O'Ree had a chance to play against the Rocket on *Hockey Night in Canada*. Beliveau, a fellow Quebec Aces alum, also featured in the Canadiens' side, as did legends like Henri Richard, Dickie Moore, Doug Harvey, and Jacques Plante.

Butterflies fluttered in O'Ree's stomach during pregame warm-ups. They settled once the game began, as O'Ree played on a line with center Don McKenney and Jerry Toppazzini, according to NHL.com.

The Bruins got goals from Johnny Bucyk, Larry Regan, and Bronco Horvath in a 3–0 win over the Canadiens at the Montreal Forum. The closest O'Ree came to a scoring chance, as he recalls, was in the third period. He received a pass from Topazzini, only to be hooked by Canadiens defenseman Tom Johnson, who was penalized on the play.

There was some media coverage but little to no fanfare for O'Ree's exploits at the time. When O'Ree was interviewed by a local television reporter after the game, he wasn't asked about being the first Black player to play in an NHL game, but instead was asked about the feeling of playing for Boston.

"I told him it was the greatest thrill of my life," O'Ree said in his autobiography.

As Dave Stubbs found in the *Montreal Gazette* for an article on O'Ree in 2017, O'Ree was introduced as the "first Negro" to play in the NHL and was described as a "fleet skater." In the *New York Times*, according to O'Ree's autobiography, his upcoming debut was written in a short graf titled "Negro Skater Will Make Debut as Bruins' Wing."

"I was expecting a little more publicity," O'Ree said in a 2007 interview with NHL.com. "The press handled it like it was just another piece of everyday news. I didn't care much about publicity for myself, but it could have been important for other blacks with ambitions in hockey. It would have shown that a black could make it."

O'Ree also went pointless in the second game of his two-game Bruins stint, also against the Canadiens. The Bruins lost that second game 6–2. O'Ree was later sent back to the Aces, where he finished the season with 13 goals and 32 points in 57 games.

O'Ree returned to the NHL three seasons later, playing 43 games during the 1960–61 season. O'Ree's first NHL goal came on January 1, 1961, in a home game against the Canadiens. It was the game-winning goal in a 3–2 victory for Boston. O'Ree ended that season with four goals and 14 points in 43 games.

It was the last season O'Ree ever played in the NHL. O'Ree's contract was traded to the Canadiens, but he never played a game for the franchise. O'Ree spent most of his remaining playing years in California with the Los Angeles Blades and San Diego Gulls of the Western Hockey League. In his final three seasons with the Blades, O'Ree had three consecutive 30-goal seasons, very nearly entering 40-goal territory during the 1964–65 season.

O'Ree also spent one season with the New Haven Nighthawks of the American Hockey League as a 37-year-old. He finished fifth in scoring on the team, outscoring future NHLer and Stanley Cup champion Bob Nystrom. The team also featured future NHLers Garry Howatt and goaltender Glenn "Chico" Resch.

"He was definitely a good player," Nystrom told William Douglas of NHL.com back in 2022. "He was very good with the puck, had tremendous speed. He was built like a racer. He looked like he could run the 100-yard dash."

Despite shattering the Black color barrier in the NHL, O'Ree experienced more racism as he continued his pro career. O'Ree said the racism was much worse in American cities compared to Canadian ones. Fans told him to "go back to the South" and asked why he wasn't picking cotton like slaves in the field, according to Grant Fuhr's autobiography.

"It wasn't a game that went by that there wasn't racial remarks directed toward me by players and fans," O'Ree said in the *Willie* documentary. "But I didn't let it bother me; I didn't let it get away from my game."

And it didn't take away from his legacy. In 1962, O'Ree was invited to an NAACP luncheon in Los Angeles. It had been four years after his NHL debut for the Bruins in Montreal and a year after scoring his first NHL goal. O'Ree was in his first of six seasons with the Blades.

The luncheon honored baseball legend Jackie Robinson, who was enjoying retirement after a stellar career that saw him win an MVP Award, a World Series, and a batting title and earn seven All-Star Game appearances.

O'Ree hadn't seen Robinson since his teenage days. But the baseball legend greeted him warmly.

"Willie O'Ree!" Robinson said, according to O'Ree in his autobiography. "I met you back in Brooklyn, and you told me you were going to be a hockey player. And so you are."

When the Bruins celebrated their centennial season in December 2024, O'Ree was featured in a video showcasing the early years of the franchise. O'Ree received a standing ovation from fans when he joined the children of past Bruins legends on the ice during their centennial ceremony, ahead of a Bruins game versus the rival Montreal Canadiens.

"I'm just so proud to be a part of the Bruins family," O'Ree said.

DEFENSEMAN E.J. EMERY WAS selected 30th overall by the New York Rangers during the 2024 NHL Draft in Las Vegas. The prospect was one of three Black players selected in the first round alongside Tij Iginla and Cayden Lindstrom, who were taken by Utah and Columbus, respectively. When each player's name was called at the Las Vegas Sphere, an announcer listed some facts as they made their way to the podium to receive their jersey and take photos with members of their new team's front office.

Some draft picks named players they would have loved to have had the chance to play alongside. If you polled several aspiring NHL players, you'd hear names like Sidney Crosby or Connor McDavid, and maybe older names like Wayne Gretzky or Sergei Fedorov.

When Emery's name was announced, the public address announcer revealed that—if given the choice—Emery would have loved to have played alongside Willie O'Ree. Emery still treasures the autograph he received from O'Ree as an eight-year-old.

"As a Black man growing up, there's not too many in hockey," Emery said. "He was finally one of those figures I was able to look up to. He's the first person I got a signature from. Just an awesome guy."

One summer earlier, defenseman Pierre-Olivier Joseph attended the 2023 NHL Awards in support of his then Pittsburgh Penguins teammate Kris Letang. Letang was that year's recipient of the Bill Masterton Memorial Trophy for "perseverance, sportsmanship, and dedication" to hockey. Joseph wore a brown custom suit, the lining of which featured photos of Black sporting legends Muhammad Ali, Serena Williams, Pelé, and O'Ree.

Joseph met with O'Ree prior to the ceremony, and the hockey legend signed the lining.

"I wanted to get to know him," Joseph told Tom Gulitti of NHL.com in 2023. "He means the world to me, and just being able to walk in his path, he opened the path for all of us. Being able to see him was nerve-wracking more to meet him, I think, than being on stage."

Emery and Joseph's reverence for O'Ree are just some examples of his impact resonating years after his NHL debut. It comes decades after a handful of players followed in O'Ree's footsteps.

Sixteen years after O'Ree's first night in the NHL, Mike Marson became the second Black NHLer when he joined the Washington Capitals in time for the 1974–75 NHL season. Marson grew up in the Toronto suburb of Scarborough and played two seasons for the Sudbury Wolves of the Ontario Hockey Association—he even scored 35 goals and 94 points in 69 games—before being drafted in the second round of the 1974 Amateur Draft by the Washington Capitals.

In Marson's first NHL season, he scored 16 goals and 28 points in 76 games. As his career progressed, he established himself as a physical, fighting, brutal force. He once racked up 101 penalty minutes. Marson's NHL career was 196 games long with 24 goals and 48 points to his name. Unfortunately, Marson was also subjected to numerous racist experiences throughout his playing days including receiving racist letters and taunts from hockey fans.

"There were places I went to as a National Hockey League player where they weren't going to allow me to stay in the hotel, where I couldn't get fed in the dining lounge," Marson told Sportsnet's Wayne Scanlan in February 2020.

Marson played in Washington alongside Black teammate Bill Riley throughout chunks of his Capitals tenure. Riley joined the Capitals three months after Marson did in 1974. The two made NHL history when they both dressed for a Capitals game on December 26, 1974, against the Philadelphia Flyers. It was the first time two Black players were featured in the same NHL game.

Riley played 139 NHL games and scored 31 goals and 61 points in that span. His NHL days ended in 1980 following a 14-game stint with the Winnipeg Jets. He also spent time in the American Hockey League, spending time with Maritime-based teams in New Brunswick and Nova Scotia.

Like Marson, Riley experienced racism during his playing days. He'd receive taunts from opposing fans and players when he went on the road.

As a member of the Dayton Gems of the International Hockey League, he remembered fans in Toledo, Ohio, singing a racist song as an organist played along. Riley even remembered a game in Toledo where his opponents picked fights with him because he was Black.

"But my teammates, to the number, were all on my side," Riley said to the CBC in a February 2021 interview. "Lots of times, when I went to fight, they pushed me out of the way, and they'd take care of it."

Just as Marson and Riley exited the NHL in 1980, Val James entered during the 1981–82 season. He made history as the first African American to play in the NHL. He was born in Ocala, Florida, but grew up in Hauppauge, New York. James was originally a 16th-round draft pick of the Detroit Red Wings in 1977 but never played any games with the franchise.

James' NHL career lasted only 11 games, split between the Buffalo Sabres and Toronto Maple Leafs. But the Florida native carved out a professional career, scoring a Calder Cup–winning goal in the American Hockey League with the Rochester Americans in 1983.

"I still got the experience I set out to do when I was younger," James said in an interview with the *New York Times* in 2015. "I got to play in the NHL. I forgot to say I wanted to stay in the NHL. I can't say I didn't get what I wanted. And the thing was, I got to do it a few times. A lot of guys don't get to ever do it once. I consider myself extremely fortunate."

James was briefly a teammate of Tony McKegney's, who was establishing himself as an NHLer with the Sabres. The Montreal native had two 30-plus goal seasons in Sabres colors and eventually became the first Black player to score 40 goals in a season when he accomplished the feat with the St. Louis Blues in 1988.

Dirk Graham made his NHL debut during the 1983–84 NHL season with the Minnesota North Stars and spent time with the franchise until the 1987–88 campaign, when he was traded to Chicago. Graham then became the first Black captain in NHL history in Chicago in 1989 and won a Selke Trophy for best defensive forward in 1991. The following season he led Chicago to a Stanley Cup Final berth against the Pittsburgh Penguins.

"He was a great captain," Chicago defenseman Eric Weinrich told Andscape in a 2018 interview. "As a leader, there aren't many better. He was a quiet leader, but when he said something, it made sense. I don't think more than 10 times a year he'd really snap, let everybody know how he felt, but everybody always responded."

Graham eventually became the first Black NHL coach during the 1998–99 season when he served as Chicago's head coach for a season.

Grant Fuhr made his NHL debut months after being drafted eighth overall in the 1981 NHL Entry Draft by the Edmonton Oilers. Two seasons after joining, Fuhr won the first of five Stanley Cups as an Oiler—Fuhr was injured and didn't play a game in the 1990 playoffs—and went on to win a Vezina Trophy and William M. Jennings Trophy. He was inducted into the Hockey Hall of Fame in 2003. Fuhr will never forget the trail paved by O'Ree for players like him to succeed in the NHL.

The list of players who have followed after O'Ree has grown since, including star talents and fan favorites like Jarome Iginla, Anson Carter, Donald Brashear, Georges Laraque, P.K. Subban, Wayne Simmonds, Quinton Byfield, and more. The same goes for the tributes commemorating the forward for his contributions to the game.

O'Ree's No. 22 has since been retired by the Bruins, one of three numbers he wore as a Bruin, according to Hockey-Reference.com. During the 1957–58 season, when O'Ree made two appearances, O'Ree wore the number 18. O'Ree wore Nos. 22 and 25 in 1960–61, the only other year he played in the NHL. Fittingly, his No. 22 was retired on January 18, 2022, 64 years after he made his NHL debut.

In 2021, a pair of skates was commissioned in O'Ree's honor thanks to player-agent Eustace King, former player Wayne Simmonds, artist Terry Smith, and hockey equipment outfitter Bauer. Proceeds went to the Black Girl Hockey Club.

"Willie is the godfather and the center of everything that's started with diversity and inclusion in the NHL," King told me in an interview for Yahoo Sports in 2021. "We wanted to make sure that we recognized and showcased him. In the same token, we wanted to integrate him on a product. It's the first time in the National Hockey League that a product line has been created [for] diversity and inclusion and then actually used in a regular season game."

O'Ree was also named to the New Brunswick Sports Hall of Fame in 1984 and was named to the Fredericton Sports Wall of Fame in 1992. O'Ree received the Order of New Brunswick in 2005. Three years later, O'Ree received the Order of Canada.

O'Ree now serves as the NHL's diversity ambassador, visiting schools and hockey programs to tell his story. The NHL even has an award in his name, the Willie O'Ree Community Hero Award, given "to an individual who—through the game of hockey—has positively impacted his or her community, culture, or society."

In 2018, O'Ree was inducted into the Hockey Hall of Fame as a builder purely off the strength of the "historical impact of his NHL career that has led him to Honoured Member status in the Hockey Hall of Fame," according to the HHOF website. But that came after columns, articles, and letters around the hockey world made the case for him to be inducted.

Local Fredericton columnist Bill Hunt wrote a column in 2018 titled "Time to Put Willie in the Hall of Fame." It led to signatures being collected at city hall by O'Ree's friends Brenda and David Sansom. It culminated in a 76-page document featuring letters expressing support for O'Ree.

When O'Ree was introduced at the 2018 Hockey Hall of Fame ceremony, Fuhr was the first to present O'Ree with a plaque bearing his face.

"You look at what Willie started," Fuhr said in October 2023 following O'Ree's stamp unveiling. "I followed Mike Marson, Tony McKegney, Bill Riley. I followed those guys. So, the game's slowly growing more and more. And that's what you want to see. You want to see progress."

O'Ree acknowledged players like Marson, Iginla, and Fuhr during his induction speech, honoring those who've continued his legacy long after his NHL playing days ended. But O'Ree also looked toward the future.

"Tonight, I am here to tell you we are not done," O'Ree said during his speech in November 2018. "Because the work is not done. We have barriers to break and knock down. Opportunities to give. I leave this with you. When you return to your communities, take a look around. Find a young boy or girl who needs the opportunity to play hockey and give it to them. You never know; they may make history."

2

Herb Carnegie

Hockey Night in Canada host Ron MacLean quickly threw to Elliotte Friedman, who stood in the Zamboni entrance at the Bell Centre ice in Montreal. It was a Saturday night in January 2008, and Friedman was assigned to cover a game between the Montreal Canadiens and Pittsburgh Penguins.

Friedman introduced a television story he had worked on in preparation for that day, more than 50 years after Willie O'Ree broke the color barrier as the NHL's first-ever Black player. But instead of focusing on O'Ree, Friedman told the story of a relatively unknown hockey figure who isn't as widely recognized compared to the trailblazing O'Ree.

When the NHL insider met with *Hockey Night in Canada* producers to pitch a story, he sold them on Herb Carnegie, a Black hockey player who spent his career in the Quebec Provincial and the Quebec Senior Hockey Leagues, scoring goals, winning individual accolades, and playing with future NHL legend Jean Beliveau. But Carnegie somehow never appeared in an NHL game.

Friedman himself didn't know much about Carnegie's story, not in the same way he knew about other Black players like Mike Marson or Tony McKegney. But he remembered a teacher from his school days mentioning Carnegie's name in passing and learned some basic details about Carnegie's unfulfilled NHL dream.

"They said that he was a player who could have played in the NHL, but just at the time, there was nobody willing to let him in," Friedman said. "I kind of always remembered his name. I didn't know a lot about him. But I remembered the name."

Friedman's producers greenlit his pitch and the reporter got in touch with Carnegie's daughter, Bernice, setting up an interview in a suite at Herb's retirement home.

He remembers Herb being "gracious" and "uplifting" as he showed off individual honors, newspaper clippings, trophies and photos, including one of a goal he scored past Jacques Plante in a game. Carnegie described the goal, using his backhand to deflect the puck off an opposing player before it beat Plante. Friedman joked with Carnegie that he should've said that he beat Plante with a wrist shot over the legendary netminder's glove from 25 feet away. Carnegie chuckled and smiled.

But the mood of the interview changed when Friedman asked about a painful memory in Herb's life.

In 1938, Carnegie was a member of the Toronto Young Rangers, a Junior A–level team in the Ontario Hockey Association. The team played their home games at Maple Leaf Gardens in downtown Toronto, the site of Toronto Maple Leafs games. The Young Rangers also used the ice for early morning practices at 6:00 AM.

During a practice, Maple Leafs owner Conn Smythe watched players like Carnegie closely. Smythe was an architect for some of the Leafs' early 20th century successes. He bought the Leafs when they were known as the Toronto St. Pats in 1927, investing $10,000 alongside other partners into the team before changing the name to Maple Leafs. Smythe also became head coach of the team, holding that position for three full seasons between 1927 and 1930 before resigning after two games during the 1930–31 season. He returned to the bench for one more game during the 1931–32 season in an interim role.

Smythe eventually made way for Dick Irvin, who won a Stanley Cup with the Leafs by season's end. Irvin was still head coach in 1938, making an appearance in a Stanley Cup every season in his tenure except for 1934 and 1937. But Smythe still remained the team's owner and general manager.

Smythe sat in Maple Leafs Gardens and watched Carnegie's skills, but knew he'd have no real future on his hockey club. A coach named Ed Wildey spoke to Carnegie that morning, pointing at Smythe sitting in the stands. Wildey then said Smythe would pay anyone $10,000 if they could turn the young Carnegie white so he could join the Maple Leafs. Another version of the story has Smythe saying he'd take Carnegie on his team "tomorrow" if someone turned him white.

"I got that statement when I was 18," Carnegie told Friedman, drawing a lengthy pause.

Carnegie then pointed at Friedman and said: "How would you feel?"

"I'd feel awful," Friedman responded.

"I can't forget it," Carnegie said, visibly emotional. "Because he cut my knees off. He broke my legs. It's horrible. So, I don't want people to go through that."

Carnegie broke down and sobbed.

"I can go back to that very moment," Carnegie continued, still sobbing. "When Ed Wildey had me at the side of the boards and was telling me the story."

Herb wiped away tears with a cloth as his daughter, Bernice, consoled him by rubbing his back. Decades after his encounter with Wildey, Carnegie was still devastated by how Smythe felt about him. Carnegie cheered for the Maple Leafs as a young boy and it was a "shattering" revelation for him, as was later written on the Hockey Hall of Fame website.

"I think it really caught me because it was such a quick turn," Friedman said. "And the emotion was so raw, like you really feel inadequate, there's nothing you can do in that moment to make someone feel better and it's a very helpless feeling."

"They always used to say sticks and stones will break your bones, but names will never hurt you. Now we know that's not true," Bernice said. "We know that what people say and what people do can make a difference, and it can last a lifetime, and you have to deal with it."

Carnegie's autobiography, *A Fly in a Pail of Milk: The Herb Carnegie Story*, was published in 1997, detailing his upbringing and racist experiences professional hockey. Carnegie expressed anger when he recounted Smythe's harmful words.

Carnegie never met Smythe, but he obsessively imagined scenarios where he physically and verbally confronted the Maple Leafs owner and GM.

"He had crushed my dream, and, in a sense, ruined my life," Carnegie wrote. "I knew I wouldn't ever play with the Toronto Maple Leafs. Smythe was a leader in the NHL at the time, and if he wouldn't cross the colour barrier, who would?"

Smythe has since become a recognizable name among hockey fans. He won seven Stanley Cups and lost six other finals as GM and owner of the Maple Leafs. In the present day, the Most Valuable Player award from the NHL postseason bears his name.

Carnegie does not have the same level of reverence. Even some Black hockey players and personalities aren't as familiar with his story.

FROM THE BEGINNING OF Herb Carnegie's autobiography, both Carnegie and his daughter/coauthor, Bernice, refuse to hold back on the racist experiences they endured.

The very first line of the book reads, "Nigger, nigger, go back to where you came from." It's a line that Herb remembered hearing from his childhood from as early as four or five years old. Herb might not have known exactly what "nigger" meant, but he was confident that he pushed back against a "hurtful" statement.

"Fortunately, I was born stubborn," Herb wrote. "It's said to be a character trait of Scorpios. So, I'm sure that I fought back and spoke with my fists."

Many of Herb's stories were a surprise to Bernice, when she read it for the first time. She wasn't told much about the racism her father faced during his upbringing and playing career.

"I found it so engaging, so conversational, so informational, so enlightening to think this is how many times you had to face that challenge and try to navigate around it," Bernice said. "I was so impressed, because what I saw in my dad was this man who kept reinventing himself so that he could make life good for him and for us."

A Fly in a Pail of Milk was originally printed in 1996 as a collection of stories from Carnegie's life as he rose up through various levels of professional hockey. Bernice added to her father's work, leading to a reprint of the book in 2019 in celebration of his birth 100 years earlier.

While they anticipated some readers would be disturbed by the language, they hoped their stories would serve as an education for those unaware of their upbringing or similar stories for Black people growing up in a certain era. According to Bernice, select Toronto-based school boards made the book available within their schools as an "educational tool."

Racism, of course, does not define the Carnegie family. But it ultimately plays a significant role in Herb's story.

Herb was born November 8, 1919, in Toronto, Ontario as the son of Jamaican parents George and Adina, who first lived in New York before moving to Canada. He was the fifth child of seven. He had three sisters: Geraldine, Bernice, and Lillian, and three brothers: Eric, Ross, and Ossie. The family eventually moved to the Toronto suburb of Willowdale when Herb was two months old, as one of the few Black families in the area.

"From the moment my grandparents arrived in Toronto in the early 1900s, they stuck out like flies in a pail of milk," Bernice wrote.

But it was in Willowdale where Herb found his passion for hockey. He learned to skate as an eight-year-old, using his brother Eric's skates on frozen ponds in the area. He took to skating quite well, eventually challenging other neighborhood kids to games with brother Ossie and other friends.

At home, Herb's love of hockey was strengthened by listening to Foster Hewitt's broadcasts on *Hockey Night in Canada*. Herb and Ossie would imagine themselves as Toronto Maple Leafs stars like Lionel Conacher, Joe Primeau, Ace Bailey, and Montreal Canadiens star Howie Morenz.

"Ossie was usually Conacher, while I, a left, was most often Primeau," Herb wrote. "We believed we were every bit as talented as the stars who dominated the game. And it was only a small step from there to imagining Hewitt calling out our names with all of Canada listening on."

Carnegie first played organized hockey either at the age of 12 or 13, according to his autobiography. He joined the team at Lansing Public School and a local midget hockey team—the Observers—in his teens with Ossie.

The Carnegies' father, George, was usually the only fan of color in the stands. But he didn't provide much support for Herb's hockey-playing dreams. Much of that had to do, according to Herb, with George wanting his son to be a doctor. Herb also feels his father's opinions were echoed by his white coworkers and bosses, thinking that racism would keep him out of professional hockey.

"You know they won't let any Black boys into the National Hockey League," George would say, according to Herb in his autobiography. "We thought Papa was deranged. Why was he saying such nasty things? Didn't he realize how well his sons played hockey? How could they not play in the NHL? What did colour have to do with it? Already, that put me in conflict with Papa."

Still, Herb and Ossie continued to play for local school teams in their teens. They spent a season at Earl Haig Collegiate before transferring to Northern Vocational School. It was at Northern where teammates, coaches, and even local media took more notice of Herb's skating, agility, and ability to maneuver past opposing players despite his smaller stature at 5'8" and 140 pounds, giving him the nickname "Swivel Hips." Herb eventually won a Junior B championship with Northern in his second year with the team.

As the Carnegies made their way up, however, the racism they faced would not cease. Herb remembers playing a game where a fan yelled "Get the Black bastard!" from the stands.

"When I skated off the ice, [coach] Bob Crosby put his arm on my shoulder and whispered into my ear, 'The way to answer that remark, Herbie, is to put the red light on.'"

It's a quote that Carnegie held dear for years on and off the ice.

In 1938, Carnegie joined the Junior A Toronto Young Rangers squad after mulling offers and opportunities from other teams. It was with the Young Rangers that Carnegie was told by his coach, Ed Wildey, that Conn Smythe would sign him if someone could turn him white.

The next year, Herb and Ossie moved to Perron, Quebec, a small mining town of Val-d'Or, to join the Perron Flyers and continue their hockey-playing ambitions. It was their first year as pro hockey players as they had aged out of Junior A-level hockey.

There are no available statistics of that season, but Carnegie writes that his team won the Northern Ontario Intermediate Championship and he and Ossie "had lots of goals and assists" while getting on the power play and penalty kill.

Herb and Ossie were in Northwestern Quebec just as the Second World War was about to begin. Herb was asked to report to a military base in Toronto to be recruited for the country's war efforts but was told he failed his medical. Ultimately, Herb was among many Black Canadians barred from serving with the Canadian Armed Forces as well as the country's naval and air force. Herb, however, was relieved "if not ecstatic" at the prospect of not reporting to war.

As the NHL lost players to conscription, both brothers anticipated getting tryouts to help teams fill in roster vacancies. Those calls never came despite their production, and other, white teammates received those call-ups instead.

"We never had an agent, we never had a lawyer, we never had a players' union, and the press was silent on the issue," Herb wrote in his autobiography. "There was no one to speak for us and we never made a fuss with anyone. There were, I suspect, some players who probably knew what was going on and said nothing, while others simply didn't even consider it. I felt that if I continue to play hard and to excel, sooner or later, I would get my chance. I continued to hope somebody out there would have a heart."

Herb made sacrifices to pursue his dreams, leaving behind his hometown and partner, Audrey, for a small Quebec town six hours north by car of Montreal and eight and a half hours away from Toronto. He grew homesick.

"The sixteen-mile road from Val d'Or (the closest train stop) was slightly curved and seemed to be cut from rock. The sides of the road were dominated by huge boulders and largely barren as a result of forest fire," Herb wrote in his autobiography. "In the town proper, mine shafts were visible. With a population between 900 and 1,200, the homes were spaced about 50 yards apart. The roads were dusty and lacked street lights. It was as desolate as the landscape, and I was ready to head home."

According to Carnegie, the town only had one department store and one movie theatre. Running water was a luxury and not the expectation for most people who lived in Perron. You'd have to buy a pail of water for a nickel each time.

Carnegie admits that this experience was his "first real taste of the loneliness and the heartache" that came with being away from his loved ones. But he tried to make the best of his situation by making friends with his hockey-playing teammates, working at the local mill, and playing fastball with the local team, the Perron Orphans.

In the summer of 1940, Carnegie received a telegram from Audrey just as he began a work shift at the mill saying to meet her in downtown Montreal at 7:30 the next morning. Carnegie got a ride with a coworker and his family, leaving Perron shortly after midnight and arriving in Montreal moments before Audrey's train arrived. The two hadn't seen each other in "several months."

In Montreal, Carnegie and Audrey decided to elope. They held a short wedding ceremony August 8, 1940, in Val d'Or and moved into their Perron, Quebec home. But later that summer, they moved to Timmins, Ontario, when Herb and Ossie joined the Buffalo Ankerites.

Herb and Ossie didn't know it at the time, but they'd become two-thirds of Black hockey history in Timmins and accomplish something not seen since the Colored Hockey League of the Maritimes.

DECADES BEFORE THE CARNEGIES were born, the Colored Hockey League of the Maritimes was established in 1895 by local Black church leaders in Nova Scotia who wanted more Black men to attend services. They enticed them to join through a hockey league that played games after church. The Colored Hockey League was formed by four Black church and community leaders: James Borden, James A.R. Kinney, James Robinson Johnston, and Henry Sylvester Williams.

The league was preceded by the Halifax City Hockey League, formed one year earlier in 1894 for whites only. In 1893, Sir Arthur Frederick Stanley, Lord Stanley of Preston and Son of the Earl of Derby, donated a trophy he purchased for 10 Guineas (the equivalent of $50 at the time, according to the Hockey Hall of Fame) to the championship-winning team of the "Dominion of Canada." We know that trophy now as the Stanley Cup.

The CHLM at its peak had over 100 players and 12 teams mostly spread out through Nova Scotia with one team in the province of Prince Edward Island. The Halifax Eurekas, the Dartmouth Jubilees, the Africville Sea-Sides, and the Charlottetown West End Rangers were among the teams who played in the CHLM. The Eurekas won nine CHLM titles throughout their existence, more than any other league franchise.

Attendance was higher than that of white teams and leagues, drawing up to 1,500 fans per game. The fast-paced, physical game played a role in the league gaining popularity in Eastern Canada.

The CHLM is also credited with notable innovations relevant to the present-day game. The slap shot, commonly attributed to Montreal Canadiens legend Bernie "Boom Boom" Geoffrion, made its debut in the CHLM through Halifax Eurekas forward Eddie Martin. Goaltender Henry Franklin dropped to his knees to make saves, in contrast to the standup goaltending style other goalies used. Franklin's style has since been modernized and innovated as the butterfly, a goaltending style and technique that has become the norm in every level of hockey. The "flying body check"—a variation of modern-day body-checking—debuted in the CHLM through George Tolliver of the Eurekas.

"He was quite a physical player," sportswriter, historian and former hockey player Bob Dawson said. "He had no hesitation in displaying that physical side of the game in the way he would fling his body into other players. At times, it created some angst among the players and some of the games became somewhat heated because of his style of playing."

Despite the talent throughout the CHLM, no teams ever competed for the Stanley Cup against white teams. Competitive teams could formally challenge the current holder of the Cup, resulting in multiple Cup-winning teams in one calendar year.

The CHLM was also not helped by real-world issues and serious economic constraints caused by tragedy. Members of the league were enlisted into World War I—a complete reversal from the Canadian military's initial decision to bar Black Canadians from joining the country's war efforts abroad. Some CHLM members eventually joined the No. 2 Construction Battalion that was formed in 1916, recognized by the Canadian government as the "first and only all-Black battalion-sized formation in Canadian military history."

The league was also rocked by the events of the Halifax Explosion of 1917. More than 1,700 lives were lost and at least 9,000 people injured after a steamship carrying explosives from France collided with another ship in the Halifax Harbour Narrows port. Many relied-upon shipping piers, railways, and roadways, especially by citizens of Africville, were destroyed as a result.

The league and some of its teams continued into the 1930s but, as George and Darril Fosty wrote in *Black Ice: The Lost History of the Colored Hockey League of the Maritimes 1895–1925*, it succumbed to hurdles that it just couldn't overcome.

"Racism, the war, the Halifax Explosion, and economic factors had all played their part in the league's demise," they wrote.

The CHLM is an integral part of Black hockey history that must be celebrated and acknowledged. The league even celebrated its 130th anniversary in February 2025.

Canada Post commemorated the Colored Hockey League and the Colored Hockey Championship with a stamp in January 2020 featuring the 1904 Halifax Eurekas—that year's championship winner.

"There's a hunk of history in that stamp," local politician Wayne Adams told the CBC in January 2020. Adams is the grandson of Augustus Adams, who helped the CHLM get off the ground and played with the Eurekas alongside his brother, George.

"I think research over the past 10, 15 years has proven that this is a significant piece of real Canadian history, and you can't have it locked away in security vaults at various universities."

In 2024, the Canadian government acknowledged the CHLM as a "national historic event."

"The history of this league and its players is one that illustrates the many remarkable ways Black Nova Scotians worked to promote equality in the Maritimes and exemplifies the enduring legacy of Black heritage in Canada," Canadian MP Steven Guilbeault said in a news release.

Black players playing alongside each other was the norm in the CHLM. It was a rarity in other professional leagues.

Herb and Ossie Carnegie spent their first season in Timmins together in 1940–41. But it wasn't until their second season that their squad acquired Vincent Churchill "Manny" McIntyre.

Manny McIntyre was born in Fredericton, New Brunswick, on October 4, 1918, in the same town as Willie O'Ree. McIntyre grew up playing baseball and hockey, later becoming the first Black Canadian to sign a professional baseball contract just weeks after Jackie Robinson joined the Brooklyn Dodgers organization. McIntyre even played for the Sherbrooke Canadiens, the St. Louis Cardinals' farm team in 1946.

Five years earlier, McIntyre joined the Carnegies in Timmins, Ontario. According to Herb, McIntyre wrote a letter to the Ankerites team manager offering his services. The Carnegies were impressed with McIntyre's play from the moment they watched him skate.

It wouldn't be long until the Carnegies and McIntyre formed the first all-Black line in hockey outside of the Colored Hockey League.

"I hoped that Manny's hockey talent would match his skating ability," Herb wrote in *A Fly in a Pail of Milk*. "If so, we'd have one formidable line. Once together, it wasn't long before our style of play brought praise for its uniqueness, not only in colour but also in talent. We soon became an attraction at the gate and the league's tills were humming a merry and profitable tune in harmony with senior hockey's only coloured line."

The trio stayed together in Timmins through 1944 when they made the move to Shawinigan Falls, Quebec, to join the Shawinigan Falls Cataracts of the Quebec Provincial League. Herb credits McIntyre for negotiating the deal that ensured all three players could move to Shawinigan. Herb led his team in goals and points that season with 24 goals and 54 points in 33 games.

By 1945, the "Black Aces" joined the Sherbrooke Randies. The trio continued to see success together in Sherbrooke through 1949—with the exception of the 1947–48 season, when Ossie and Manny spent a season in France—with Carnegie winning three consecutive MVP titles from 1947 to 1949.

"My own game was rooted in speed and puck control," Herb wrote. "Ossie was a dogged positional player with a blazing shot, and Manny was the mucker who battled for the puck in corners and then placed a perfect pass onto one of our sticks. Manny was also a gifted positional player."

After scoring 48 goals and 127 points during the 1947–48 season, Herb was offered a training camp invitation by the New York Rangers. Carnegie accepted the invite and traveled to Saranac Lake, New York, to skate alongside 80 other players vying for roster spots.

Partway through Carnegie's training camp, the Rangers prepared an offer for him to play for their minor league affiliate in Tacoma, Washington. According to Herb, he was offered $2,700. It was less than the $5,100 he earned during his 1948 season with Sherbrooke. After Herb declined, the Rangers countered the next day with another offer: $3,700. Herb would play in St. Paul, Minnesota—the site of another minor league Rangers affiliate.

Finally, the Rangers offered Carnegie $4,700 to play in New Haven, Connecticut, in the American Hockey League. But Herb was adamant that he belonged in the National Hockey League. While players offered support for Carnegie, management would not acquiesce to Carnegie's desire to play NHL hockey. He left the Rangers' training camp and returned to Sherbrooke "satisfied and angered."

That was Carnegie's final chance at making an NHL roster. Despite showing he could play with NHL talent in camp, the Rangers would only make him a minor leaguer.

"The scars of that experience mark my soul to this day," Carnegie wrote in his autobiography. "The Rangers training camp was the end of my dream to play in the NHL. I was deeply hurt and frustrated by the realization of what had happened. Now I was certain that I had the talent, the skill and the attitude to play in the NHL. The only thing I lacked, to the everlasting shame of the NHL, was white skin."

Carnegie played one more season in Sherbrooke before joining the Quebec Aces for four seasons starting in 1949. His head coach was George "Punch" Imlach, who spent four seasons as a player before assuming duties as coach, general manager, vice president, and part owner of the Aces.

Carnegie eventually became teammates with a young Jean Béliveau before he joined the NHL. As Beliveau led his team in scoring during the 1951–52 and 1952–53 seasons, Carnegie registered consecutive 50-plus point seasons from 1949 through 1952—his first three seasons with the Aces. Carnegie played one final year with the Aces in 1952–53 before joining the Owen Sound Mercurys of the Ontario Hockey Association's Senior A League for the 1953–54 season. It was Carnegie's final professional season before retiring at the age of 34.

Decades after both their playing careers ended, Béliveau wrote the foreword for Carnegie's autobiography. He echoed the sentiments of many who had seen Carnegie play by saying he belonged at the sport's highest level.

"It's my belief that Herbie Carnegie was excluded from the National Hockey League because of his colour," Béliveau wrote in his foreword. "How could the NHL scouts overlook not one, but three most valuable players for a player on a team in a top senior league?"

Even Willie O'Ree, who accomplished what Carnegie could not, felt his compatriot was denied an NHL dream. O'Ree has stated in multiple interviews that Carnegie should have broken the Black color barrier.

"Herbie Carnegie was the one," O'Ree said in an interview with the Associated Press in 2000. "It should have been Herbie."

In retirement, Carnegie fulfilled his athletic passions through golf—a sport he enjoyed in his youth. Carnegie won several golfing championships including two Canadian Senior Golf Championships in 1977 and 1978 and three Ontario Senior Golf Championships in 1975, 1976, and 1982. Carnegie also worked for the Investors Group as a financial planner for more than 30 years.

But his legacy post-retirement is best remembered for his founding of the Future Aces hockey school in 1955. According to the Future Aces Foundation—which came into existence in 1987—it is believed to be the first registered hockey school in Canada. At the heart of Future Aces, whether through its school or foundation form, are the values that Carnegie wanted to live by and hoped to instill in students from his school and through the foundation: attitude, courage, example, and service (ACES). While the hockey school ceased operations in 1964, the foundation still exists today. As of Summer 2024, they've handed out nearly $1 million in scholarships to hundreds of deserving student applicants and helped form numerous anti-bullying and anti-racism initiatives across school boards in Ontario.

"And so that Future Aces philosophy jumped from the hockey school, which ran for 10 years, into the education system," Bernice said. "It became a movement, a movement of how to empower young people to become the best of who they can be."

Bernice continues to advance her father's legacy through the Carnegie Initiative, a nonprofit organization which encourages diversity and inclusion in hockey through informative panels, events, and a monthly newsletter. Bernice and Bryant McBride, a film producer and former NHL vice president of business development, co-founded the initiative in 2021.

Despite not making it to the NHL, Carnegie received support from the media and the wider hockey world to be included in the Hockey Hall of Fame. Carnegie's call to the Hall of Fame came posthumously in 2022, a decade after he passed away at the age of 92 in March 2012. Carnegie was inducted into the hall's builder category in a class that featured Daniel Alfredsson, Roberto Luongo, Daniel and Henrik Sedin, and Riikka Salinen.

"The one regret I have is that he didn't, he wasn't alive for the Hockey Hall of Fame," Bernice said. "He had been inducted into 13 Halls of Fame before 2022 happened.

"They had a chance to recognize him while he was alive."

Carnegie's Hall of Fame induction is now part of a long list of honors and accomplishments that he's received since his playing career ended. He was named to the Order of Ontario in 1996 as well as the Order of Canada in 2003. Carnegie was named to the Canadian Sports Hall of Fame in 2001 and the Ontario Sports Hall of Fame in 2014.

Carnegie was also named an honorary chief of police of York Regional in 2005 and obtained an honorary doctor of laws degree from York University in 2006. Carnegie was even a character in two issues of *The Amazing Spider-Man*, appearing in *The Amazing Spider-Man: Skating on Thin Ice* and *The Amazing Spider-Man: Double Trouble*, both from December 1992.

The Herbert H. Carnegie Centennial Centre, a multipurpose arena formerly known as the North York Centennial Centre, is named in his honor. A public school, Herbert H. Carnegie Public School, also bears his name.

While Carnegie's NHL dream was never realized, his achievement of playing on an all-Black line in professional hockey has since been replicated throughout numerous levels of hockey, including the NHL.

DANIEL WALCOTT'S PHONE RANG the night before history was made.

The Quebecer was enjoying his day off in Florida, one day before the Tampa Bay Lightning were supposed to close out their season with a matchup against the rival Florida Panthers. It would cap off one of the strangest years in NHL history, as the league managed to play through a worldwide pandemic by forcing its teams to only play opponents in rearranged divisions. The schedule was baseball-esque, with teams playing consecutive games in cities to limit travel.

The Lightning and Panthers had played the first of two games the previous day. Florida was about to defeat its rival when then Panthers defenseman Brandon Montour speared then Lightning forward Pat Maroon in the groin. Despite a linesman trying to separate Maroon from Montour, the man known as the "Big Rig" dropped his gloves and fought the Panthers defenseman. Maroon was assessed a one-game suspension and would miss the regular season finale against Florida.

Walcott was on the Lightning's taxi squad. That season, NHL teams were allowed to carry up to six players that they could use if they found themselves in need due to injury or "pandemic-related issues." And that's what led to the phone call from Lightning head coach Jon Cooper.

"Wally, hope you didn't spend your day at the pool bar," Walcott remembered Cooper saying. "Because with what happened, there's a chance you're going to play tomorrow."

To that point, Walcott was an American Hockey League lifer. Walcott joined the Lightning's minor league affiliate after being traded by the New York Rangers for a seventh-round pick in 2015. The former defenseman turned forward played 249 games in the AHL before he received that phone call from Cooper.

Making his NHL debut would have been special enough for Walcott. Then, Cooper said, "Also I'm thinking of potentially playing you with Smitty and Jo."

Smitty is Gemel Smith and Jo is Mathieu Joseph, two of Walcott's best friends in the Lightning organization. Two players who have spent time with Walcott with the Syracuse Crunch. All three men are Black. Not only was Walcott about to make his NHL debut, but he'd be able to play with some of the closest hockey friends he's made along the way.

The following night, at the BB&T Center in Sunrise, Florida, all three men took their spots on the ice ahead of the opening faceoff. The trio is believed to be the NHL's first-ever all-Black line, coming decades after Carnegie lit the lamp alongside his brother Ossie and Manny McIntyre.

"It's important to show it and a make a big deal out of it because it should be a normality, but it isn't," Walcott said. "The fact that it isn't a normality. The fact that there aren't a lot of Black guys playing or even on the same team. That's a big deal."

Decades before the Lightning iced an all-Black line of their own, Willie O'Ree made history as the NHL's first Black player. He was also part of an all-Black line with the Quebec Aces during the 1958–59 season, playing alongside John Utendale and Stan Maxwell one season after O'Ree made his NHL debut with the Boston Bruins.

Other NHL teams have had a handful of Black NHLers on their team, including the 2011 Atlanta Thrashers, who had Dustin Byfuglien, Anthony Stewart, Evander Kane, and Johnny Oduya. The 1999–2000 Calgary Flames had an all-Black goalie tandem of Fred Brathwaite and Grant Fuhr, in addition to forward Jarome Iginla. The following season, the Edmonton Oilers boasted a roster with Georges Laraque, Mike Grier, Sean Brown, Joaquin Gage, and Anson Carter.

But there is no record of any NHL team playing an all-Black line until the Tampa Bay Lightning did on May 10, 2021. To make matters more special for Walcott, then Panthers forward and fellow Black Quebecois Anthony Duclair started the game for the opposition.

"It was like a reuniting of all my buddies," Walcott said. "And so happens that we're all Black players. It was fun. In the moment I wasn't really thinking, 'Oh my god, this is such an awesome experience.' I was just going out there with my buddies in my first NHL game, and I was comfortable around the people I was [with]."

"It was great, man," Joseph said after the game, via the Associated Press. "A step in the right direction. It was fun to have some progress, and it was great to see and I was glad I was part of it.

"Any players of color in this league want to showcase to our families or other people of color. I thank the coaching staff for doing this."

That game's result did not go Tampa Bay's way; the Lightning lost 4–0 to Florida. But the meaning was not lost on members of the organization, including head coach Jon Cooper.

"As we move forward as a league, you hope this isn't a story," Cooper told Joe Smith of The Athletic after the game. "Maybe it's a story today. But as the league gets more diverse, you hope it's not going to be a story. You hope it's going to be the norm, that it is a league for everybody."

Two months prior, the Ontario Reign of the American Hockey League played a line featuring Akil Thomas, Quinton Byfield, and Devante Smith-Pelly in a March 21, 2021, game against the Bakersfield Condors.

Smith-Pelly played 395 games in the NHL and won a Stanley Cup with the Washington Capitals in 2018—scoring the game-tying goal against Vegas in the Cup-clinching game—before joining the China-based Kunlun Red Star of the Kontinental Hockey League. He sought a return to North America in 2021, with COVID delays across the hockey world keeping him out of game action for more than a year. He eventually signed a professional tryout contract with the California-based Reign on March 13, 2021, joining a roster that had Thomas, Byfield, and Bokondji Imama.

Days later, Smith-Pelly was slotted on a line with two young budding prospects in their first professional seasons for the Los Angeles Kings organization. There was Byfield, who was drafted second overall by the Kings during the 2020 NHL Entry Draft, making him the highest-drafted Black player in NHL history. And then there was Akil Thomas, who scored the game-winning goal for Canada in the 2020 IIHF World Junior Hockey Championship against Team Russia and was a second-round pick of the Kings back in 2018.

"I just thought it was exciting to play with two younger guys who were having good years," Smith-Pelly said. "It was just exciting. I think at times during that year some of the games were a little bit of a drag to get involved in because no fans. We were playing at a practice rink.

"Getting a chance to play with Q and Akil, two guys who are friends. Two guys who are trying to make it and try to get to where I already was. That chance to be on a line with them was exciting.

And I honestly didn't really think of it as three Black guys on a line. Although that was pretty obvious."

The trio combined for six points in a 5–4 shootout win for Ontario over Bakersfield. Byfield opened the scoring with an assist from Smith-Pelly nearly five minutes into the contest. However, Ontario was chasing most of the game.

A win for Ontario was far from certain when they found themselves down 4–1 in the third period. But with 3:07 to play, Akil Thomas elevated his game.

Thomas scored his first goal by wiring the puck past Condors goaltender Stuart Skinner with a fast shot from the right-side faceoff circle, wasting no time shooting after a failed clearing attempt from a Condors defenseman. Almost 90 seconds later, Thomas scored his second of the game from the slot, taking a pass from behind the Condors net before quickly snapping it toward goal.

Finally, with 23 seconds to go in the game, Thomas used his quick trigger again to beat Skinner and tie the game at four goals apiece. It was his first-ever hat-trick as a pro player. Thomas added another goal via shootout en route to victory for good measure.

"It was a cool experience," Thomas said. "I don't think we even noticed what was happening in the moment. But just to win that game and see all the media after that was pretty cool. And hopefully some other Black kids out there were able to see that and able to believe that they can be on a Black line too."

The game was reported as the first time an all-Black line played in a professional game since the original Black Aces were led by the Carnegie brothers and Manny McIntyre in the 1940s.

But it turns out Akil's father, Kahlil, played on two all-Black lines during his minor league career, according to NHL.com. Kahlil Thomas played on a line with Daniel Hickman and Tyrone Garner as a member of the Jacksonville Barracudas during the 2006–07 Southern Professional Hockey League.

The Jacksonville Icemen, an ECHL franchise, claim that Thomas was on the first-ever all-Black line in professional hockey as a member of the Flint Generals of the United Hockey League. The line consisted of Thomas, fellow forward Nick Forbes and former Cincinnati Cyclones head coach Jason Payne, who is also Akil's godfather. Payne had also watched Smith-Pelly, Byfield, and Smith grow up as youngsters playing hockey in Toronto and Newmarket, Ontario.

As coach of the Cyclones, Payne was the architect of an ambitious idea that one-upped the Lightning three years after they made history. He fantasized about it weeks before it happened, even writing out jersey numbers for his starting lineup on a dry-erase board. But he needed some stars to align first.

Payne kept an eye on two Black players who were playing collegiate hockey at the start of the 2023–24 ECHL season. Kyle Bollers spent three seasons playing in Toronto for Toronto Metropolitan University (formerly known as Ryerson) but had previously taken part in the Cyclones training camp. Payne encouraged him to continue pursuing his education and to dominate while playing hockey for his school team. Bollers achieved that by winning team MVP and even male athlete of the year.

Elijah Gonsalves spent five seasons at the Rochester Institute of Technology before joining the Cyclones. In his final season at R.I.T, he was named a third-team All-Conference player and the Atlantic Hockey Conference tournament's most outstanding player. Gonsalves scored four points (two goals and two assists) in the tournament's championship game, leading R.I.T to a 5–2 win over American International.

Once they finished their collegiate seasons, both men signed pro contracts with the Cyclones within days of each other. The same day Gonsalves signed his contract and was added to the pro roster, March 30, 2024, Gonsalves and Bollers were in the Cyclones' starting lineup alongside Josh Burnside, Landon Cato, and Jalen Smereck. It was the first time an all-Black lineup was fielded in professional hockey.

The Cyclones won the game 3–2 in overtime over the Wheeling Nailers. Smereck, who was named an ECHL first-team All-Star that season, earned an assist in the victory, establishing a team record for most points by a defenseman in the process. The Detroit native ended the 2023–24 campaign with 14 goals and 71 points in 70 games played.

"To watch the look on their faces when I told them [they'd be starting], it was of pride and knowing that they'd be part of something special," Payne said. "For me, it was something I took pride in. One, I know it's never been done with five players. But I think the fact of the matter is it's five players with a Black head coach.

"That'll come with a lot of scrutiny, because people will think you're doing it because you want Black players on your team. Well, no, because I don't play that. I want good players on my team. I want great people of character on my team. All of these guys here can play and they can play really well. They're good. That, to me, didn't discredit what we were going to do."

Payne is no stranger to making Black history in hockey, becoming the first person of color to become head coach of the Cyclones when he was unveiled on August 31, 2021. Payne's hiring made him the third coach of color in league history and the sixth in professional hockey history. The following season, Payne's Cyclones faced off against the Kalamazoo Wings, coached by another Black coach in Joel Martin. According to Sportsnet, it is believed to be the first time two Black coaches have ever coached against each other at the pro level.

Approximately a decade after the Carnegies and Manny McIntyre did it in Timmins, Ontario and less than a decade before Willie O'Ree made his NHL debut, another trio of Black players came together in Mount Forest, Ontario. Arthur Lowe, Gary Smith and Howard Sheffield all played for a team in the town located about two hours northwest of Toronto. According to the CBC, fans packed arenas to see the three men play, eventually earning the nickname "the Black Flashes."

Similarly to the Paris family, hockey history flows through the Lowes as well. Arthur's son, Darren, became the first Black player to ever represent Canada in men's hockey at the Olympics when he joined the squad ahead of the 1984 Olympic Games in Sarajevo.

"There weren't a lot of people of color playing hockey back then, so it's quite unique," Darren told the CBC in 2020 when asked about his father. "To be able to follow in those footsteps is kind of nice."

Finally, a Canadian university boasted an all-Black line of its own in the 1960s.

Before becoming a hockey historian and writer, Bob Dawson made history as the first Black athlete to play in the Atlantic Intercollegiate Hockey League as a member of the Saint Mary's Huskies men's hockey team when he joined in 1967. Dawson primarily played defense for the Huskies until one night in 1970 against the Mount Allison Mounties. Huskies head coach Bob Boucher called on Dawson to center a line with fellow Black players Percy Paris and Darrell Maxwell, causing all three players to look at each other in "bewilderment." And that's how Paris, Maxwell, and Dawson made history.

"[Boucher] was socially aware of the times that we were living in at that time, in terms of race relations within the area, within the province," Dawson said. "Knowing him, he was wanting to send a message in the fact that here are three good Black hockey players. And [he] seized the moment and the opportunity to showcase our contribution to the game and the fact that we were good hockey."

Hockey history doesn't stop there for the Paris family, however. Percy is the brother of John Paris Jr., the first Black man to coach a pro hockey team and win a league championship as coach—four years before Dirk Graham was the first Black man to coach in the NHL in 1998.

Paris Jr. was named head coach of the Atlanta Knights of the International Hockey League, leading them to a Turner Cup victory in 1994. Paris Jr. also holds the distinction as the first Black male scout in pro hockey as well as the first head coach and general manager in Quebec Major Junior Hockey League history. A petition has even been launched by Hockey Nova Scotia to get Paris Jr. inducted into the Hockey Hall of Fame as a builder.

In February 2023, brothers Percy and John coached against each other in a game marking the 128th anniversary of the Colored Hockey League of the Maritimes. Both men coached all-Black rosters representing the Halifax Eurekas and Dartmouth Jubilees, the two teams who played in the first-ever CHLM game.

"We were just playing hockey like the other kids did, like our dad taught us to do," Paris Jr. told the CBC in a 2023 interview. "We already knew what color we were, but we were playing the game simply because it was a game that kids played, adults played, fans loved."

The Paris brothers imagined themselves as hockey players who weren't solely defined by their skin color, as O'Ree and Carnegie did before them.

3

Jarome Iginla

The party began once Jarome Iginla got to his feet on a Sunday evening in February 2010.

Tens of thousands of fans packed in a Vancouver arena jumped to their feet to celebrate Canada being golden, again. Those celebrations spread to bars, restaurants, and homes across the city, country, and the world.

Sidney Crosby's hands were already in the air, his gloves floating above his head as he jumped with jubilation. The weight of an entire nation was thrown off his back. Crosby's teammates Scott Niedermayer and Drew Doughty were the first to catch him once gravity brought him back down.

Iginla soon joined the growing dogpile of red-and-white sweaters, with each man achieving Olympic immortality. Many remember the gold medal, overtime winning moment as the "Golden Goal."

"Those are the most fun games to play in," Iginla said. "It was intense the whole time, back and forth. You're a fan when you hit the bench and you're almost a little bit nervous. You get out on the ice, and you go as hard as you can and then you get off and recover.

"But when that went in, it was one of the coolest memories because it was everything. It was relief, it was elation. You can't believe it. It was like a minor hockey moment like in peewee where you imagine when you're on the outdoor rink. It's over. In overtime. Guys throwing their gloves everywhere. It was awesome."

The "Golden Goal" is the apex of Canada's 2010 Winter Olympic Games, where they set a record for most gold medals won in a single Olympics. It erased the bittersweet taste of the 2006 Turin Olympics, when Canada finished seventh, their worst-ever finish at an Olympic tournament.

All it took was an iconic call for the puck: "Iggy!"

"I remember a play in the corner and Sid yelled for the puck," Iginla said. "We always talk communication as coaches and players and how important it is. When players yell for it, there's a different type of yell when you're open. Like, 'Iggy, I'm with you!' or 'Iggy! Yeah, yeah, now!'

"I was just doing everything I could to try to get it to him because, obviously, he had a step on somebody. So I got it, diving, falling and just made the play over to him coming down and he made a great five-hole shot and finished it."

"It was four-on-four, and I had a rush," Crosby said, reliving the goal. "It was kind of like a one-on-two, I think. It got broken up. The puck went in the corner. I tried to take it up the wall. Just kind of got stuck along the wall. And when it was stuck, Jarome was coming there to help out.

"I just jumped to the middle and called for it. Just tried to get it away as soon as it hit my stick, and it went five-hole."

As Crosby called for the puck, Iginla did the dirty work in the corners. Iginla then fell to the ice and made the perfect pass to Crosby. Two American defenders tried to stop the magic. Ryan Suter was the defender on Iginla's back, trying to limit his space. Brian Rafalski stuck out his stick to cut off Iginla's pass. They were left helpless as the puck deftly reached Crosby's stick blade.

"It's the 'Iggy' heard 'round the world, right?" hockey reporter Chris Johnston said. "You can go back and listen to any of the broadcasts in any of the languages. You can hear Crosby calling up for that pass. And I think when you look at how significant the moment was, the whole country is calling for that pass."

"It's his nickname," Crosby said. "I saw an opening there. I wanted to let him know that I was there. It was kind of a broken play in the corner. It's just a reaction, more instinctive than anything."

The goal has been watched worldwide, including one YouTube video with more than 2.5 million views. You can even find YouTube compilations of different play-by-play calls in numerous languages and reactions across the planet. According to Hockey Canada, 22 million people tuned in to watch the goal on television and over 26 million tuned in to watch the game that fateful Sunday.

"That's actually why my dog's name is 'Iggy,'" popular hockey YouTuber Steve Dangle said. "Because that's what Sidney Crosby shouted right before the Golden Goal. He shouted for Jarome Iginla to give him the puck."

Just as older generations had Paul Henderson's 1972 Summit Series winner, giving Canada a win over the Soviet Union, younger Canadian hockey fans will always have Crosby beating United States goaltender Ryan Miller short side, sending an entire nation into a frenzy.

No one had a better front-row seat than Iginla, whose primary assist secured his second-ever Olympic gold medal. All while falling to the ice. The goal that made it happen will live on forever in Canadian history. But we must not forget the assist from one of the greatest players the sport has ever seen.

Iginla, as is his default, deflected any of the praise thrown onto him. He instead commended Crosby, who had massive expectations in his Olympic debut. Team Canada had already lost to the United States in the round-robin. In the prior game, the Canadians needed a shootout-winning goal from Crosby to upend Switzerland. In the semi-finals, Canada needed late saves from Roberto Luongo to preserve a 3–2 win to advance to the final. And just when it looked as if Canada would win over the U.S. in regulation, Zach Parise's last-second goal sent it to overtime. The Canadians weren't exactly dominant in 2010 and Crosby bore a significant chunk of that pressure despite playing at his first Olympic Games.

Iginla knew everything about the pressure, having experienced something similar in 2002 when he joined Team Canada at the Olympics as the NHL's leading scorer at the time. Following a tournament-opening loss to Sweden, Iginla swapped lines to join Joe Sakic and Simon Gagné. Iginla credits Sakic as the savvy veteran who helped find his place on the team. In 2010, Iginla was able to extend that comfort to the Penguins' superstar.

"The whole Olympics, it didn't seem like goals were coming easy," said Crosby, who scored four goals and seven points in seven tournament games. "And he just said stay with it, keep going. And he was really supportive. As a young player at the time, and obviously a lot of pressure playing in Vancouver at home at the Olympics, he was just so good to me. So, to be able to connect with him on that goal was pretty big.

"For him to continue to encourage me, to be supportive, to stay positive through that, to get that was huge. When there's that much pressure when all that stuff [is] happening, that sure can make a big difference.... So many guys on that team like[Scott] Niedermayer and [Chris] Pronger. All these guys. But when you're playing with someone with Jarome with all that experience, it gives you a certain sense of confidence too."

"I thought it was just awesome to be on there and so excited to see [Crosby] put it in and score that big one," Iginla said. "He had so much pressure on him. And for him to come through, it was really fitting to see him score."

For so many athletes, that play would be career-defining. In the case of Henderson, the '72 Summit Series is the most iconic moment of a respectable and successful career with two All-Star Game appearances, 236 goals, and 477 points in 707 career NHL games for the Detroit Red Wings, Toronto Maple Leafs, and Atlanta Flames. Henderson also succeeded in the World Hockey Association with the Toronto Toros and the Birmingham Bulls.

Some pundits and sportswriters have advocated for Henderson to be inducted into the Hockey Hall of Fame purely off the strength of his 1972 heroics, but Henderson himself has said he wouldn't vote himself into the Hall.

"So many Canadians get upset that I'm not in the Hall of Fame, and I tell them all the time if I was on the committee, I wouldn't vote for me," Henderson told Stu Cowan of the *Montreal Gazette* in 2012. "Quite frankly, I didn't have a Hall of Fame career.

"There's a lot of guys who had a lot better careers than I did and they're not in the Hall of Fame. So if they ever put me in, there would be somebody else who wouldn't get in, and I would feel bad about that."

For Iginla, his assist on the Golden Goal is just one of many signature moments that built up his case for the Hall of Fame. By 2010, he already won a World Championship, a World Cup, two Maurice "Rocket" Richard trophies, an Art Ross Trophy, a Lester B. Pearson Award, and a handful of NHL All-Star Game appearances. Some would argue that a Hart Trophy should also be on his mantle for his 2001–02 season in which he led the league in goals (52) and points (96). Iginla even became the first Black player in NHL history to score 50 goals in an NHL season.

Despite his success, Iginla still fell short to Montreal Canadiens goaltender José Théodore for the honor. It is rumored that an unnamed Montreal reporter left Iginla off their MVP ballot. But Iginla doesn't feel he was robbed of the honor and felt Théodore was "deserving" of the MVP.

"To some people, being a part of a playoff team was a big part of whether you can be up for the Hart or should win the Hart," Iginla said.

"I sure would have loved that extra vote. But at the same time, I get that that is part of it."

But with respect to Théodore's trophy case, Iginla's own is crammed with hardware from his junior and professional career. Not to mention a historical first. Iginla is the first Black male athlete ever to win a Winter Olympics gold medal when he won in 2002 with Team Canada. Iginla's worldly assist on the Golden Goal in 2010 wasn't even his first time delivering in an Olympic gold-medal game. By then, Iginla was already one of the premier power forwards in the NHL and as one of the league's best captains, setting an example on the ice for others to follow.

"Jarome Iginla is everything that everyone my age was taught to love in a hockey player," Dangle said. "He was the captain of his team, a heart-and-soul player, he would hit everything that moved, he would fight if he had to, and basically always win the fights, rarely ever punched down. And on top of all that he was his team's best player."

"On game days, especially before the game, he put a towel above his head and he does what he needs to do to get ready," former teammate Craig Conroy said. "So, he's not a big rah-rah guy in the room. He does his talk mostly on the ice.

"But the one thing about Jarome, as he became captain, as he moved along, he spoke more. When he had to talk, he talked. When he spoke in the room in between periods, he did. His mindset was, I don't need to be talking every day. When I talk, I need it to be meaningful and important."

Iginla's aggressive style of play allowed him to battle with the league's best players whether through board battles or throwing punches. But Iginla's lethal shot also allowed him to score 30, sometimes 40 or even 50 goals in a season.

Crosby marveled at Iginla's game in his youth. The superstar first saw Iginla live in Calgary while in town with his school team, Shattuck St. Mary's, as part of the Mac's Midget-AAA hockey tournament.

"He was just a pure goal scorer, and he played with a certain toughness, too," Crosby said. "He was physical, he could fight. He really thrived in those high-intensity environments."

"He was a prick to play against," Doughty said. "A little bit scary in some ways because he could hit. He could fight. He could score. He could do anything."

His on-ice meanness and toughness were in stark contrast to his off-ice demeanor, which came across as friendly and generous.

"As a teammate, he was one of the best," former junior hockey teammate Ryan Huska said. "Whether you were like a younger guy, if you were one of the so-called lower-end players. If you were one of the top players, he had time for everybody and he cared about everybody. So, he made it very welcoming for people to be around him and make you feel like you're a valued person."

"Jarome was a capital-S superstar," former national hockey writer Craig Custance said. "When you sat down with him and you spent time with him, he was humble and thoughtful and an incredible teammate."

"One of the nicest human beings out there," Doughty said. "Like almost awkwardly nice at times. If you met at the door at the same time, he would not go first. There's nothing you could do to make him go first.

"You just had to lose the battle because he would not go first."

Play-by-play man Gord Miller remembered visiting Canadian troops stationed in Kandahar, Afghanistan, alongside Iginla, women's hockey stars Marie-Philip Poulin and Jayna Hefford, and then Prime Minister Stephen Harper in 2011. Iginla met up with the group on a midday Sunday in Athens, Greece, then traveled with the group to Qatar before landing in Afghanistan.

When the group landed in Kandahar, it was already 40-plus degrees Celsius outside at 10:00 in the morning. It didn't stop Iginla from joining in on a ball hockey game at the outdoor rink in the area.

"Jarome played ball hockey for like an hour in that heat. I lasted 10 minutes maybe," Miller said. "We all posed for pictures, but he posed for hundreds of pictures. And people went to the photo shop and got them printed so at night, he spent most nights signing them. But he must have been exhausted. I was.

"He was so authentic and genuine and just kind to everyone. I was awestruck by it. We flew back from Kandahar direct to Athens and then back to Ottawa. I think he slept the entire way. I was worried his head was going to fall off. It was incredible. He was just so amazing to all those soldiers."

Iginla's exploits didn't always generate an insane amount of attention because the Calgary Flames teams he played on in the late 1990s and early 2000s consistently missed the postseason. But many consider him the franchise's best player, even besting Lanny McDonald, who won the Flames' lone Cup in 1989. Iginla's No. 12 jersey hangs in the rafters of the Scotiabank Saddledome. No other Flame has scored more goals (at even strength or on the power play) and points or played more games than he has.

"I always thought of him as an all-around player," play-by-play broadcaster Gary Thorne said. "He was an outstanding skater, scorer. And he did his part at the other end of the ice too. And a real competitor. This was a really great competitor. I'm not sure he [got] as much recognition as he should've received in his playing days. It's almost like he received more recognition after he retired than he did while he was playing. Although he had a good deal of it, I'm not sure all around the National Hockey League his skills were appreciated."

Iginla's rise to national stardom was helped by his 2001–02 season, but it was also propelled by a dream 2004 Stanley Cup Final run with the Flames. The postseason appearance also broke a seven-year playoff drought. Iginla scored 13 goals and 22 points throughout that 2004 postseason, coming up huge in prime moments for the Flames. Calgary upset three division winners before reaching the Stanley Cup Final against the Tampa Bay Lightning.

"The one thing he could do was elevate his game," Conroy said the day Iginla retired in 2018. "We didn't have a bunch of stars. We had [Miikka Kiprusoff] and Jarome. When we had needed him to do something, he did it."

Iginla even fought Lightning captain Vincent Lecavalier in Game 3 of that year's Cup Final.

"I thought I did OK," Lecavalier told The Athletic in a May 2024 interview. "I think Jarome is probably more of a fighter than me. He was a righty and a lefty, and he could really fight. But I feel like I've never backed down from anybody. It doesn't mean that I thought I was going to win. I think Jarome is probably tougher than me, but I thought the fight went pretty well. I thought I had a pretty good start. If we would have fought for five minutes, I think he would have beaten me up pretty good."

"I think it got a little bit more hype because there's not that many fights in the playoffs let alone the Stanley Cup Finals, because there is a risk to it," Iginla said. "But we didn't really think of it in those terms."

Iginla also provided a game-winning assist in Game 5 of the Cup Final while showing off his skill and physical prowess with no helmet. Flames fans know that moment as "the Shift."

"What an absolute athlete," Dan Gallant of hockeyfights.com said. "The epitome of everything that you would've wanted. The best player to never win a Stanley Cup. I don't know how that doesn't come up more often."

Ultimately, the Flames came up short in their seven-game Cup Final series against the Lightning. Martin Gélinas thought he had a game-winning goal in Game 6 of the series. But NHL officials determined the puck never crossed the line. Iginla, like many of his teammates and Flames fans to this day, believed the puck went in. Instead, Martin St. Louis won the game in double overtime and sent the series back to Tampa Bay for Game 7, where the Lightning won on home ice.

"I honestly always thought I was going to get to be part of winning a Stanley Cup," Iginla said. "That's your goal, that's your dream. That's what you work for in the summers when you do extra workouts. You're pushing to get better to help your team in those moments and you imagine you're going to be part of winning. Growing up, I was very blessed. I won a lot. I won provincials. I got to be at the World Juniors with Canada. I got to be at the World Championships. I got to be at the Olympics. I won Memorial Cups. I was very, very blessed. You just always think you're going to find a way to be part of a winning team in the NHL and it just never happened.

"Unfortunately, we didn't get a chance to be that close again. But I feel fortunate to [have gotten] to be a part of it. Because you get to get to learn a lot as a player. And when people talk about teams and when they won, and how special that group was. Well, that was our group. I mean we were one goal, maybe even one overheard camera and three extra minutes [away], and that was our group."

Despite the Stanley Cup missing from his mantle, Iginla was inducted into the Hockey Hall of Fame in 2021. The legend of "Iggy" has been celebrated and commemorated the hockey world over for his achievements at the professional, junior, and minor league levels.

In the present day, Jarome's hockey-playing children are continuing the Iginla legacy. Eldest child Jade is playing NCAA hockey at Brown University. She spent a season at Shattuck-St. Mary's, the famous Minnesota-based boarding school where hockey stars past and present like Crosby; Nathan MacKinnon; Jonathan Toews; Amanda Kessel; the Lamoureux twins, Jocelyne and Monique; and Blayre Turnbull have played. Jade also won a gold medal at the U18 Women's World Championship in 2022 for Team Canada and was named a Second-Team All-Ivy conference player after her sophomore season in 2024.

Middle child Tij was drafted sixth overall by the Utah Hockey Club at the 2024 NHL Draft in Las Vegas. Months before the draft, he won a U18 Men's World Championship for Team Canada. Tij even outscored his father in his draft year, scoring 47 goals and 84 points with the Kelowna Rockets of the WHL compared to Jarome's 33 goals and 71 points. Flames fans hoped their team could draft young Tij during the 2024 NHL Entry Draft, but he was taken three picks before the Flames' turn. Jarome, who works as a special adviser to Flames GM Craig Conroy, spent draft night in the stands with his son instead of on the draft floor.

"I'm happy for Tij and Jarome," Conroy said after the first night of the draft. "You would've loved to have seen him as a Calgary Flame. But I get it. We knew it was a long shot going in. He just played so well this year."

Finally, youngest son Joe was drafted in the first round of the 2023 Western Hockey League bantam draft by the Edmonton Oil Kings. In his first five games with the team, he scored three goals and five points. Joe will be NHL draft eligible in 2026.

For as long as they'll be playing, each child will be faced with mounting expectations in line with their father's Hall of Fame career, which in itself was a journey.

"I guess there's comparisons and that, but I think they really enjoy it," Jarome said. "I think they love the game, they love competing. I think back to when I was going through my draft year. It was a lot of pressure, and I wasn't trying to live up to anybody. I just wanted to get to the first round and go as high as I could."

IF JAROME IGINLA HAD his way with his nickname, "Iggy" would have been buried in the sands of time following his junior hockey days with the Kamloops Blazers. But there's a reason why that short yet catchy nickname has followed the Hall of Famer.

Hockey nicknames are shortened by nature, typically with a "y" at the end. Combine that with the popularity of The Stooges frontman Iggy Pop, "Iggy" stuck as a name before he entered the NHL. But to his friends and family growing up, Jarome is "Joe," the same name as his youngest son.

"Hockey players aren't that smart," junior teammate Shane Doan said. "I was 'Doaner,' he was 'Iggy.' It was just the way it was."

"I didn't like [Iggy] at first," Iginla said. "It made it sound like they were saying 'egg.' 'Eggy'. I don't want to be egg. E-G-G. It sounded to me like that. But you don't have much say in your nickname."

Iginla can't quite remember which teammate came up with it. Teammate and future Calgary Flames head coach Ryan Huska denied it was him, while Nolan Baumgartner says he and Huska might have done it together.

"I don't know what he wanted to be called, and he should've said something," Baumgartner said.

"I just probably assumed that everybody called him 'Iggy,'" Huska said. "When he came to Kamloops, that's what I remember. There wasn't a lot of Joe. It was always Iggy."

Joe was shorthand for Jarome's full name: Jarome Arthur-Leigh Adekunle Tij Junior Elvis Iginla. He was born on Canada Day 1977 in St. Albert, an Edmonton suburb nearly 30 minutes northwest of the provincial capital. Jarome's parents, Elvis and Susan, divorced when he was young.

While Elvis lived in Edmonton with a new family, Jarome grew up with his mother and grandparents, Rick and Frances, in St. Albert. When Jarome's family realized their son was a highly energetic child—he'd even wrestle with his cousins from time to time—they turned to sports as a way for him to channel that energy and to keep him out of trouble. Through school, Iginla also enjoyed playing tennis, basketball, volleyball, and bowling. But his two biggest loves were hockey and baseball.

Iginla played T-ball in his youth before graduating to baseball. He continued playing the sport into his teens, playing pitcher, catcher, and shortstop. As a preteen, he dreamed of playing both baseball and hockey—similar to what Bo Jackson had done as a baseball and football star. But once Jarome realized he was better at hockey, he transitioned to hockey full-time. He began through floor hockey as a five-year-old.

"I was not very good to start," Iginla said. "I got most improved player. I remember that award. As the youngest [in the league], they probably just gave it to me. I don't even know if I scored one goal that year or what."

Iginla had only skated one time before joining a local novice-level team at the age of seven. He visited an outdoor rink down the street from his grandparents' place when he was six years old. It was enough for him to give the sport a try. On the day of tryouts, Iginla had his equipment ready but no jersey or socks to wear over his gear.

"I'm skating around doing the drills," Iginla said. "I tried to do the crossover circles. I got no, no socks and no jersey on, and I can barely skate. Could you imagine how I looked?"

Meanwhile, Jarome's grandfather raced to a local sports store to buy a jersey and socks. He found socks, but he found only one jersey that would fit his grandson. A jersey in Calgary Flames colors, only missing their flaming C on the front.

Iginla, who grew up an Oilers fan, wasn't "thrilled."

"Calgary wasn't too popular up in that area," Iginla said.

The Flames were first founded in 1972 as the Atlanta Flames, one of two new teams entering the National Hockey League alongside the New York Islanders. The NHL was maintaining its footing as the rival World Hockey Association sought rapid expansion of its own. According to Ryan Pike's *On the Clock: Behind the Scenes with the Calgary Flames at the NHL Draft*, the Flames' name is a reference to the city burning during the Civil War in 1864 thanks to U.S. general William Tecumseh Sherman.

Also in 1972, the Alberta Oilers played their first season in the WHA. They became the Edmonton Oilers the following season and joined the NHL in 1979 as part of the NHL-WHA merger with three other teams, the New England Whalers (now the Carolina Hurricanes), the Quebec Nordiques (now the Colorado Avalanche), and the Winnipeg Jets (now the Utah Mammoth, though another iteration of the Winnipeg Jets was created in 2011 and still exists today).

The Flames remained in Atlanta until 1980, when they were sold to Canadian business owner Nelson Skalbania and moved to Calgary. The Battle of Alberta, the rivalry pitting the Flames against the Oilers, started October 22, 1980, with the Oilers besting the Flames that day 5–3. Since then, a genuine hatred has formed between both sides with regular season and postseason meetings.

By the time Iginla turned seven years old, the Oilers won back-to-back Stanley Cups in 1983 and 1984. When he watched hockey with his grandfather, it was the Oilers or whoever they were playing that night. But Iginla was more than familiar with their Smythe Division—named after Conn Smythe—foes in Calgary, Los Angeles, Vancouver, and Winnipeg. But the Oilers were Iginla's team, and he marveled over their superstars of the 1980s.

"As kids, you'd say who's your favorite player? Gretzky. Well, who else?" Iginla said. "Because everybody loved Gretzky. So mine was Messier and Grant Fuhr."

As Iginla pushed further into minor hockey, so grew his dreams of playing in the NHL. But Iginla was commonly asked one question. How could he make it in a white-dominated sport?

"It came up a lot," Iginla said. "It was normal. I didn't take offense to it. It was normal. People would bring it up and say, 'Well, there's not many Black players in the NHL. What are the odds? So, it really helped."

Seeing Black NHL players fueled Iginla's desire to play the sport. But Iginla watched players like Fuhr and Dale Craigwell, who played 98 NHL games—all with San Jose—but made history as the first Black player to represent Canada at the World Juniors. Craigwell scored a goal and added two assists in seven games for Canada, who won gold in 1991. Another goaltender, Claude Vilgrain, became one of the first Black players to ever represent Canada at the Olympics when he played at the 1988 Games in Calgary. That was the same year Tony McKegney scored 40 goals in a season, the first Black player to accomplish that feat.

Iginla was so enamored with Fuhr, he played goalie during his first two years in minor hockey with the Novice-C team. When his mom would drive him to his grandparents' to play street hockey with the other neighborhood kids, he'd put on goalie pads and a glove before taking his place in goal.

All it took was one bad game for Iginla to quit as a goalie.

"We played a team [where] everyone was scoring," Iginla remembered. "I got like five shots. I'm like, this sucks. Never again."

Iginla soon made the switch to forward, taking extra steps to improve his abilities. Iginla was in hockey schools and skating courses, thanks to his grandfather. And if the youngster wasn't shooting pucks in his grandparents' carport, he was at his neighborhood rink.

After dinner with his grandparents, Iginla—in full gear—waddled to nearby Braeside Rink one block away. Iginla stood and patiently waited as local teams used the ice. If it was too cold, he'd stay in the rink's shack. When the ice was free to use, Iginla skated and shot pucks for almost an hour before the rink's lights went off for the night.

"It was really, really fun," Iginla said. "Christmas Day, any day. I'd just go every day. Literally every day."

Just for fun, Jarome's grandfather would pay him a dollar, sometimes two, every time he scored a goal during his minor league days. As Jarome progressed and won provincial titles through the St. Albert minor league hockey system, it's fair to assume that Iginla collected more than enough coin. Despite his success, however, Iginla wasn't guaranteed to be taken in the Western Hockey League Bantam Draft at the beginning of his teenage years.

On draft day, Iginla sat by the phone with family waiting to be selected. As the draft went on, Iginla heard from teammates who also hadn't been called. But they eventually got picked. They'd keep Iginla's spirits up by reassuring him he'd get drafted.

But that call never came. Iginla broke down and cried when he wasn't selected in the Bantam draft.

"It was one of the harder days," Iginla said.

Iginla learned decades later that his lack of size led to teams not picking him in that year's draft, according to a junior scout who wasn't happy his team passed him. But Iginla still found ways to win puck battles in corners and produce consistently despite not being big enough.

Iginla later joined the Kamloops Blazers, who added him to their negotiation list after the draft, according to the Edmonton Sun. Before joining the Blazers, as a 15-year-old, Iginla lit the Alberta Midget Hockey League ablaze with a 34-goal, 87-point season on the St. Albert Raiders U18 AAA team. His point totals led the entire league that year.

Iginla joined the Blazers in time for the 1993–94 season, where the "Iggy" nickname took hold. But there were some growing pains for the young forward. He only played 48 games that season and scored just six goals and 29 points as a 16-year-old. He remembers playing a game that year where he scored two points but was promptly benched the next game by his head coach, Don Hay. It was just part of Hay's development strategy according to Iginla, with older players gaining more time in the regular season.

The 1993–94 Blazers, meanwhile were led by older, future NHL mainstays in Baumgartner, Darcy Tucker, Hnat Domenichelli, and Tyson Nash. Tucker was one of three 100-point getters on the team alongside Rod Stevens and Jarrett Deuling. The team won a WHL championship and the Memorial Cup in the same season for the second time in three years.

Despite the inexperience, Iginla surprised older teammates with his work ethic.

"I think he learned in a hurry how to make sure he's competitive each and every night, every practice that he was on the ice," Huska said. "But a lot of that came natural to him. So, I was more impressed with how he showed up as a young guy as mature as he was."

It wasn't all hard work and no fun for Jarome, however. He bonded with and endeared himself to his teammates. Iginla built a friendship with fellow future NHLer Shane Doan, with both men competing over activities like golfing, shooting pucks, and building the better snowman.

"It's always fun to compete against Jarome," Doan said. "It's not going to be just for fun, it's going to be for real and that's what makes it the best."

"Whatever the competition was, it was, 'I could do that better than you,'" Huska said. "It was everything. The two of them wrestling, carrying bags, sprinting down a hall. Whatever the case was, they would always go at each other. It made for some entertaining times for us.

"There's a reason why they were so good at that young age and why they became such good players as they aged."

Iginla and Doan both improved on their 1993–94 seasons. Iginla scored 33 goals and 71 points in 72 games during the 1994–95 WHL campaign. Doan scored 37 goals and 94 points in that span, getting the better of his friend statistically. For the second consecutive year, both men were WHL and Memorial Cup champions.

NHL teams took notice of both prospects during their WHL playoff and Memorial Cup runs. That included the Dallas Stars' scouting staff, headed by director of scouting Craig Button. As Button recalls, they continued scouting prospects as the league endured the 1994–95 lockout so they wouldn't fall too far behind. They studied both Doan and Iginla. As good as Doan was, and turned out to be, there was something about Iginla that caught the Stars' eye.

"Because there's so many things he did well in the game and yet there was very little flash in his game," Button said. "He wasn't somebody that raced up and down the ice, he wasn't somebody that dazzled you with blinding speed. He played a straight-line game, he was powerful. He was smart, he could score, he could make plays. So, we really looked at him as just a really well-rounded player."

Two months after Iginla and Doan won their second Memorial Cups as Blazers, they both became first-round picks in that year's NHL Entry Draft. Doan went to the Winnipeg Jets at seventh overall. Doan played 21 seasons with the Jets/Phoenix-Arizona Coyotes franchise with over 1500 games to his name and 972 points.

Four picks later, Iginla fell to Button and the Stars. But as excited as the Stars might have been to draft Iginla, he never played a game for the franchise.

Entering the 1995–96 season, Calgary Flames star Joe Nieuwendyk was in a contract holdout seeking a new deal. Then-Flames GM Al Coates sought trade partners to offload the disgruntled star in exchange for a top prospect. The New York Rangers, Dallas Stars, and St. Louis Blues were three primary teams in the running for

Nieuwendyk's services, according to a 2019 The Athletic story by Eric Duhatschek about the trade.

"It had to be someone that, in our estimation, would be an A prospect for the National Hockey League," Coates told Duhatschek. "I remember saying this repeatedly: If we trade Joe Nieuwendyk, we want to be watching his replacement play at some level in the National Hockey League for the next 10 or 12 years."

Button watched Iginla play a game against the Tri-City Americans during the 1995–96 WHL season, his final junior year with fellow front office staffer Les Jackson. Impressed by Iginla's play, both men spoke postgame about his tantalizing abilities and felt he was NHL ready.

The Stars were far from a powerhouse in 1995–96. A so-so start followed a dreadful December—they only won two games that entire month—put them on course to miss the playoffs. They were eager to acquire another center to bolster their depth led by Mike Modano. But it was going to cost them a quality young prospect from their stable. The Stars resisted as much as they could, but Coates pushed the team repeatedly to acquire Iginla.

Once the dust settled, an agreement was made. The Calgary Flames acquired Iginla and forward Corey Millen in exchange for Nieuwendyk on December 20, 1995, just before the NHL's annual roster freeze.

"We knew that either way we went there was going to be pain and disappointment involved," Button said. "Whether it was the pain and disappointment of not finding that complimentary center and an excellent player in Joe Nieuwendyk. Or the pain and disappointment of losing a really good young player in Jarome Iginla. Because we had so many young players, we felt that the move at that time was to add Joe Nieuwendyk.

"A lot of people think, 'Oh yeah, well, you won a Stanley Cup [in 1999].' We made that trade in December of 1995. We were the fifth-worst team in the National Hockey League that year. We weren't one player away from competing for a Stanley Cup. We were not at that stage. But we knew in the Western Conference, you had Yzerman and Fedorov, you had Sakic and Forsberg. We knew we had a superstar in Modano and there was no way that we were going to be able to compete unless we found a really good center to be the 1–2 punch and that's what Joe provided."

Iginla was at Team Canada's World Junior team camp ahead of the 1996 World Junior Championship in Massachusetts when the trade was completed. A phone call at those camps usually brings bad news. Players chosen for that year's roster would normally get a knock on their room door and a visit from their coaches. A phone call meant they were cut. Fortunately for Iginla, he had already made the team, so his nerves didn't spike when the call came to his hotel room that December morning.

Team Canada head coach Marcel Comeau told Iginla the news over the phone that he had been traded. Iginla's first thought was that he'd be changing Western Hockey League teams and leaving the defending WHL and Memorial Cup Kamloops Blazers behind. It would mean finding a new billet, moving to a new team and city.

Instead, Iginla would only swap NHL jerseys—though he had never played for Dallas—for a familiar outfit in Calgary. If he wasn't watching his beloved Oilers on television, the Flames were likely on. Even Jarome's father, Elvis, was a fan.

It turns out that fateful day where Jarome's grandfather bought him a Flames jersey ahead of minor hockey tryouts would prove to be cosmic foreshadowing.

"I was excited after talking to Al Coates [to know] that they wanted me and that I could be part of a trade for such a good player," Iginla said. "After you think about it, you're going to get a good opportunity. Looking back, I probably got to play younger than I would've. I don't think I would've gotten the chance to play at 18 and play in the playoffs. They were a pretty stacked team. Who knows how long I'd play in the minors or whatever. All things worked out."

The Flames can certainly say the same. While Nieuwendyk spent seven seasons in Dallas and even won a Cup and playoff MVP honors in 1999, Iginla was a mainstay and emerged as a franchise player and captain through a 16-year tenure in Calgary, accumulating a handful of individual awards and achieving international success along the way. That includes his performance on an iconic day in both Canadian sports and Black hockey history.

WHAT WOULD YOU DO if you got a phone call from Wayne Gretzky? And how would you feel if you missed that phone call?

Gretzky was part of Hockey Canada's executive team for the men's program ahead of the 2002 Olympic Games in Salt Lake City. Canada was seeking its first gold medal win in 50 years. Gretzky himself suffered heartbreak at the Games when he was infamously not used in a shootout for Canada during the 1998 Olympic Games in Nagano and Canada fell to the Czech Republic in that year's semi-finals. Canada failed to medal in 1998, losing to Finland in the bronze medal game.

Hockey Canada named Gretzky to its executive team in November 2000 as executive director. Long-time teammate Kevin Lowe was named assistant director as well. Pat Quinn would lead the Canadians behind the bench.

Team Canada assembled a camp of more than 30 players in September 2001, months before the Games, in Calgary. Iginla wasn't originally invited. That changed when Simon Gagné suffered a shoulder injury, taking him out of a pair of scrimmages at camp. So, Team Canada sought Iginla to replace him, and Gretzky decided to give him a phone call.

Gretzky couldn't get a hold of him.

But Iginla's future wife, Kara, picked up the phone. Jarome was at a dinner with friends in Edmonton.

When Jarome was eventually notified that one of his favorite players of all time invited him to the Olympic camp, he was skeptical. Could this have been a prank from a former teammate? Iginla pictured himself frantically grabbing his equipment at home and driving three hours south to Calgary to practice, only to be told he wasn't needed.

Sure enough, Iginla got in touch with Lowe and was invited to the September camp. He made the drive to Father David Bauer Olympic Arena, approximately 10 minutes northwest from downtown Calgary.

"I was the last invite," Iginla said. "I still wonder if I was just the closest call for a fill in."

Once Iginla put on his gear and stepped onto the ice, his eyes lit up at the star power that surrounded him.

"For me to be on the ice with all the players there," Iginla said. "[Eric] Lindros was there. [Steve] Yzerman's there and shooting on Patrick Roy, who was there at that camp. I know he didn't play [in 2002] but he was there. Lindros was just flying around. All those people you look up that I've watched since I was in bantam. I'm playing against them but now I'm on the same ice and on the same team. It was a really good confidence boost going into that season."

Iginla had played five full NHL seasons when he got the call-up for September camp. His star was rising. He won a World Junior Championship with Canada in January 1996. Three months later, he suited up for the Flames for the first time in a playoff series against Chicago during the 1996 Western Conference quarterfinals. He scored his first assist by keeping the puck in the offensive zone, leading to a Theoren Fleury goal in Game 3 of the series. In Game 4, he opened the scoring with a shot from the slot after taking a pass from German Titov in front of the Flames faithful. Calgary lost the series in four, but there was reason to be hopeful with their young prospect.

In 1997, his first full season, Iginla scored 21 goals and 50 points in 82 games with the Flames. He then played for Canada at the World

Hockey Championship, where he won gold. Entering the 2001–02 season, he was coming off his best statistical year when he set career-highs in goals (31) and points (71) in 77 games. Flames fans who might have been skeptical about the trade were changing their tune, marveling over Iginla's growing potential. He also proved to be an emerging bright spot in an otherwise dark, empty time for Flames fans who yearned for postseason action.

The beginning of the 2001–02 season proved to be the start of a breakout campaign for Iginla. From mid-October of that year through to late November, Iginla amassed 18 goals and 31 points in a 15-game points streak. It didn't take long for him to catch Gretzky's eye.

"Jarome Iginla right now might be the best forward in the NHL," Gretzky said in an October 2001 CBC story.

Once the NHL reached its Olympic break in mid-February 2002, Iginla had already surpassed his single season best in goals with 34 and had 59 points.

"This guy was just scoring at will," said Ryan Pinder, the co-host of the FlamesNation podcast *Barn Burner*. "It was him, Dean McAmmond, and Craig Conroy. It was just like, get the puck to Iggy and let him shoot. He was in one of those zones."

"I think, for Jarome, it was a time of discovery," Button said. "And he was discovering just how dominant and what a superstar he was becoming."

When Gretzky announced who would fill out the roster in February 2002, beyond their first eight selections known to the public—Colorado's Joe Sakic and Rob Blake, Detroit's Steve Yzerman, St. Louis' Chris Pronger, San Jose's Owen Nolan, New Jersey's Scott Niedermayer, Anaheim's Paul Kariya, and Pittsburgh's Mario Lemieux—Iginla was the first name called. Gagné, who was injured in September, was also added to the 2002 team.

"When it happened, you know, people in Calgary were super excited about it," said Pat Steinberg, a Calgary-based sports radio host for Sportsnet. "I don't think anybody at that time expected a Flames player, being [from] this team that had missed the playoffs. It was like almost every year it was a foregone conclusion that they weren't going to make the playoffs. They'd finish with 75 or 80 points and be eliminated in March.

"And so, all of a sudden this guy gets added to the Olympic team, and this is something to be excited about. Not only are Flames fans ready to cheer for Canada and watch this team play in the right time zone and see if they can avenge what happened in 1998. But there's also a Flames player on the team."

When Iginla arrived at the E Center in Salt Lake City he remained starstruck. Iginla was astonished at the players' names that flashed on the back of their jerseys as they hung from their lockers. Lemieux. Sakic. MacInnis. Brodeur. These were players he admired watching from afar before his own career began. Now, he could say they were his teammates and linemates. Iginla began the 2002 Games alongside Brendan Shanahan and Steve Yzerman.

Despite the star power, Canada fell at the first hurdle in their road to glory. After Blake scored to give Canada a 1–0 lead, they allowed five unanswered goals against Sweden in a 5–2 loss.

It meant the Canadians would have to lean on their veteran leadership much sooner and much earlier than anticipated. Iginla felt down after the tournament-opening loss to the Swedes but was surprised to see his older teammates already eager to move on to their next game.

"You watch guys like Lemieux and Sakic, and it was no big deal," Iginla remembered.

A team meeting followed, and lines were juggled. Iginla was soon flipped to a line with Simon Gagné and Joe Sakic. Sakic was originally with Lemieux and Paul Kariya, and Iginla was originally nervous about the Avalanche captain having to go from two established veterans to playing alongside two younger players.

"Right after the meeting he comes over and he says, 'Oh, I'm excited to play with you two young bucks,'" Iginla said. "'You guys are going to have lots of energy. We're going to be a great line.' It was so helpful that he did that. It was really, really good leadership. I can't speak for Simon but for myself, you're wondering if you even fully belong on this team. How is he going to feel? Now he's playing with us, he was playing with Mario Lemieux before."

Sakic responded with a goal in Canada's next game, assisted by Gagné, in Canada's 3–2 win over Germany. The two combined for another goal in a 2–1 Olympic quarterfinal win over Finland. Iginla would have to wait a little longer before recording his first point of the tournament, a 7–1 blowout win over Belarus in the semi-finals. He scored Canada's seventh and final goal with an assist from Brendan Shanahan. Iginla saved his best performance of the tournament in the gold medal game, a matchup against rival and host United States.

A win for Canada would give the men's team its first gold medal in ice hockey since 1952—when the Edmonton Mercurys, a senior-level hockey team—won at that year's Olympics in Oslo, Norway.

Fifty years to the day of the Mercurys' win, Canada and the United States battled. A "back-and-forth" contest pitting the two best teams standing featuring a handful of the world's best players.

"You felt like Canada was watching at home," Iginla said. Every play was big. You're so nervous. You get on the ice, you go as hard as you can, and it was really cool."

Tony Amonte sent the crowd to its feet with a game-opening goal on an odd-man rush, wristing the puck past Canada goaltender Martin Brodeur. But nearly six minutes later, Chris Pronger sent a pass through Mario Lemieux's legs before Paul Kariya shot the puck past American goaltender Mike Richter.

Almost four minutes later, Iginla gave the Canadians their first lead of the game. Sakic fed Iginla with a pass from the faceoff circle.

Camped in front of the goal, Iginla swiped at the puck and beat Richter with less than 90 seconds to play in the first period.

Both teams traded chances and missed opportunities into the second period as the hockey world held its collective breath. The Americans equalized in the second period thanks to a goal from Brian Rafalski. But almost three minutes later, Sakic played hero again and beat Richter to give Canada a 3–2 lead.

The Canadians spent much of the third period clinging to their one-goal advantage. But it was Iginla who gave Canada the breathing room it needed. Sakic rushed up ice and entered the offensive zone. As two defenders closed in on him, he passed the puck back to Yzerman. The Red Wings captain sidestepped around a defender before finding a wide-open, streaking Iginla, who immediately shot the puck toward goal. Richter tried to catch it with his glove but couldn't hold it cleanly.

"It went up in the air and it barely rolled over the line against Richter," Iginla said.

When the puck crossed the line, Canadian fans celebrated in the stands and across the world. Members of Canada's executive team, including Gretzky, hugged one another. Gretzky pumped his fists in celebration as he looked down onto the ice.

Canada needed one more goal, from Sakic, to put the game out of reach for the Americans and secured a 5–2 gold-medal-winning victory.

The Canadians celebrated as the final buzzer sounded, pouring onto the ice mobbing Brodeur. Canada earned its first men's hockey gold medal in 50 years. Canadian men's hockey history was achieved. But a unique piece of history didn't get the same amount of attention.

In victory, Iginla became the first Black male athlete to win a Winter Olympics gold medal. Following in the footsteps of Darren Lowe and Claude Vilgrain, who played in the Olympics before him, Iginla succeeded.

"I thought it was really cool," Iginla said. "It's one of those ones that, with my kids and stuff, it's kind of neat to mention it now and then again. It's pretty special. It is hard to believe but I guess it's not, too. It's definitely very special."

If Iginla had to choose between his 2002 gold medal and his 2010 gold medal, which one would he pick? He wavers back and forth. Sometimes, it's the 2010 gold medal, where he played a role in an iconic moment with Sidney Crosby while providing leadership along the way. Other days, it's the 2002 gold medal, when he learned from veterans like Lemieux and Sakic as a younger player while helping Canada win a gold medal for the first time in 50 years.

But more importantly for Iginla, it's just a blessing to have experienced Olympic glory at all—let alone twice.

"You think back to all the things that fall into place from starting hockey to my grandparents' support and getting to be a part of it. [Hockey's] not just a sport for me. It's been my life and it's been an awesome thing to be a part of."

4

Grant Fuhr

Many Black hockey fans or players have a Black NHL player they first saw, or idolized, in their early days enjoying the sport. Jarome Iginla, Wayne Simmonds, Georges Laraque, and P.K. Subban are prominent examples. So are newer players like Quinton Byfield, K'Andre Miller, and Anthony Duclair.

But for an entire generation, Grant Fuhr was that player. Unlike some of his contemporaries like Mike Marson or Val James, who either played sparingly or weren't cast in prominent roles on their teams, Fuhr was the first Black hockey player to be seen as a genuine superstar.

"He was a great goalie, and he was very fun to watch," former goaltender Kevin Weekes said. "He was electric. He looked different in the net. Plus, he was a southpaw. Plus, his gear always looked sweet."

"It's nice that the fans see you that way," Fuhr said about being recognized as hockey's first Black superstar. "Obviously, when you're playing, you're not really worried about it. You're just worried about trying to be successful. And then you sit back and you look at it after you're done. I think it has more prevalence after you're done because when you're playing you don't really worry about it.

"When people see you that way, obviously, you've done something right. And it's always an honor."

Fuhr nearly convinced Iginla to be a goaltender full-time thanks to his performances with the Edmonton Oilers in the 1980s. Iginla put on pads and gloves, emulating an early hockey hero in street hockey and minor hockey.

"I loved watching him," Iginla said. "It was very important for me to follow him and to see him be an All-Star. You go into McDonald's and he's up on the wall. Do you remember that save when he did the splits in the air? I remember in McDonald's that'd be up there."

Fred Brathwaite, a former journeyman NHL goaltender, was briefly Fuhr's teammate as a member of the Calgary Flames during the 1999–2000 season. Both men would soon become friends. When Fuhr met Brathwaite's parents in Ottawa, Brathwaite's mother mentioned that her son had photos of Fuhr on his bedroom wall as a child.

"I'm like 'Mom, I'm friends with this guy,'" Brathwaite said. "He doesn't have to know that I have stuff on my wall."

When TV personality Cabral "Cabbie" Richards collected hockey stickers, the covers of those sticker books were littered with Edmonton Oilers, including Fuhr. When Richards played street hockey and was told by other children that he couldn't be players like Pavel Bure or Jaromír Jágr, he played goalie to channel Fuhr. Even as Richards got older and refused to be told that he couldn't play like other white players such as Steve Yzerman, Richards still held Fuhr in high regard.

"Seeing someone that looked like me was hella important," Richards said. "Grant Fuhr was a premier goaltender. There's someone cool. There's someone who's really good. So, I just had a lot of pride."

Fuhr wasn't just a simple backstop who helped the Edmonton Oilers win multiple Stanley Cups. His athleticism led to incredible saves, which proved useful on those offensive-minded Oilers teams.

"Grant Fuhr, really, he existed on an island," Edmonton journalist Mark Spector said. "That team was all about going north until the games really mattered. They weren't that much worried about what was going on their own end, and that was kind of left up to Fuhrsie.

"The beauty of that team was, you go to the rink on a Tuesday night against the Minnesota North Stars and you got to see this historically elite offensive team that was on its way to scoring 400 goals in a season. But at the same time, you got to see Grant Fuhr left on his own on so many occasions that he was forced to be the most acrobatic goalie in the game."

Fuhr's first Stanley Cup win in 1984 made him the first Black player to win the sport's ultimate trophy. When you combine that with his various mask styles throughout the 1980s—he was among the first NHL goaltenders to wear the fiberglass face masks originally designed by Dave Dryden and Greg Harrison according to the Canadian Encyclopedia—Fuhr became one of the most influential NHLers of his time.

"He's a guy that won Cups and made big saves when needed," Brathwaite said. "I mean, there was games where it was probably 5–5 and he would even up having a 2-on-0 at the end and he'd make that big save. And then they would come back and win. So, he was always, for me, always able to win those big games in his prime."

If you're trying to pick the best save of Fuhr's career, you would have an easier time finding a needle in a haystack. There is a long list of larceny from the Spruce Grove, Alberta native. Fuhr made two key saves on penalty shots in the 1985 Stanley Cup Final against the Philadelphia Flyers en route to a Stanley Cup win. You could always take your pick there. But what about his Game 1 Stanley Cup Final debut performance against the New York Islanders? In 1993, as a member of the Buffalo Sabres, Fuhr made an incredible save against the Winnipeg Jets. Fuhr's glove stole a puck out of the air as an opposing player had an open cage.

"He's completely out of position and out of nowhere, he darts out and saves it with his glove," broadcaster and columnist Shane Malloy said. "How do you do that? I tried to emulate that kind of stuff as a kid in road hockey. I thought Grant Fuhr was the greatest."

The Hockey Hall of Fame wasted no time inducting Fuhr during his first year of eligibility in 2003, making him the first Black hockey player to enter the Hall of Fame. A 19-year-career packed with five Stanley Cup wins, a Vezina Trophy, a William M. Jennings Trophy, two All-Star Team appearances, and two Canada Cups to his name. Fuhr is also the Oilers all-time leader in wins by a goalie. The goaltender was inducted in the Hall of Fame alongside longtime Buffalo Sabre Pat LaFontaine, longtime Detroit Red Wings owner Mike Ilitch, and legendary coach Brian Kilrea.

When Fuhr addressed those in attendance during his speech, he made sure to thank Willie O'Ree, a man he'd celebrate when it was his turn to make it to the Hall of Fame 15 years later.

"It's an extra special honor to be the first man of color in the Hockey Hall of Fame," Fuhr said. "It just shows that hockey is such a diverse sport that anybody can be successful in it. And I'm proud of that, and I thank Willie for that."

FUHR'S RISE TO PROMINENCE began in Spruce Grove, Alberta, a small community that has risen in population since Fuhr was born in the 1960s. Fuhr was born to a Black parent and an Indigenous parent. But 18 days after being born, according to the book *Grant Fuhr: The Story of a Hockey Legend*, Fuhr was adopted by two white parents named Bob and Betty Fuhr, who were initially concerned about adopting a mixed-race baby. But those fears quickly dissipated when they held Grant in their arms for the first time.

It was through his upbringing with the Fuhr family that Grant learned to love hockey. If he wasn't watching *Hockey Night in Canada* at home, he was playing on an outdoor rink on the grounds of Spruce

Grove Composite High School with other children in cold Alberta winters until his feet froze. Even if it meant missing the odd class or two.

"You're sort of missing class, but at the same time, you're sort of at school," Fuhr said.

"We had a really supportive vice principal where he knew where to find us. So if we got marked absent, he would walk over to the rink and there'd be 10 or 12 of us skating. I was pretty fortunate that way."

As other children weren't interested in playing in net, Grant quickly took to the position. It helped that equipment looked cool and that it meant more playing time. Fuhr would fill in for older age groups who needed a goalie in a pinch and even, sometimes, his dad's teams.

"I could play with two or three different age groups, and I get to play seven days a week," Fuhr said.

From the age of seven, Fuhr knew he wanted to be in the NHL. He grew up idolizing goaltending legends like Glenn Hall, Tony Esposito, Roger Crozier, and Maple Leafs legends Johnny Bower and Terry Sawchuk. Fuhr was a fan of the Maple Leafs in his early days. With his heart set on making the league, he told his parents, "I am going to be a goaltender in the NHL," according to *Sports Illustrated*.

"He said that more than once, too," Betty Fuhr told *Sports Illustrated* in a January 1988 interview. "Grant had a natural ability from a tender age. He was very well coordinated. He went to grade one, and the teachers were astounded at his coordination. Playing NHL hockey was a dream Grant had very early on. In concentrating on it so much, he never really liked school."

But hockey wasn't Fuhr's sole sport. Fuhr spent part of his teenage years playing catcher for a local baseball team in nearby St. Albert, almost 30 minutes northeast of Fuhr's hometown. One of the coaches on Fuhr's team just happened to be Rick Schuchard, Jarome Iginla's grandfather. The young Iginla even made an appearance as a bat boy on Fuhr's team.

As Fuhr continued to play both hockey and baseball, he had to make a choice. Fuhr's ambitions and athletic ability helped him get on the radar of local hockey scouts and by 15, he had already participated in his first WHL camp with the Victoria Cougars. The Pittsburgh Pirates of Major League Baseball drafted Fuhr as a 16-year-old in 1979. But because "hockey was in," as was said in the 1988 *Sports Illustrated* interview, Fuhr opted for hockey instead. The same year he spurned the Pirates' organization, he joined the Cougars for their 1979–80 campaign—his first full-time junior hockey season. The Cougars were a relatively new franchise, only joining the league in 1971 when the WHL was known as the Western Canada Hockey League.

In Fuhr's two seasons with the Cougars, he was a first-team WHL All-Star both years. He won 30 games in 43 games played with Victoria in his rookie season, winning WHL Rookie of the Year and helping his team to a WHL final appearance where they lost to the Regina Pats. Only three goalies, according to QuantHockey.com, won more games than Fuhr that season. It is also around the time when Fuhr's nickname "Coco" came to be, given to him by older teammates.

Fuhr improved his win total to 48 in 59 appearances in his second and final WHL season, leading all Canadian Hockey League goaltenders in victories. The young goaltender helped the Cougars to a President's Cup win after rallying from a 3–1 series deficit against the Calgary Wranglers and also earned a Memorial Cup tournament berth in Windsor, Ontario, that season. Fuhr's 48–9–1 record with a 2.78 goals-against average and a .908 save percentage also earned him the Del Wilson Trophy for WHL Goaltender of the year.

At the 1981 Memorial Cup, the Cougars played in a round-robin style tournament against the Ontario Hockey League champion

Kitchener Rangers, led by 16-year-old Brian Bellows, winger Jeff Larmer, and a future teammate of Fuhr's in St. Louis, defenseman Al MacInnis. The Quebec Major Junior Hockey League was represented by the Cornwall Royals, led by future No. 1 overall draft choice Dale Hawerchuk and future NHL coaches Marc Crawford and Scott Arniel. The Cougars had Fuhr and three 100-point scorers in Barry Pederson, Rich Chernomaz, and Torrie Robertson.

Victoria won its first game of the tournament, defeating the Rangers 7–4. It was the Rangers' second loss of the Memorial Cup, having already lost to Cornwall in their first game. Unfortunately for the Cougars, that win proved to be their high point at the tournament. The next night, Victoria lost its first game of the Memorial Cup against the Royals. Two nights later, Kitchener exacted revenge with a 4–2 win. On the Cougars' final night at the Memorial Cup, they allowed eight goals in an 8–4 loss against Cornwall.

NHL scouts traveled to Windsor to see the incoming class of talent for the upcoming draft. They included Edmonton Oilers head scout Barry Fraser, who was bullish on Grant Fuhr as a goaltending prospect. He believed Fuhr would be destined for the Hall of Fame "some day." Oilers head coach and general manager, Glen Sather, felt much differently about Fuhr's future prospects.

"I remember going to see Fuhr play once and he was dreadful," Sather told the *Edmonton Journal*'s Jim Matheson in 2022. "I saw him a second time and same thing. I said to Barry, 'Are you sure?' Barry said he'd seen Grant play 25 or 30 times, and yeah, he was sure."

During the Cougars' 8–4 loss to Cornwall, Fraser was in attendance alongside Oilers defenseman Paul Coffey, who was also less than impressed with the young goaltender.

"I remember saying to Barry, 'I don't block shots,'" Coffey said in the 2018 Grant Fuhr documentary *Making Coco*. "If you're expecting more blocked shots, I'm not going to be doing it. We need a better goalie."

Despite a sour end to the Memorial Cup, Fuhr entered the 1981 NHL Draft as a highly touted prospect, and Fraser wouldn't budge off his opinion of the young goaltender. That year's class featured numerous Hall of Fame talents including Hawerchuk, Ron Francis, Al MacInnis, Mike Vernon and Chris Chelios.

When it was the Edmonton Oilers' turn to draft at eighth overall, landing there wasn't a possibility in Fuhr's mind. The Oilers had just finished their second-ever NHL season after leaving the World Hockey Association in 1979. Fuhr grew up attending Oilers games at the Northlands Coliseum when the team was a WHA mainstay. In 1980–81, the Oilers won their first-ever playoff round—a preliminary round sweep of the Montreal Canadiens where Andy Moog was near perfect. He only allowed six goals all series and posted a .938 save percentage. Edmonton had also used five different goaltenders that season, including Moog, who was drafted by the Oilers in 1980.

"So, the last place I thought I was going was Edmonton," Fuhr said.

But at eighth overall, Sather made the decision—at Fraser's urging—to select Fuhr. It wasn't expected, but Fuhr got his chance to represent his hometown team in front of his loved ones. After Fuhr put on his jersey, beaming with pride over the selection, a young Oilers teammate approached him to introduce himself. That man would come to appreciate his netminder and recognize him as the best goaltender he had ever played with.

"One of the first people I met was Wayne [Gretzky]," Fuhr said. "So it doesn't get a whole lot more special than that."

THE OILERS WERE ONE of 12 founding teams of the World Hockey Association when it got off the ground in 1971. They began as the Alberta Oilers but only for a season, before changing their name to the Edmonton Oilers. The Oilers were a nickname for the local junior team, the Edmonton Oil Kings. But when the WHA placed a franchise in Alberta, the nickname stuck for the new team.

The Oilers were a playoff team for the majority of their WHA tenure, culminating in a 1979 Avco Cup Final appearance against the Winnipeg Jets. The Oilers fell in six games to the Jets in their final year in the WHA before joining the NHL for the 1979–80 season.

Wayne Gretzky was an 18-year-old rookie for the Oilers during the 1978–79 season. He was originally property of the Indianapolis Racers, having signed a seven-year, $1.75 million contract as a 17-year-old. His very first pro goal was against his future team, the Oilers. But Gretzky's tenure as a Racer wouldn't last very long; he played just eight games for the franchise. Nelson Skalbania, then the owner of the Racers, needed to make up for financial losses of $1 million—according to the *Edmonton Journal*—and was close to sending Gretzky either to Winnipeg or Edmonton.

Gretzky, alongside teammates Eddie Mio and Peter Driscoll, soon boarded a plane with no knowledge of where their future home would be. All three knew they'd be departing Edmonton but were mostly left in the dark. It turns out then Oilers owner Peter Pocklington acquired Gretzky's contract alongside Driscoll and Mio for $825,000.

"We landed in Minnesota before we officially got the word where we were going," Gretzky told Daniel Nugent-Bowman of The Athletic in a 2018 interview. "It was an interesting flight."

Gretzky then played 72 games with the Oilers in 1978–79, scoring 43 goals and 104 points to cap off an electric season where he won rookie of the year honors. He finished third in league scoring behind Réal Cloutier and Robbie Ftorek before losing the AVCO Cup final to Winnipeg that year.

When the Oilers entered the NHL in 1979, much of their young core was still in development. Gretzky was well ahead as an 18-year-old. Other players like 20-year-old Kevin Lowe and 18-year-old Mark Messier hadn't yet turned into the All-Star-caliber players Oilers fans would come to love in the 1980s. But there was promise. The Oilers then added youngsters Paul Coffey, Jari Kurri, and Glenn Anderson in time for the 1980–81 campaign.

Oilers owner Peter Pocklington was quite confident in his core, so much so that he told the media that his team would win a Stanley Cup "within five years" of them entering the league.

"We were all young," Fuhr said. "So we were all kind of growing into the game. Most everyone was within a couple of years. I think I was the baby of the group by a couple of years, but we all got to grow up together pretty much. And Glen Sather wanted it more like a family than a team as well. He made a point of stressing to us that you're going to spend more time with the guys than you will with your family. That's just the way hockey is."

Through the team's first two seasons, the Oilers established themselves as a playoff team. They lost in the preliminary round in 1980 against the Philadelphia Flyers. During the 1981 postseason, the Oilers stunned the Canadiens before losing to the New York Islanders in the quarterfinals. The Oilers were just getting started on the makings of their dynasty when they held training camp in 1981. It wasn't about to be derailed by having a rookie goaltender in Grant Fuhr, whom some expressed some doubts about prior to him being drafted. But Fuhr made an impression on his Oilers teammates in camp and earned a spot in a three-man goalie rotation alongside Ron Low and Andy Moog as a 19-year-old.

"When you don't have goalie coaches, your partner is the guy you get to bounce things off of. Pick his brain," Fuhr said. "So, I was pretty fortunate to have really good partners. And the fact that we battled to have ice time, I think made all of us better."

It was Moog who opened the season for the Oilers, starting his team's first two games before Low got the start in the Oilers' third game of the season. Fuhr made his first career NHL start on October 14, 1981, against the Winnipeg Jets. He allowed three goals on 36 shots in a 4–2 loss, dropping the Oilers' record to 2–2-0 on the season. But history was made at the Northlands Coliseum in Edmonton that night: It was the first time a Black goaltender played between the pipes in an NHL game.

After the game, Fuhr and his family went to Coliseum Steak & Pizza for dinner to celebrate, according to his autobiography. As he sat in the restaurant thinking of the game, he was "disappointed" to not get the win. But he couldn't help but think of the accomplishment of playing an NHL game, a dream he voiced to his parents when he was seven years old and spent the next 12 years of his life working toward it.

"I actually don't remember the goals they scored that night," Fuhr said in his autobiography. "That's the great thing about being a goalie—you don't have to remember. You're like a relief pitcher in baseball or a cornerback in football: you can only think about the next play. All I knew was I'd played in an NHL game."

Fuhr wouldn't see another loss on his record until January 16, 1982. He would only lose five games that year, ending the regular season with a 28–5–14 record to go along with a 3.31 goals-against average and an .898 save percentage. The goals-against average and save percentages might not look impressive compared to present day standards, but Fuhr battled in an era with more scoring and offense. And perhaps no team represented that era more than the high-flying Oilers.

"The only number that mattered back then for goalies was wins," journalist Mark Spector said. "We didn't even have save percentage back then, right? We had goals against average. That was it."

In between his first career game and that January loss, Fuhr went unbeaten for 23 consecutive games. He registered 15 wins and eight ties in that span of games with a .902 save percentage. To date, it is the longest unbeaten streak by a first-year goaltender in league history. Fuhr would only return to the losing column in a 7–1 January loss against the Toronto Maple Leafs, a loss in which Fuhr allowed all seven goals. When interviewed after the game, Fuhr shrugged off his bad performance.

"I had to lose sometime," Fuhr said after the game, per the *Edmonton Journal.* "It's nothing serious. I was sloppy in the game."

The Oilers entered the 1982 postseason as Smythe Division champions. Gretzky led the way with 92 goals—the most anyone has ever scored in an NHL season—and 212 points. Glenn Anderson was the next highest point-getter for the Oilers with 105. Mark Messier was a 50-goal scorer for the first—and only—time in his career. Paul Coffey exploded with a 29-goal, 89-point season. Good enough to finish third among Oilers in points, as a defenseman. As for Fuhr, his season was good enough to be nominated for both the Calder and Vezina Trophies.

The Edmonton Oilers had every reason to be considered a contending team in 1982. But most young teams experience a major hurdle en route to greatness. That year, the Oilers were stunned in the Smythe Division semifinal series against the Los Angeles Kings, which included a legendary Kings comeback in Game 3 of the series dubbed as the "Miracle on Manchester." The Oilers raced to a 5–0 lead and looked well on their way to winning it before the Kings responded with six unanswered goals, including an overtime winner from Daryl Evans.

"It was a 'last shot wins' game," Fuhr said in his autobiography. "There weren't many saves made. It was one of those games where the harder you chased it the farther away it got from you."

The Oilers tied the series with a Game 4 win, forcing a Game 5 back at the Northlands Coliseum. Both teams flew to Edmonton together on the same chartered flight, with the Oilers sitting at the back of the Kings' plane. In Game 5, Edmonton found itself in trouble minutes into that series-deciding game. Los Angeles struck first thanks to a goal from Charlie Simmer after a failed clearing attempt by Glenn Anderson led to a Dave Lewis shot from the point. Fuhr couldn't corral the rebound cleanly, and Simmer was first to the puck. He then went to his backhand and lifted the puck over a sprawling Fuhr and into the net. Simmer scored a second goal nearly three minutes later, off another Fuhr rebound.

The Oilers finished the period down 3–2, but a disastrous second period in which they allowed three goals ultimately doomed them. A fourth unanswered goal was scored a little over three minutes into the third period. Edmonton tried to come back with two more goals, but the ending had already been decided. It would be the Kings who'd move on to Round 2 when the final buzzer sounded as the scoreboard flashed a 7–4 score in their favor.

"Well, I'll tell you one thing, I don't think it's an upset," Kings forward Marcel Dionne said after the game on television. "We were very confident. All I can say is that all the people at home that stuck with us, my wife, all the players' wives, my friends for the last seven years, we proved it to everybody."

As the Kings celebrated in triumph and clearly still riding high off a magnanimous comeback in Game 3, Fuhr and the Oilers felt sadness and disappointment.

"I thought, I'm not going to be here very long if that's the way the playoffs are going to go," Fuhr said in his autobiography. "We should have beat L.A. Wow, I didn't play very well in that playoff series."

Fuhr's first two seasons provided eye-opening lessons for the young goalie. Following the heartbreaking loss to Los Angeles in his rookie year, Fuhr entered the 1982–83 training camp 20 pounds overweight and failed to properly rehab his shoulder after offseason surgery. When the season began, he had four losses in his first six starts and a record of 9–8–3 entering a January 9, 1983, contest against the Detroit Red Wings. Fuhr allowed four goals on 30 shots in a 4–3 loss later that night, and he vented his frustrations to the media.

"I'd like to get the fans out of my system," Fuhr said after the game. "I could care less what they want to do…they're all jerks. I've given up on them.

"The fans here all over my case…I've not had good luck in this building. For me, it's a lot easier to play on the road than here."

Oilers head coach and GM Glen Sather responded by having a one-on-one talk with his netminder, advising him on how to talk to the media. Sather then sent Fuhr to the Moncton Alpines of the American Hockey League for a 10-game stint, returning before the end of the month. But it did not result in significant improvement for Fuhr at the NHL level. Fuhr went 4–3–2 in his final 10 starts of the season with an .860 save percentage.

Fuhr was not the Oilers' first choice goaltender that postseason. Instead, Moog reestablished himself as the team's No. 1 netminder with a 33–8–7 record, a 3.54 goals-against average, and an .891 save percentage. Fuhr made just one playoff appearance in 1983, playing under 12 minutes in relief of Moog in a blowout Oilers win over the Calgary Flames in Game 3 of the Smythe Division Finals. Unfortunately for Fuhr and the Oilers, Edmonton was swept in its first-ever Stanley Cup Final appearance against the New York Islanders.

Fuhr, however, battled back the very next season and reasserted himself as a reliable option in goal for Edmonton. He went 9–0–1 in his first 11 appearances that season. After the Oilers' final game of 1983, a 2–0 shutout, over the Boston Bruins, Fuhr had a record of 16–3–3. By season's end, Fuhr reached the 30-win mark for the first time in his career and notched 14 assists. It is the most points ever recorded by a goalie in a single season.

Fuhr was the Oilers' choice for Game 1 of the 1984 playoffs against the Winnipeg Jets in their opening-round series. The Oilers swept the Jets in three games before defeating the rival Flames in a seven-game, second-round series. Edmonton brought out the brooms once more for their conference series, quickly disposing of the Minnesota North Stars. It set up a rematch against the Islanders, who sought a fifth consecutive Stanley Cup Final victory and second straight at the expense of the Oilers.

Game 1 of the series featured one of Fuhr's finest goaltending performances of his career. With the Oilers offense struggling to score on Islanders goaltender Billy Smith, it was on Fuhr to hold the line. In his first ever Stanley Cup Final appearance, Fuhr made 34 saves while working to preserve a shutout. In the first period, Fuhr saved a breakaway chance from Greg Gilbert. Fuhr was also brilliant on a pair of chances from Islanders legend Bryan Trottier in the game. The Oilers got one goal, but it wasn't from any of their superstars. Kevin McClelland scored his third of the postseason—he had eight goals that regular season through 52 games—early in the game's final period. Thanks to Fuhr's heroics, it was the only goal Edmonton needed that night. It was also the Islanders' first Cup Final loss in 10 games.

Nine days later, with Fuhr sitting on the bench in favor of Moog, the Oilers were on the verge of toppling a dynasty.

The Northlands Coliseum was amped for celebration as they prepared to watch a center-ice faceoff following an empty net goal from Dave Lumley. His teammates—and even fans—jumped onto the ice to celebrate and hugged one another as fans celebrated with sparklers in the crowd. Balloons and streamers fell to the ice with the game well in hand. The Oilers held a commanding 3–1 series lead and a 5–2 lead in Game 5 of the Stanley Cup Final series over the Islanders.

Oilers players and trainers were already high-fiving each other on the bench once play finally resumed, and only the clock kept them from clearing the bench to celebrate with Moog. At last breath, those players and more fans spilled onto the ice. The game served as a transition of power after four years of Islanders dominance. It was the Oilers' turn to stand on top and commence a new era of hockey royalty. Five years after Pocklington said his team would be champions within that span of time, they accomplished their goal.

Even if Fuhr didn't play in the championship-clinching game, NHL history was made that day. Fuhr became the first Black player in NHL history to win the Stanley Cup. Fuhr played an integral role in the Oilers' championship run, posting an 11–4 record with a .911 save percentage. Fuhr's dream at seven years old was to make it to the NHL. Now, three seasons into his career, he had already ascended to the mountaintop as a Stanley Cup champion with his prime years still ahead.

Another dream was realized.

"You grow up dreaming of it as a kid, especially growing up in Canada," Fuhr said. "That's kind of the ultimate thing in hockey. Everybody as a kid, you played street hockey, you played ball hockey. You all talk about winning a Stanley Cup. But to actually do it. It's pretty much a kid's dream come true. And we were all bunch of big kids playing a game. And we love the game. We love everything about it. There's nothing better than winning a Stanley Cup."

GRANT FUHR CAN SAY he played a significant role in four out of five of the Edmonton Oilers' championship runs. After a successful 1984 campaign that resulted in his first Cup, he finished the 1985 season with a 26–8–7 record to go with an .884 save percentage and a 3.87 goals-against average while mostly splitting net duties with Andy Moog. The Oilers ended the season as the best team in the Smythe Division with 109 points, only four points less than the league-best Philadelphia Flyers. That season, Flyers goaltender Pelle Lindbergh was the NHL's best goaltender with 40 wins, more than any other netminder that year. For his efforts, he was awarded the Vezina Trophy.

Edmonton made quick work of Los Angeles and Winnipeg in the postseason, sweeping both teams in their opening two rounds.

Fuhr drew praise from his teammates and media through both rounds and was an early contender for playoff MVP.

"If the voting for the Most Valuable Player of the Stanley Cup playoffs were held today, Edmonton Oiler goaltender Grant Fuhr would be the unanimous choice of his teammates and the Winnipeg Jets," reads the top graf of a United Press International file story from April 1985.

"He single-handedly beat L.A.," Glen Sather told the *Los Angeles Times* in 1985. "He got the team going when we weren't playing well. Grant was the reason we beat L.A."

"Grant is the most underrated goalie in the league," Wayne Gretzky also told the L.A. Times. "We know that if we break down, he's going to make the big save for us. I've never seen a goalie like him. He never points the finger at anyone."

Edmonton didn't lose its first postseason games until Games 3 and 4 of the Clarence Campbell Conference Final against Chicago, resulting in a series tied at two games apiece. The Oilers responded by scoring a combined 18 goals in Games 5 and 6 en route to a Cup Final berth against Lindbergh and the Flyers. The Flyers won Game 1 of the series but eventually fell in five games to the Oilers. Fuhr's biggest contributions were two saved penalty shots in the series. He stopped Ron Sutter in the first period of Game 4, helping to preserve a 5–3 win over the Flyers. In the third period of Game 5, Fuhr was tasked with saving a Dave Poulin penalty shot. He was up to the task with a stacked pad save.

If Oilers head coach and GM Glen Sather somehow hadn't already been won over by Fuhr before that Cup Final, his comments in *Sports Illustrated* after Game 5 certainly affirmed his affinity for the goaltender. He referred to him as "the best goalie I've ever seen."

The 1986 Oilers looked primed for a three-peat. They entered the season as the best team in the regular season and were the first-ever winners of the Presidents' Trophy, awarded to the team with the most points in the regular season. Fuhr ended the year with a 29–8–0 record to go along with an .890 save percentage and a 3.93 goals-against average. He finished third in Vezina Trophy voting that season.

But not all was well for Fuhr that spring. He lost his father, Robert, to cancer in the middle of his team's opening-round series against the Vancouver Canucks. Fuhr missed Game 2 but helped the Oilers close out the Canucks with a near-perfect win in Game 3.

"I did want to play [in Game 2]," Fuhr said in his autobiography. "It would have been easier. Less thinking. And as a tribute to my dad."

And then, Fuhr and the Oilers fell victim to one of the biggest blunders in sports history.

The Edmonton Oilers met the rival Calgary Flames in the second round, battling all the way to Game 7. That's the game in which defenseman Steve Smith accidentally shot the puck off Fuhr's skate and into his own goal. The Flames eventually won the series and went on to represent the Clarence Campbell Conference in that year's Final.

"It's one of those things where s—t happens," Fuhr said on *Hockey Night in Canada* in 2021.

But while dreams of a three-peat were dashed, it didn't stop the Oilers from returning to glory in 1987. That calendar year, and parts of 1988, gave us the peak of Fuhr's goaltending career.

Fuhr's win total decreased following the 1986–87 regular season—29 wins in 1985–86 compared to 22 in 1986–87—but his goals-against average dropped from 3.93 to 3.44. For the second consecutive year, Fuhr finished third in Vezina Trophy voting. The Oilers made it to the Cup final for a rematch against the Flyers, only this time both teams would meet each other in a seven-game clash. Edmonton raced out to a 3–1 series lead before the Flyers won Games 5 and 6. Fuhr shut the door on the Flyers in Game 7 with a 19-save performance, allowing one goal in a 3–1 victory. While Fuhr emerged as the winning goaltender, Flyers goaltender Ron Hextall emerged as playoff MVP after a dominant postseason run that saw him record 15 wins, two shutouts and a .908 save percentage.

Fuhr and Hextall, alongside Kelly Hrudey, were teammates for Canada at the 1987 Canada Cup tournament in late August to early September of that year. The Canada Cup was an international tournament that served as an alternative for professional players who were unable to represent their countries at the Olympic Games. The 1987 edition was the fourth-ever iteration of the tournament. Canada had won two of the last three. Fuhr represented Team Canada in 1984 but was used sparingly after he injured his shoulder. Fuhr returned in 1987 and was used in all nine games of the competition.

"We'd just come back from winning a Cup in 1987," Fuhr said in his autobiography. "You win a Cup and all of a sudden it's August, and it's serious hockey. Playing for your country—you don't take that lightly. You maybe didn't have the same urgency that you would have had if it was back in May or June for the final rounds of the playoffs. But you also had the same urgency to win. It's the same but different, if that makes sense."

Canada reached the final of the Canada Cup against the Soviet Union, and all three games were high-scoring affairs ending with the same score of 6–5. Canada and the Soviets each split the first two games with overtime victories. Despite the goals allowed, Fuhr's goaltending was a key to Canada earning victories in the final series.

"If you look at that Game 2, they had three or four glorious chances to score in overtime and eliminate us. But Grant was just cool under pressure," Team Canada head coach Mike Keenan told The Hockey News in a February 2024 interview.

"He played out of his mind in that series, and he let in five a night," journalist Mark Spector said.

Finally, after Canada came back from 3–0 and 4–2 deficits in Game 3, they secured the 1987 Canada Cup thanks to an iconic Gretzky and Mario Lemieux back-and-forth resulting in the game-winning goal late in the third period. Fuhr was named to the tournament's All-Star Team.

Fuhr continued his stellar goaltending into the 1987–88 NHL season, his best year in the league. He won 40 games for the first time in his career, more than any other goalie that season. Fuhr also lowered his goals-against average to 3.43—down from 3.44 the year previous to go along with a .881 save percentage. After being nominated for the Vezina Trophy in back-to-back seasons, the 1987–88 campaign proved to be his year, as he won the honor for the first time in his career. Fuhr also finished second in MVP voting behind Lemieux and ahead of Gretzky.

In the spring of 1988, Fuhr's dominance continued into the postseason with a 16–2 record. The Oilers swept the Boston Bruins in four games, giving Fuhr and the Oilers their fourth Stanley Cup of the decade. The championship capped off a successful eight-month stretch for Fuhr dating from the Canada Cup victory to his fourth Stanley Cup win.

"I think I added up all the games I played, I think I played about 103 games that year, which at that time, nobody had really done," Fuhr said. "So, lots of things to be happy about that season."

When Fuhr joined his teammates at center ice for a commemorative photo to celebrate the Cup win alongside teammates, coaches and trainers—a tradition that began after the victory and continues to this day—Fuhr was at the peak of his powers.

Months before his fourth Stanley Cup victory, a *Sports Illustrated* feature story from Ralph Wiley described Fuhr as "the best on earth." Gretzky even described Fuhr as the "best goaltender in the history of the NHL."

"Bar none, Grant Fuhr is the best goalie in the league," Canucks forward Barry Pederson said in Wiley's story. "He has the fastest reflexes. Sometimes his concentration might drift during inconsequential games. But in the big-money games Fuhr is the best. He's the Cup goalie. It's sure not by luck."

From Fuhr's debut in 1981 to 1988, he had a record of 188–80–42 with a 3.68 goals-against average and an .884 save percentage. Four Stanley Cups, one Vezina Trophy, and a runner-up for regular season MVP, along with two Canada Cups. It's a résumé that made him worthy to stand among the NHL's best between the pipes.

But unbeknownst to Fuhr during the celebrations, a period of decline and controversy was to come.

NEW HAVEN, CONNECTICUT, IS a long way from the bright lights of the NHL.

The New Haven Coliseum seated more than 11,000 fans in its heyday, a much smaller venue compared to NHL rinks and thousands of miles away from Grant Fuhr's home province of Alberta. If it wasn't hosting the local hockey team, the Nighthawks, it played host to basketball games and wrestling events. The Nighthawks were once the affiliate of the Los Angeles Kings, a near-six-hour flight away from coast to coast.

If Fuhr wanted his NHL career to restart, he'd have to play at the Coliseum in a Cape Breton Oilers jersey—the minor league affiliate of the Edmonton Oilers.

Fuhr would also have to stave off fans who were well aware of why his career had suffered a setback. They reminded him of how far he'd fallen by throwing bags of sugar onto the ice.

"I expected it," Fuhr said. "Once you've made a mistake, people love to jump and thrive on your mistake. So, coming back, I prepared myself for it. Mentally, it didn't bother me at all. I actually kind of found it funny after a while."

After winning the Stanley Cup in 1988, Fuhr's career experienced more turbulence and changes. First, some of his teammates from those Oilers championship teams were being moved to other teams. The Oilers had already moved on from players like Paul Coffey,

Dave Semenko, and Andy Moog prior to the 1988 championship—Moog was on the Bruins squad that lost to the Oilers in 1988. But no transaction was as earth-shattering as Wayne Gretzky being traded to Los Angeles in August 1988, nearly three months after winning his fourth Cup with the Oilers.

The Oilers lost in the opening round of the 1989 postseason against the Los Angeles Kings. Fuhr then represented Canada at the 1989 World Championship in Sweden where the Canadians left with a silver medal after losing to the Soviet Union.

Edmonton returned to glory in 1990, only to do so without Fuhr. The netminder only played 21 games that season after persistent injuries to his shoulder. Months before the playoffs, Fuhr had an emergency appendectomy as well. Fuhr would miss most of that year's regular season and all of the 1990 postseason. The Oilers, however, still managed to win the championship that season, again at the expense of the Boston Bruins. Fuhr's name was still engraved on the Cup. Another Black goaltender, Eldon "Pokey" Reddick, was also part of the Oilers squad that won the Cup that year.

The following season is when things took a turn for the worse.

After years of rumors and denials, a report in the *Edmonton Journal* surfaced through Fuhr's ex-wife, Corrine, about his drug usage. She claimed Fuhr used cocaine "heavily" when they met in 1983 and tried to hide it from her and his teammates, but she still found drugs in Fuhr's clothes and in parts of the house. Corrine also fielded "angry" phone calls from drug dealers, according to Grant's autobiography. Fuhr told the *Edmonton Journal* that he used a "substance" and that he lied to Oilers GM Glen Sather about his drug usage.

On September 27, 1990, NHL president John Ziegler handed down a one-year suspension following a hearing the day prior. Fuhr was given the lengthy sentence despite no official penalty for drug usage made by the league and despite the goaltender coming clean with his drug usage prior to the hearing.

"We didn't think that I was going to get slapped on the fingers that hard," Fuhr wrote in his autobiography. "I would have been better off to have been caught rather than to have admitted it and sat through that hearing. I'd have gotten less punishment."

Fortunately for Fuhr, Ziegler reduced his suspension to 59 games after the goaltender maintained good behavior. Fuhr played four games with the AHL Oilers in February 1991, including that night in New Haven, to get himself back into game shape. He eventually returned to the Oilers on February 18, 1991. Fuhr made 27 saves in a 4–0 shutout victory over the New Jersey Devils for a victory in his first game back after suspension.

"It's nice to get the shutout," Fuhr said after the game, according to the Associated Press. "It's a real good feeling and a long time coming. It's nice to be back."

Fuhr played just 13 games during the 1990–91 season, ending the year with a 6–4–3 record with a 3.01 goals-against average and an .897 save percentage. He was used as the Oilers' No. 1 netminder for the playoffs that year and helped the team reach the Clarence Campbell Conference Final, including a victory over Gretzky's Kings in the second round. But the Oilers' magic ran out in the conference final, where they lost to the Minnesota North Stars.

When the Oilers skated off the ice after a Game 5 loss at Northlands Coliseum in Edmonton, it was Fuhr's final time suiting up in an Oilers jersey during his playing career. The rest of his playing career featured stops in Toronto Buffalo (he won the William M. Jennings Trophy along with Dominik Hašek as a Sabre), and a brief 14-game cameo in Los Angeles, where he reunited with Wayne Gretzky.

Fuhr signed with the St. Louis Blues as a free agent ahead of the 1995–96 season and was used heavily by his new team, playing 79 games. It's the most games ever played by a goaltender in one season, a record that holds up to the present day. Fuhr finished sixth in voting for the Vezina and Hart Trophies that season after a 30–28–16 campaign, a 2.87 goals-against average, and a .903 save percentage.

Unfortunately, Fuhr's 1996 postseason was cut short after two games. Blues defenseman Chris Pronger pushed Toronto Maple Leafs forward Nick Kypreos into Fuhr. Fuhr suffered a torn anterior cruciate ligament, a torn medial collateral ligament, and a torn meniscus, ending his playoffs.

"He fell on me," Fuhr said. "I just happened to have my leg in a bad spot."

The Blues, who had Wayne Gretzky and Brett Hull on their team, found a way to beat the Maple Leafs in six games without Fuhr. But they fell to the Detroit Red Wings in the Western Conference semi-finals, losing via double overtime goals from Steve Yzerman in Game 7.

Despite the serious injury, Fuhr still managed to return to the Blues in time for the start of the 1996–97 season. He spent the offseason rehabbing with Bob Kersee, the track and field coach and husband to American Olympic legend Jackie Joyner-Kersee. The coach spent a month with Fuhr helping him rehab his knee and slicing his recovery time in half.

"It's a lasting memory, ACL reconstruction and having the rehab that goes with it," Fuhr said. "One, it hurts. Two, there's nothing fun about it. And to do it in three months, to be able to play, when everybody said was going to be six months to a year.

"It's a mental thing."

Fuhr rejoined the Blues and played 73 games during the 1996–97 campaign, the third-most games he has ever played in a single season. Fuhr improved his record to 33–27–11 with a 2.72 goals-against average and a .901 save percentage. The Blues, however, did not experience more playoff success with a healthier Fuhr. Once again, they lost to the Detroit Red Wings in the opening round of the playoffs. The Red Wings went on to win the Cup in 1997.

But Fuhr, despite being seen as well past his prime, had now proven he still had more in the tank after bouncing around from team to team after his Oilers days ended.

"Most of it is mindset," Fuhr said, when asked about how he maintained his career longevity. "And you have to believe in yourself. There's going to be ups and downs. The downs, everybody gets kicked. And the ups, it's easy. So you've got to have the mindset of trying to keep everything even keeled. And when things were bad, you stay positive. [When] things are good, you just don't get over the moon with it. You just kind of try and ride a steady wave."

Fuhr spent four total seasons in St. Louis before being traded to the rival Calgary Flames in 1999 where he'd share the net with Fred Brathwaite to form an all-Black goaltending tandem. Fuhr only won five games with the Flames, but one of those five was his 400th career victory. To some, it was strange to see a longtime Oiler join a rival in the final moments of his career.

"I'll never forget him putting on a Flames jersey," journalist Mark Spector said. "The look on his face was like, even he couldn't believe he was putting on a Flames jersey that day."

The 1999–2000 season proved to be Fuhr's last, his résumé already worthy of Hockey Hall of Fame induction and legend status. The final tally: 403 wins, 295 losses, and 114 ties and overtime losses. An .887 save percentage to go with a 3.38 goals-against average. Five Stanley Cups to his name alongside a Vezina Trophy, two Canada Cups, a silver medal at the IIHF World Hockey Championship, a William M. Jennings Trophy, and two NHL All-Star Team appearances.

By October 2003, Fuhr's No. 31 was retired by the Edmonton Oilers. He watched the ceremony on the ice in full goalie garb with his family. One month later, Fuhr was the first Black player to be inducted into the Hockey Hall of Fame.

"I don't think one [accomplishment] stands out over the other," Fuhr said. "They're all different. But they're all very cool. I mean, if you'd told me that I'd accomplished that when I started. I'd have laughed. The fact that I lasted as long as I did, and we managed to accomplish as much as we did in Edmonton, and you get all the accolades afterward. It's all special, and it all kind of blends into each other."

Fuhr takes pride in knowing that his play inspired future Black players who came after him and went on to have successful pro careers like Kevin Weekes, Fred Brathwaite, and even Jarome Iginla, who opted to play forward instead of goalie.

"Anything that I can do to grow the game you have to be proud of," Fuhr said. "I'm proud [of] the fact that players want to follow and the fact that I can help grow the game. I think that's one of the biggest honors you can take out of the game. For all your on-ice accomplishments and everything, I think it's the recognition that other guys feel like they could play. I think that's something that you want to accomplish over the course of your career. You want to give people hope."

5

P.K. Subban

The media scrum grew around P.K. Subban after Game 6 of the 2014 Eastern Conference semifinal at the Bell Centre, as it tends to for players under the spotlight in a Montreal Canadiens uniform. That spotlight beams even brighter in a postseason series, and especially against a heated rival like the Boston Bruins—the Canadiens' most frequent playoff matchup in NHL history.

Subban was already fielding questions as more reporters put their recorders and microphones in his face. You could tell that he was in the thick of a grueling war against a heated rival with his lowered energy when talking to the media horde.

"I can't tell the difference between games now," Subban said in the scrum. "Every game is physical. Every game is high intensity. And that's the way we expect it to be."

This was Subban's second-ever playoff series against the Bruins, dating back to the 2011 postseason. That year, in Game 7 at Boston's TD Garden, Subban unleashed a slap shot from just below the faceoff circle and tied the game at three goals apiece. The Canadiens, however, were beaten in overtime by a Nathan Horton blast. The Bruins won the Cup that season.

Three years later, Subban was still producing in high-pressure moments in the postseason. In the first game of the 2014 series, the defenseman scored a double-overtime winner past Bruins goalie Tuukka Rask. His celebration was a simple stare toward the opposing bench, arms stretched out wide in recognition of his playoff heroics. You could hear audible groans and expletives from the Bruins fans in the arena. But online, spews of racist social media posts toward Subban flooded internet feeds. The Bruins denounced those posts, and Subban responded by saying it wasn't a "reflection by any means" of the NHL or the team.

In Game 3, Subban sat in the penalty box serving a roughing penalty. But when the Bruins couldn't capitalize on the ensuing power play, out came Subban rushing to receive a pass from teammate Lars Eller. One-on-one with Rask, Subban's headfake and deke left the goalie helpless as the puck entered the back of the net. It sent the Canadiens' faithful in a frenzy and remains an enduring memory from the Canadiens–Bruins rivalry, as well as Subban's own highlight tape.

"Coming out of the box, Larry [Lars Eller] made a good play in the neutral zone," Subban told Sean Gordon of *The Globe and Mail* after the game. "I just went in at Tuukka. To be honest with you, I was pretty surprised, a little bit nervous; he's a good goalie. Just tried to bury my head, make a move, the puck went in for me."

Subban had also battled with Bruins enforcer Shawn Thornton at various times in the series, ducking hits and being sprayed at with a water bottle—prompting a chuckle from Thornton on the bench. Whenever Subban touched the puck in Boston at the TD Garden, fans booed him to get the defenseman off his game. It didn't quite work as well as the fans hoped.

So, there was every reason for media to talk to Subban in the locker room after Game 6 of that series. The Norris Trophy–winning defenseman—the very first Black player to accomplish the feat—featured prominently in another chapter of the Canadiens–Bruins rivalry while asserting himself as one of the best players at his position.

"P.K. loved the big moments," former teammate Daniel Brière said. "Loved being the guy who would make the difference and really believed that he was going to be the guy that would make the difference in every game. His personality's contagious. Gave us a lot of swagger. Was also excellent at disturbing the opponent and the fans in other buildings. P.K. was certainly a treat to play with."

With that spotlight on Subban, he had no issue adding fuel to the fire.

"It's going to be great. I can't wait for the crowd, the noise, the energy in the building," Subban said after Game 6. "I can't wait to take that all away from them."

"The single greatest quote that I've ever been present for," reporter Chris Johnston said.

In a one-on-one interview with NBC's Pierre McGuire, Subban delivered another quotable in anticipation of the must-watch Game 7 in Boston.

"I hope their crowd is louder than in [Montreal]," Subban said in the interview. "I hope it gets nasty, I hope it gets dirty. Because at the end of the game when you're shaking hands, whoever wins, that's what the feeling's all about. It's knowing that you battled, you went through a war, and you know what? We're going to be at the end there standing tall."

Subban didn't register a point in the game, but he was the most-used player on the ice. (Teammate Andrei Markov played one second fewer than Subban's 26:17.) Brière scored a goal and an assist in a 3–1 Canadiens win over the Bruins to advance to the 2014 Eastern Conference Final. He didn't allow a goal while on the ice and did his best to keep the Bruins at bay. The Canadiens helped him back up his end of the bargain.

As disgruntled Bruins fans jeered, Subban smiled alongside his teammates in the handshake line.

"It's rare you get a guy who is so brash, so confident in himself. I don't want to call him cocky, because I don't think he was," The Athletic's Arpon Basu said. "But he just had extreme confidence in himself and also delivered when it counted, like he backed it up almost every single time."

Moments after the game, Subban was interviewed again by McGuire. Subban remained stoic and composed as he answered his questions. That's the norm for hockey players in most situations on camera. But when McGuire ended his interview by congratulating Subban on reaching the Eastern Conference Final, Subban flashed a wide grin. He immediately turned toward McGuire and yelled, "Yeah, baby!" before planting a kiss on McGuire's cheek. McGuire laughed as he watched him trot back to the locker room to continue celebrating a series victory.

"He was a showman," Johnston said. "He almost had the spirit of what we see in professional wrestling. He had the idea of promoting the game and he kind of leaned into the chaos."

That is Subban in a nutshell. His skating, flashiness, physicality, and penchant for making plays gave the NHL world something to talk about while putting him among the league's best rearguards at his absolute peak. While Subban doesn't often talk about race—he's even said he'd rather not be defined by it—he was an undeniable, modern-day Black NHL superstar during his best years. In the present day, he's since used his platform to grow the game through the NHL's Player Inclusion Coalition—designed to "advance equality and inclusion in the sport of hockey on and off the ice."

Subban's boisterous off-ice personality, combined with being a minority in a white-dominant sport, made him a lightning rod in those same NHL circles. While some white players are typically characterized as reserved and spotlight-averse, Subban was unafraid of the bright lights. He expanded his own personal brand beyond hockey, establishing friendships with fellow superstars in Kobe Bryant and

Novak Djokovic. He was even engaged to Winter Olympian Lindsey Vonn, though they ultimately called it off.

The kiss on McGuire's cheek was just one of many on-camera moments that placed the defenseman in the limelight. Later in Subban's career, as a member of the Nashville Predators during the 2017 Stanley Cup Final, he walked around with a Listerine bottle in response to Sidney Crosby saying his breath stunk after an on-ice confrontation. (Crosby denied saying that and video has since revealed that they both just shouted expletives at one another.) Subban's triple-low five celebration with Canadiens goaltender Carey Price was another sign of his flair that went against the grain of the conservative NHL. Subban and Price's triple-low five was eventually banned by then Canadiens head coach Michel Therrien in favor of more team celebrations.

"Just think about how inclusive, how important, how powerful, how exciting this was, and that there were still conversations in the team that it's too flashy," former *Hockey Night in Canada* host George Stroumboulopoulos said. "And Carey who was so understated and would present so calmly all the time, to see him so excited and engaged and to have any of the narrative around that be anything other than how exciting it is.

"Those two together should have hoisted the Cup in Montreal and then the whole country would've been doing that. All the Habs fans would've been doing that triple-low five and it would've been perfect. It would've been perfect. So, I see that, and I remember how fun it is to look at that. But, as always, because I'm a hockey fan who is used to watching my team lose more than win, it reminds me of what could have been."

Subban's off-ice philanthropy was also a massive talking point in Montreal. He pledged $10 million over seven years to the Montreal Children's Hospital in 2015. At the time, it was described as "the biggest philanthropic commitment by a sports figure in Canadian history." To this day, an atrium at the hospital still bears his name. The pandemic slowed some of that fundraising, resulting in only $6.3 million of the $10 million being raised by January 2023. In response, Subban extended his target end date to 2025, according to the *Montreal Gazette*.

While generous, many people remarked at the fact Subban accomplished this independent of the Canadiens. Another sign of Subban's stardom, but in this case dwarfing the Canadiens' own name and brand power.

"I remember when I was speaking to Devante Smith-Pelly," TV personality Cabbie "Cabral" Richards said. "He was on the Canadiens at the time. Nobody knew. P.K. was just absent from practice. There wasn't this big rollout with the team."

Subban did tell The Athletic, however, that he spoke to members of the Canadiens' front office prior to the announcement.

The defenseman's personality endeared him to many fans, but it also gathered a fair share of detractors, too. Hall of Fame center Doug Gilmour once said Subban was "a little too flashy for us old-school guys." Former coach and GM turned hockey analyst Mike Milbury was annoyed by Subban dancing during a pregame warm-up, saying he acted like a "clown." In an interview with ESPN in 2017, NHL enforcer John Scott referred to Subban as a "piece of garbage" for thinking "he's better than everybody."

Hockey Night in Canada's Don Cherry warned that Subban's presence and overconfidence could make him a target for retribution, which was eventually echoed by then-Philadelphia Flyers forward Mike Richards. It was difficult not to interpret those comments as threats or general annoyance at a player breaking from the NHL's traditional norms. Intentional or not, a critique of Subban was usually viewed under the guise of racism. TV analyst Darren Pang once compared then St. Louis Blues defenseman Alex Pietrangelo to Subban by saying the former played the "white way"—a Freudian slip, instead of saying the "right way." Pang apologized.

"P.K. had to face a lot of shit that was so unnecessary," Stroumboulopoulos said.

Speculation suggested that Subban's relationships with select teammates, coaches, and management was not completely amicable and that his overexuberant personality didn't always mesh with certain teammates. But much of that had to do with how Subban's persona was counterculture to the average hockey player, and that includes his Blackness.

"I think the hockey world in general is a very conservative world," Brière said. "I think because of the fact that since an early age, we're always taught that hockey is all about the team. It's never about the individual. It's always team comes first. I think the personalities in hockey are more conservative, and we always try to temper things down. Where P.K. just wasn't afraid of it and then wasn't afraid to be in the limelight and welcomed that attention.

"For some people, yeah, it would rub some people the wrong way. But there was also a lot of good with that and the way he was playing and how dominant he was at the time. You have to appreciate the talent, and you have to love the fact that he's on your team and gives you a better chance to win."

While Subban might not have been close with every teammate, it didn't necessarily mean that he was at odds with them. Reports surfaced that Subban and teammate Max Pacioretty weren't always on the best of terms throughout their tenure together, with some wondering if there was tension after Pacioretty earned the Canadiens captaincy ahead of Subban through a player vote before the 2015–16 season. But to date, there hasn't been any tangible evidence—at least any that has emerged beyond the realm of speculation and rumor—that both players hated each other. Subban even playfully interviewed his former teammate on ESPN in December 2022, asking about Pacioretty's family and Christmas plans.

"I never got the sense he had a problem with P.K.," Basu said. "Some of the other people who were rumored to have a problem with P.K., like Andrei Markov. For crying out loud, P.K. literally went to Andrei Markov's wedding in Russia. They were very close. Tomáš Plekanec. A lot of people assume he had a problem with P.K., and he really didn't. Maybe personality wise, it didn't really mesh. But Tomas had a great appreciation for what he could do on the ice, how much he could help the team win, and that's what it came down to."

However, Subban's relationships with head coach Michel Therrien and general manager Marc Bergevin were rocky, and there are receipts to back that claim up.

Subban drew critiques from Therrien for his on-ice mistakes, usually giveaways, bad defensive positioning, and unnecessary penalties. An infamous clip from 24CH—the TV series that followed the Canadiens behind the scenes—showed Therrien chewing out the defenseman in between periods of a game against the Calgary Flames.

That tension between Subban and the Canadiens also extended to management. Bergevin was months into his Canadiens GM tenure in 2012 when he had to handle Subban holding out for a handful of games during the 2012–13 lockout-shortened season. It led to a two-year bridge deal. When that deal expired in the summer of 2014, Subban eventually elected for salary arbitration against the Canadiens. The *Montreal Gazette*'s Jack Todd reported that Canadiens owner Geoff Molson "overruled" Bergevin to ensure his defenseman got signed during that process. But according to Michael Farber of *Sports Illustrated*, Molson contacted Subban during negotiations and denied going over his general manager's head.

"I would never do that," Molson told Farber in November 2014.

"I'm just speculating," Stroumboulopoulos said. "But I remember saying to my friends back then [that] this must've really pissed Bergevin off."

Subban eventually signed an eight-year, $72 million deal. But the defenseman didn't finish out his contract in Canadiens colors as he was eventually dealt to the Nashville Predators in a trade for Shea Weber, one of three massive transactions made in a 23-minute span on June 29, 2016.

"In an instant, I was overcome by an all-consuming, primordial sense of dread," actor and Canadiens superfan Jay Baruchel said in his book *Born Into It: A Fan's Life*. "The kind that manifests itself in squalls of cold rushing through your blood and hordes of asshole butterflies swarming your stomach. My eyes went into wide shock as my hand flew to my mouth.

"And then I clicked on P.K. Subban's name and my whole world threw up."

Subban's career wasn't just defined by a league-shattering trade, media soundbites, and wanting to be in front of the camera. There is a reason why he has a Norris Trophy in his cabinet and why he was nominated for the trophy two other times in addition to three All-Star Team appearances.

"I think at times it overshadowed how good he was as a player because of how much he loved the stage and wanted to be a team player in important times," hockey insider Elliotte Friedman said. "He craved it. I think he wanted to be great. He wanted to be a great player in the big moments."

"He was never nervous," NHL insider and former goalie Kevin Weekes said. "It was just like the same kid at [my] hockey camp. I got to say that's a really huge quality. Especially for all of some of thc vitriol that he had to endure at different points in his career."

Subban's career had its fair share of ups and downs, and that spotlight followed him everywhere he went. Not that he completely minded. The peaks and valleys of his 13-year NHL tenure didn't stop Subban from embracing that spotlight, making him one of the most fascinating players to ever play the game.

"The biggest personality in the history of the sport," Richards said. "I think Jeremy Roenick is a close second. But, authentically, P.K. Subban is the biggest personality in his sport."

MALCOLM SUBBAN AND HIS older brother, P.K., would sometimes spend their days playing each other in tennis. You could find them at a local court in the community of Humberwood, a neighborhood in the Toronto suburb of Etobicoke. Even with their five-year age gap, they'd compete against each other. Malcolm remembers P.K. constantly getting the edge on him and never letting him win.

One day, Malcolm had enough.

On his next serve, Malcolm whacked the ball well over P.K.'s head and cleared the fence behind him. P.K. was beside himself. Enraged, he demanded Malcolm retrieve the tennis ball he'd lost. Defiantly, Malcolm refused.

"No, I'm going home," Malcolm said.

He immediately ran off the court and made his way back to the Subban residence. What was normally a 7–10 minute walk turned into a full-on sprint. Once he'd leave the park and run past the bus station, Malcolm went around a bend and ran down past three streets. The fourth one is where he'd be home free. He just needed to make it to the last house on the left.

But as Malcolm ran for his life, P.K. was catching up. Not only did he retrieve the ball, but P.K. followed his younger brother in pursuit. By the time Malcolm made it onto his home street, P.K. had him in his sights. As the elder Subban brother crept closer, Malcolm eventually gave in and fell to the ground. P.K. shook his brother in anger.

"What the hell are you doing?" Malcolm laughed as he remembered his big brother was yelling when he finally caught him. "He didn't hit me. He was just so mad. He just grabbed me."

It was one of the many adventures the Subbans had in their youth. If it wasn't playing sports like tennis or hockey outdoors, they'd play video games against each other, whether EA Sports NHL or the Dragon Ball Z series. The brothers reenacted their games in real life, playing hockey in the hallway or wrestling each other on their parents' beds.

"Looking back to childhood, it's crazy," Malcolm said. "It's awesome, but it's so sad because of how much you miss those times. They're the best times of your life. We're just all coming up. Our dad taking us to run hills, taking us to shoot in the front yard, in the basement. Just all the time the fun times we had playing video games and going to the park playing tennis, basketball. You grow up and then everyone's busy. Everyone's off. P.K., he's busy all the time now doing all of his stuff. I don't get to see him as much anymore. And I'm busy doing my career too, right? So, we don't get to see each other as much now. Growing up, you miss those times. Skating on the backyard rinks, skating on the outdoor rinks.

"If there's one thing in my life that I wish I could go back and do over, because of how fun it was, it was that. It's growing up in our household. It was really fun."

P.K. was born May 13, 1989, in Rexdale, a Toronto-based suburb, as one of five siblings. He has two older sisters, Nastassia and Natasha, and two hockey-playing younger brothers, Malcolm and Jordan. Malcolm has played NHL games for Boston, Vegas, Chicago, Buffalo, and Columbus, while Jordan spent the bulk of his pro career in the AHL. Their father, Karl, spent 30 years as a teacher and principal in Toronto after immigrating from Jamaica. Their mother, Maria, immigrated from Montserrat.

Both parents fell in love with hockey when they moved to Canada and soon found themselves on opposite sides of hockey fandom: Maria cheered for the rival Toronto Maple Leafs. Karl was an avid Canadiens fan growing up in Sudbury, Ontario, but also enjoyed watching players around the league like Wayne Gretzky, Mike Foligno, and Randy Carlyle. The family came together to watch Canadiens–Leafs games, but that wasn't the only rivalry that spurred them on.

"The craziest games were Boston–Montreal," Malcolm said. "No one liked Boston, because they were just rivals of the Leafs and the Habs. We used to love watching those games."

Young P.K. took up skating when he was four years old thanks to his father's insistence on having him skate every day in the winter. But the Subbans had to be creative with their son and father's own school schedules—Karl was once a teacher and a vice principal for two different schools. According to *The New Yorker*, Maria would put P.K. to sleep in snow pants so that when Karl woke him up at 10:00 PM, he'd be ready to go skating at Nathan Phillips Square in downtown Toronto. Sometimes, the two would skate until 2:00 AM.

NHL insider and former goaltender Kevin Weekes remembers a young, "highly energetic" P.K. at one of his hockey camps he attended as a child.

"He had a little snotty nose, and he had that kind of grin on his face," Weekes said. "He was just like a little Energizer bunny."

P.K. also took after his father and cheered for the Canadiens. Growing up, P.K. even played for the North York Canadiens triple-AAA novice team with two future NHLers in Steven Stamkos and Chris Tanev. But while P.K learned to hold the Canadiens legends in high reverence, his favorite player of all-time never wore the famed colors of the *bleu-blanc-rouge*. Subban was enamored with Bobby Orr, the smooth-skating, offensive dynamo whose trophy cabinet was littered with Norris, Hart and Art Ross trophies. Let's not forget his two Cup rings and two playoff MVPs for good measure alongside nine NHL All-Star Team appearances, a Lester B. Pearson Award and the Calder Trophy for Rookie of the Year.

"I just like his style," Subban said in an interview with HabsTV as a Canadiens prospect. "Because he is the best defenseman that's ever played the game. The way he changed the style of play for defensemen was just unbelievable. I like his style, his spin-o-rama. I loved the way he played offense, defense. He's just a great player."

According to *The New Yorker*, Subban got the book *Bobby Orr: My Game* for Christmas as his dad pushed him—and his brothers—to play defense. In fact, defense is one of Karl's five D's for success for his children according to the CBC: destination, dedication, discipline, determination, and defense.

Subban stuck to the position and eventually caught on with the Belleville Bulls of the Ontario Hockey League. Subban had a 15-goal, 56-point campaign in his second year as a Bull in 2006–07. The Canadiens eventually selected Subban in the second round of the 2007 NHL Entry Draft. After being chosen by the Canadiens, he shook hands with members of the team's front office at the draft table and told them, "You guys made the right choice," according to *Sports Illustrated*.

Broadcaster Gord Miller remembered seeing P.K's father, Karl, a longtime Canadiens fan, show so much pride in his eldest son being drafted, he hugged then Canadiens GM Bob Gainey and lifted the Hockey Hall of Famer off the ground.

"Bob is the most taciturn guy you've ever met," Miller said. "And there was Karl Subban, just hugging him."

When Subban spoke to the media after being selected, he made an ambitious declaration that instantly won over factions of the Canadiens' fanbase.

"I think I'm ready to play and I'm going to camp with the idea of making the Canadiens and helping them win the Stanley Cup," Subban said in 2007.

"As a fan at the time, it was like that kid cares as much as I care," analyst Andrew Berkshire said.

Following four seasons with the Bulls of the OHL and two World Junior gold medals with Team Canada, Subban spent most of the 2009–10 season with the Canadiens' minor-league affiliate in Hamilton. He made his NHL debut on February 12, 2010, the first of two games against the Philadelphia Flyers. It did not take him long to make an impression with his older teammates.

"I remember in his first game, we're at home," former teammate Mathieu Darche told me in an interview for Habs Eyes on the Prize in 2020. "Chris Pronger goes to run [him]. He ducks, he misses him. First game in the NHL. Pronger was a dirty player too. Hall of Famer. [Subban] turns around and says, 'Suck on that, Prongs.' Right away, he had that confidence."

Later that spring, Subban was called up by the Canadiens in the 2010 playoffs. He got more playing time after teammate Andrei Markov was injured in the team's second-round series against the Pittsburgh Penguins. Subban made an instant impact, scoring the first goal of the series. He spent the bulk of it going toe-to-toe against superstar Sidney Crosby.

"[Subban is] brand new to the NHL," former teammate Michael Cammalleri told me in another interview for Habs Eyes on the Prize in 2020. "And Crosby comes through the neutral zone and P.K. kind of steps on him in the neutral zone and jams him and jams him. And then Crosby goes offside. The whistle blows and I'm backchecking, so I'm like right there, within a couple feet. P.K. says to Crosby, 'You got nothing and you ain't gonna get nothing.'

"I remember that moment looking at [P.K], looking at Sid. Sid was kind of looking at him, confused, like, 'Is this guy talking to me?'

I remember thinking, 'Wow, like [P.K.] actually believes it. He actually is gonna play this guy, heads up, like this.' I remember feeling at that moment, like, this guy's a special player."

Despite the Canadiens losing in the conference final to Philadelphia that year, Subban had established himself as an everyday NHLer that postseason. The following year, Subban began his first full NHL season in 2010–11 with the Canadiens, scoring 14 goals and 38 points in 77 games. In a March 2011 game against the Minnesota Wild that season, Subban became the first-ever Canadiens rookie to score a hat-trick in an NHL game. Subban finished sixth in Calder Trophy voting for Rookie of the Year and was named to the NHL's All-Rookie Team by season's end. That spring, he scored two goals and four points in seven playoff games including a game-tying goal in Game 7 of the Canadiens' first-round series against the Boston Bruins.

After Subban nearly matched his 2010–11 season point totals with a 36-point season during the 2011–12 campaign, he was destined for a payday at the expiration of his entry-level contract. Subban held out for a new deal at the beginning of the lockout-shortened 2012–13 season. But instead of a long-term contract, Subban signed a two-year, $5.75 million bridge deal. Some teams would rather sign star talent to lengthy contracts, gaining team control over a player for as many years as possible before they become unrestricted free agents. It also ensures that if a player reaches their potential over the course of the deal, the team could have them on a cost-effective contract for longer.

When Subban joined the team after signing, he launched himself to the top of his position. He began the season with points in his first four games. After his early four-game points streak was snapped against the Toronto Maple Leafs, he scored a goal and an assist in a 4–3 Canadiens shootout win over the Tampa Bay Lightning. By season's end, his 11 goals and 38 points in 42 games matched his then-career high points output. His 26 power-play points led the league and helped the Canadiens attain the fifth-best power play rate on the season. The Canadiens finished the season with the second-best record in the Eastern Conference.

According to Hockey Reference, Subban was on pace for a 21-goal, 72-point campaign in a full 82-game season. Subban's performances were enough to win the Norris that season as the league's best defenseman, earning one more first-place vote than Minnesota's Ryan Suter while also edging out Pittsburgh Penguins defenseman Kris Letang, according to the Professional Hockey Writers Association.

His ascension continued into the 2013–14 year, a full season—10 goals and 53 points in 82 games. Subban was even added to Team Canada's squad at the 2014 Olympics in Sochi, Russia. He only played one game but was part of the Canadian squad that won gold for the second consecutive Olympic Games. Subban's solid play continued into the postseason, achieving a seven-game points streak across the first and second round matchups against Tampa Bay and Boston. The Canadiens advanced to the Eastern Conference Final against the New York Rangers where they lost the series in six games.

Subban's last two seasons set the table for an intriguing contract negotiation between him and Canadiens management. The defenseman elected for salary arbitration later that summer as a restricted free agent. Local fans and pundits were mostly dismayed that the Canadiens and Subban were unable to come to terms beforehand and lamented that the Canadiens hadn't signed Subban to a long-term contract years earlier. Subban even told Arpon Basu of The Athletic that he was willing to sign a contract extension after his Norris Trophy–winning season.

"Can you imagine how different Montreal history would be if P.K. was making five million a year instead of nine?" Berkshire said.

Subban wanted a contract that paid him $8.5 million per season while the Canadiens only wanted to pay $5.25 million, according to USA Today. Depending on what the arbitrator decided, Subban would have to play on a one-year deal with the contract term that they deemed the most fair. It appeared the Canadiens were willing to make some concessions, according to insider Elliotte Friedman, who reported that the Canadiens offered Subban an eight-year contract with an annual average value between $8 and 8.25 million before arbitration proceedings began. But a deal wasn't consummated.

"The arbitration process by its nature is difficult," insider Chris Johnston said. "Players have to hear some candid thoughts from the organization negatively about their game or things they do on the ice."

Once Molson assured Subban that a deal would be done, the Canadiens finally signed Subban to that eight-year deal worth $9 million annually in August 2014.

"I spoke to Geoff on that day and before the arbitration process, and he made it clear to me that I'd be a Montreal Canadien for a very long time. He told me that, and he was a man of his word," Subban told *Sports Illustrated.*

Subban's Canadiens tenure lasted only 697 more days—a few months short of two calendar years—after he signed that contract.

THE DAY-TO-DAY LIFE OF a hockey insider basically requires being ready at a moment's notice. The constant phone calls and texts with sources. The writing and on-camera work when a big story breaks. It's no wonder insiders like to hide away in their summer cabins as long as possible once the doldrums of the offseason are in full swing. But even the best of them try to sneak in a nap on their work day when they get a chance. Hockey insider Chris Johnston is one of them. Considering how busy he is, he earned that nap on a June summer day, completely unaware what was to come.

Johnston slept through the massive shockwaves that rocked the hockey world. By the time he woke up, all he could do was process the aftermath.

"I remember that I was the dumbest insider on the earth that day, because I missed the fireworks in real time," Johnston said.

In the span of 23 minutes, three significant transactions had hockey fans and media on the edge of their seats. The Edmonton Oilers traded away their 2010 No.1 overall pick, Taylor Hall, to New Jersey in exchange for defenseman Adam Larsson. Moments later, the Canadiens upped the ante when they flipped P.K. Subban to the Nashville Predators in exchange for defenseman Shea Weber. Not long after, the Tampa Bay Lightning signed Steven Stamkos to an eight-year, $68 million contract extension—putting to bed any talk of the Bolts captain changing addresses that summer.

The Subban trade resonated heavily in Montreal. A popular player whom many earmarked as a future Canadiens great was traded away for a leader and future Hall of Famer in Shea Weber but didn't provide nearly the same amount of excitement and flair as his predecessor. Some fans, notably Canadiens superfan Jay Baruchel, compared the situation to Canadiens great Patrick Roy being traded to the Colorado Avalanche in December 1995.

"Subban's and Roy's individualism was revered until it was resented," Baruchel wrote in his book *Born Into It: A Fan's Life*. "Their passions were encouraged until they were punished. Our fervour stoked the fire of their brilliance, and then we used that fire to burn them down. This is the quintessentially Catholic life cycle of la Sainte-Flanelle. This is Montreal in transaction."

The wheels for a Subban trade were put in motion months before it happened. Sportsnet's Nick Kypreos, who first reported the trade, knew the Canadiens wanted a "different look" for their defense and that the relationship between the team and player had strained. One specific example from the prior season occurred after a February 2016 game against the Colorado Avalanche when Subban was stripped of the puck, leading to the eventual game-winning goal with minutes to play.

Subban held the puck at the blue line and tried to cut across the offensive zone to create a play. However, Avalanche forward Mikhail Grigorenko tapped the puck away from the defenseman. Subban slipped and eventually fell into the boards, leaving Grigorenko to pick up the puck and begin an odd-man rush. Jarome Iginla finished the play with a goal, giving Colorado the lead with 2:03 left in the game. Coach Michel Therrien benched Subban after the mistake, and the Canadiens went on to lose.

"It's disappointing that we lost because of an individual mistake," Therrien said after the game. "As a coach, I thought he could've had a better decision at the blue line. He moved the puck behind, and he put himself in a tough position."

"I was going up the wall and I crossed over and lost an edge," Subban said after the game, according to Postmedia.

Months later, ahead of that year's draft, Subban was subjected to trade rumors. One particular rumor, according to Friedman, circled around Subban being traded to Vancouver for a top draft pick that would've allowed the team to draft forward Pierre-Luc Dubois. The Predators weren't even in the picture until GM David Poile caught wind of Bergevin speaking about Subban at the draft.

The final trade, which saw the Predators flip away their longtime captain who was also on a long-term contract, was a surprise to many when it surfaced as a possibility. But by June 29, 2016, the deal was announced.

"I don't remember hearing any whispers of that at a time. And that itself was kind of a bombshell," Johnston said. "I think a lot of us thought, quite frankly, that Montreal lost the trade big time the day it was made. With some time, there might be more debate about it. But in the moment, it really felt like Montreal was trading a younger player, a better player, and one that was going to go on to have a better career."

Former teammate Dale Weise did not mince words when he was asked his opinion about the trade after it happened in 2016.

"I think they were looking for an excuse, and I think he was the guy that could be targeted as a guy that could be a distraction," Weise told Amanda Stein, then of TSN 690, in October 2016. "You see his personality, you see who he is. He is who he is all the time. What you see on camera, on the ice, that's P.K. Subban all the time. He doesn't change. I never saw one guy have a problem with it in the locker room.

"I think the team was trying to make an excuse. I think he's an easy scapegoat."

When asked by The Athletic about why he was traded, Subban was in the dark.

"The reality is I'll never know 100 percent why I was traded unless I sit down with [Canadiens GM Marc Bergevin] and Geoff Molson and ask them what happened and where it went," Subban said to Basu in a 2017 sit-down interview.

But even P.K.'s own father, Karl "was not surprised" that his son was dealt from his childhood team. As he wrote in his book, *How We Did It*, Karl tried to make the most of a significant change in his eldest son's life.

"When I think about my emotional state regarding P.K's trade, I liken it to the experience of bringing home a new baby. You love the new baby, but its arrival doesn't change your love for the children you already have. The Canadiens were the team that drafted P.K., allowing him to live his dream to play hockey 'like those guys on TV.'"

Subban made his first return to Montreal following the trade on March 2, 2017, at the Bell Centre. The Canadiens played a video tribute for their defenseman, showing his game highlights and off-ice moments with teammates and fans. As the video ended, the crowd cheered and tears flooded Subban's face. One of the many in attendance was Élise Béliveau, the widow of Canadiens legend Jean Béliveau—an idol of Subban's. Subban built a relationship with Élise throughout his time in Montreal, even blowing kisses to her in the stands.

Fans booed Subban whenever he touched the puck, as is custom whenever any player leaves a team through trade or free agency. But there were just as many, if not more fans, who showed love to a polarizing yet entertaining figure in Canadiens hockey through the 2010s.

After the game, Subban tweeted a photo of him waving his stick to the Canadiens while teary-eyed with the caption "Montreal, je t'aime!"

"I wasn't really sure how I was going to feel, but I've played a lot of hockey games in this building and a lot of great things happened in this building and in this city while I was here," Subban said after the game, according to Sportsnet. "All those memories come back, whether it was stuff to do with the hospital or kids, family, teammates, whatever it is, hockey games, emotional games, and I felt that I shared that with all the fans and the community here and I guess that's how it all came out."

The debate has long raged over whether the Canadiens or the Predators won the Subban–Weber trade. It will continue even with both Subban and Weber no longer active in the NHL. Both teams reached the Stanley Cup Final with their new acquisitions and managed to get production from both players until they either stopped playing or moved on to another team. But it's a limited way to view the trade.

Thanks to his rising profile in Montreal, Subban earned endorsement deals with companies like RW&CO, Air Canada, Gatorade, and Scotiabank while emerging as one of the NHL's most prominent personalities. Sportsnet even used him in promotional ads for its hockey coverage.

"So sort of my, I don't want to say popularity, but everything with me, the brand, everything around me sort of grew. And it jumped in a small period of time," Subban told The Athletic in a 2018 interview.

When Subban swapped jerseys and was welcomed to Nashville, his exposure grew. Days after the trade, Subban sang karaoke and met fans at a local Nashville bar. The defenseman eventually established the "Blue Line Buddies" foundation to have better relations between youth in Nashville and local police. It certainly helped that in his first season with the Predators, he played an instrumental role in bringing them to the Stanley Cup final against the Pittsburgh Penguins, which allowed his personality to shine for American audiences.

Later that summer, Subban was a guest at the ESPY Awards alongside other athletes across the sporting world. He's since been profiled in *GQ*, appeared on Comedy Central's *The Daily Show*, briefly had a podcast, and raised money for the family of George Floyd, who was killed by police in 2020. Subban is also part of the NHL's Players Inclusion Coalition, working to encourage diversity and inclusion in the sport of hockey,

"It's great, this stuff's really, really important," Subban said to the Associated Press in 2024. "It's important to the growth of the game. Whenever you're dealing with kids, it's always a priority. They're the future and we have to continue to be there for them."

Subban's high-rising profile during his playing career and post-retirement in 2022 laid the table for the current stage of his career: broadcasting. Following retirement, he joined ESPN as an analyst and even worked with the network during the 2024 Stanley Cup Final between the Edmonton Oilers and Florida Panthers.

"It's a tremendous responsibility," Subban said ahead of the 2024 Stanley Cup Final in a conference call. "ESPN is a massive platform. But the NHL is a game that's given back to me and my family so much.

"To be able to step out of the game and instantly be put in a position to help grow the game and celebrate the players and the product on the ice. I think that's the most important thing, is that you understand really quickly that what's best for the game is understanding that you aren't the product anymore. People are getting to watch you play, it's they're paying to watch Connor McDavid, and these guys play."

Subban's role with ESPN has expanded since joining the broadcast team in 2022. He makes regular appearances on ESPN's Get Up with Mike Greenberg and First Take with Stephen A. Smith. Subban also worked with ESPN as part of its 4 Nations Face-Off coverage in 2025, where he drew criticism for a polarizing social media post. Subban posted an old photo of him and U.S. President Donald Trump, wondering aloud if he'd attend the 4 Nations Face-Off final between Canada and the United States. Trump has openly advocated for Canada to become the United States' 51st state, among other controversial policies and rollbacks during his tenures in the White House.

Despite Subban's misstep leading to outrage, his influence remains in hockey—particularly on what players wear, their personalities, and their brand awareness. While still miles behind what players in the NFL or NBA do, it's a much different world for NHL players compared to Subban's time in the league.

"I think a big part of his legacy is just growing the game," P.K's brother Malcolm said. "You look at the game and now it's people having brands. He's one of the only guys to have one million followers and he's not Connor McDavid by any means. He does have a Norris Trophy.

"It's OK to be a good player and to show your personality and have personality."

The sport has also changed in terms of its diversity of voices who speak about the game, and Subban is part of that change. But some don't think his post-playing days could only be limited to NHL broadcasting. Stroumboulopoulos sees Subban as a future part-owner of an NHL team or potentially part of a team's management staff. But maybe that's too limiting for him, even if his hockey story is "not done."

"There's more to P.K.'s story than just hockey," Stroumboulopoulos said. "You couldn't find a lot of athletes coming through the NHL at the time where you would say it would be more than just hockey and golf tournaments when they retire. P.K., I think he's sort of blazing a different trail for people now, I think, on what a hockey player could be. I'm excited to see what he does."

As Subban drifts further away from his playing career, the love for him in Montreal remains. The mural of Subban in Canadiens and Predators colors can still be found on the side of the old "Chez Serge" building on Saint Laurent Boulevard. Some fans still wear Subban shirts and jerseys when they go to Canadiens games.

Even the Canadiens themselves have played a role in mending fences.

The team invited Subban to a Canadiens-Predators game during the 2022–23 NHL season, honoring him before puck drop and giving fans an opportunity to celebrate him one more time. The Canadiens introduced him as "one of the most electrifying players to ever don the Canadiens jersey." Months earlier, he retired after a 13-year career that took him through Montreal, Nashville and New Jersey. Winning a Norris Trophy and an Olympic gold medal stand among his biggest accomplishments. At center ice, Subban addressed the crowd alongside a patient, Mila, from the Montreal Children's Hospital.

"To all the fans, to all of you guys who are here today and have continued to support me," Subban said during his speech. "I've always felt that we had an understanding. That when you wear the Montreal Canadiens jersey, when you wear the CH, that you play with the same passion that you fans bring every single night to this building. That we see around the city and globally.

"All I wanted to do when I put that jersey on was play with that passion. I hope that's a message to the current players and players that are going to put on the jersey in the future. That these guys will love you no matter if you leave it on the ice every night. So, leave it on the ice every night."

When Subban finished his speech, he waved to the crowd one final time as Mila was helped off the ice in her wheelchair. Meanwhile, a familiar face walked down the tunnel toward the ice in an all-black ensemble. Black suit, black cowboy hat, dark gray shirt, and black tie. When fans realized who it was, they cheered and gasped.

"What do you guys think about Carey Price?" Subban said, pointing to the franchise goaltender.

Price and Subban met and got low. They tapped hands three times. The triple-low five was back for one night. There was no better way to end Subban's return to the Bell Centre spotlight than by bringing back an enduring symbol of his Canadiens tenure, riding out into the sunset with a fellow teammate.

6

Anson Carter

No one knows for sure how long the referees needed to review the play in Helsinki. It could have been 15 minutes. But players felt like they were waiting for hours. Anson Carter was sure that puck was in the net. He hoped the referees would see things his way. It meant he wouldn't have to play the rest of the gold-medal game on a sprained knee.

Moments earlier, Carter—nicknamed "Ace" after originally being nicknamed "AC," for his initials—sped into the offensive zone as Canada battled Sweden for the gold medal in the 2003 International Ice Hockey Federation World Championship final in Finland. Canada sought its first World Championship win in five years but needed an overtime period against the Swedes to secure the victory. The Canadians were tired and would've benefitted from an overtime winner sooner than later, but were already planning ahead for a shootout if necessary.

"Krys Kolanos was really good in shootouts, and he hadn't had a shift the entire game," Team Canada's Shane Doan remembered. "Underneath the stadium was another practice sheet. And so [Canada head coach Andy Murray] tapped Krys Kolanos and was like, 'You haven't skated here in like three hours. Go take a couple drives and start getting warmed up for if we go to a shootout. You might have to go in it.'"

Carter fired the puck on net, trying to beat Sweden's Mikael Tellqvist. The forward grabbed the rebound and raced behind the net with a wraparound attempt. When he slid the puck into Tellqvist's pad, Carter immediately celebrated the goal. His teammates followed suit, flooding the ice and throwing their sticks and gloves in the air.

"When I shot the puck initially and I saw the rebound, I came around and had so much momentum and speed coming around the net," Carter said. "My only concern was, will [the referees] have the vantage point or the viewing point, or the technology, to show that puck was in. Because I clearly saw the separation between the puck, the white, and the goal line."

As Canada's bench cleared, a cluster of players jumped atop Carter at the blue line. But the Swedes tried to keep playing.

"They had a two-on-one or a three-on-one going the other direction," teammate Shane Doan said. "We were like 'Oh, oh.' We just all jumped on the ice because the best way to stop this was to jump on the ice and start celebrating."

Carter's knee felt every bit of the growing dogpile.

"I tweaked my knee in the celebration," Carter said. "I don't think people understand that the weight of 20 players jumping on you when you're trying to support everyone. When they're jumping on you, something's going to have to give."

A referee skated by the Canadian celebration and cautioned that they needed to look it over. Canadian faces went from joyfulness to confusion. As time went by, with officials looking over every possible angle, doubt crept into the minds of the Canadians.

"We're just all sitting there," Canada's Daniel Brière said. "It felt like we were there for two hours just waiting for the call to come. We had a replay that would show the puck was in. And at first you're like, 'Okay, this is over, they're gonna find it. It's a win.' We knew the puck crossed the line.

"But then the longer it takes us, then you start wondering, why are they taking so long? What's the problem? What are they looking at? Maybe they don't have this replay that our video coach was relaying in?"

All eyes fell on referee Vladimír Šindler, who had a handheld phone to his ear listening to goal officials pore over the instant replays. One point of his hand toward center ice would give Canada the gold they felt they deserved. Otherwise, more hockey would be needed, and Team Canada would have to soldier on without one of its better scorers.

Seven seasons into his NHL career, Carter was a perennial 20-plus goal scorer who found success with a handful of teams. He spent the 2002–03 season with the Edmonton Oilers and the New York Rangers. But his career also featured stops in Boston and Washington. Carter even won a World Championship with Canada back in 1997, also in Finland. His style of play and NHL success made him a worthy addition for the Canadians in 2003.

"I always felt like he was underappreciated," former national hockey writer Craig Custance said. "Anson Carter had one of those careers where I'm like, 'Why is he bouncing around?'"

"He could score, he could skate, very good on the forecheck," Brière said. "Strong on the puck. Could make plays."

"I remember how fast he was in his ability to get to the net," Doan said. "And if he got the lane, he could drive the net so well."

Carter's journey was one review away from adding another gold medal to his trophy case. A long way from his humble beginnings in Scarborough, Ontario, trying to convince his parents to take up a sport he'd fallen in love with.

THE CARTER FAMILY, LIKE many Canadian families, first bought hockey equipment for their son Anson at a Canadian Tire. For the uninitiated, the retail store offers just about everything you'd need for day-to-day living. Kitchen appliances and housewares, tools for home improvement, and even a garage to get your car fixed. If you were your own mechanic, the store offers car parts and tools—and yes, tires.

Sports equipment can also be purchased, including for young hockey aspirants wanting to be the greats who came before them. Helmets, sticks, skates, mouthguards, water bottles, hockey tape, chest protectors, gloves, masks, you name it.

Anson's parents, Horace and Valma—immigrants from Barbados—loaded up their cart with hockey equipment. A pair of gloves from Bauer or CCM. A jock strap, garter belt, hockey pants, shin and shoulder pads, a hockey bag. There was also a Titan TPM stick just like the one Mike Bossy had—a right shot stick instead of the left-shot like most of his friends. Bossy was one of Carter's earliest sports heroes alongside Michael Jordan and Bo Jackson. Carter even received an authentic Bossy jersey from an uncle once. At least he thought it was, until he put the jersey to wash. The jersey had ironed-on numbers that peeled off after tumbling around in the dryer.

There were no skates in the Carter family shopping cart that day. His parents had already bought their son a $10 pair of skates from a garage sale. They might as well have been Willie O'Ree's.

"Tan skates, no ankle support, no nothing," Carter said.

But despite the notable omission from the cart, a hefty bill still awaited the Carters at the cash register.

"All my gear cost $3,000," Anson remembered. "I look at my parents' faces. Their mouths hit the ground. I remember thinking, 'What the hell did I just do?'"

Anson was a late starter into ice hockey at eight years old. He loved playing floor hockey in gym class at school and street hockey with friends in his hometown of Scarborough, Ontario. Carter's neighborhood friends would match up against other street kids for local supremacy after school. Meanwhile, Anson's sister, Michelle, was about to start playing soccer. So, it was only fair that Anson got the opportunity to play an organized sport, too.

Anson enjoyed the sport in its other forms, but there was a learning curve for ice hockey. The first time he ever stepped into a locker room, playing minor hockey for the local Agincourt Lions, he opened his hockey bag and stared at the equipment inside. He had no idea where any of it went on his body. How do you put on shoulder pads? How do you strap on your shin guards? Carter needed help from his mother and another hockey dad to get himself sorted.

When Carter first stepped on the ice, he kept falling. The lack of ankle support on his "Willie O'Ree" skates did him in. He spent the first half of his debut minor league season falling many times, unable to catch up to the puck. He says his inability to skate properly held him back. What happened to him next was straight out of a movie. Specifically, the movie *Like Mike*, in which the lead character—played by Bow Wow—obtains a hand-me-down pair of Nikes marked "MJ" and becomes a child basketball star. If you flip shoes for skates, Carter believes his story went similarly as youth hockey player.

"I got those new skates, and I was scoring five and six goals a game," Carter remembered. "I just missed out on the league's scoring title by one point."

As Carter got better, he continued his climb through minor hockey. But his friends started playing other sports like football or basketball and wondered why he continued to play a predominantly white sport.

"They got on me and said I shouldn't be playing a white man's game," Carter told *Sports Illustrated* in October 1999. "It was like they'd become too black to play hockey. I didn't understand it."

The Black hockey players who were notable in Carter's youth were mostly tough guys and fighters. The only player who broke that mold was the first Black hockey superstar to exist: Grant Fuhr. Carter once imagined himself as a goaltender just like Fuhr, and he wasn't the only successful future NHL star to do so. But when the Carter family saw the exorbitant price of goaltending equipment, those dreams were dashed.

"My mom and dad were like, 'Hell, no. You're not playing that. It's not happening.'" Carter said.

Despite not taking after Fuhr, the goaltender still carried some influence on Carter in his youth as a Black hockey player. Carter pushed back against those who wondered aloud about Fuhr's complexion, pointing to him being biracial—Fuhr is part Black and part Indigenous—and not being as Black as Carter's complexion. Instead, Fuhr was a Black player whom he and his friends looked up to while watching the NHL.

However, Carter didn't have many NHL role models who were offensive threats. Even if players like Tony McKegney existed, they weren't always accessible for Carter to watch on television while playing in cities like Buffalo and St. Louis.

"I think that's a big reason why, when I played in the National Hockey League, I made a point not to fight all the time," Carter said. "I probably could've fought a lot more. But I made a point because I never had a lot of players to look up to that were offensive players that didn't fight.

"I made a point not to fight all the time because I thought there could be other Black kids coming up that are watching me play. I want the parents, in particular, to understand that you could be a Black hockey player. You could be a skilled hockey player. You could score and not be the team tough guy all the time."

Carter leaned all the way into being an offensive presence as a teenager, scoring 18 goals and 40 points with the Wexford Raiders of the Metro Junior A Hockey League in Ontario as a 17-year-old. It was enough to get him drafted in the NHL; a 10th-round draft choice by the Quebec Nordiques in the 1992 NHL Entry Draft, an unexpected predicament for the teenager. Carter and fellow teammate/future NHLer Bryan Muir traveled to Montreal in support of other teammates who were supposed to be selected that year.

"We stayed for maybe three rounds, not even that long, and we drove back to Toronto," Carter said.

The next day, as Carter remembers, he received a phone call from a scout who wanted to let him know the Nordiques chose him.

No, you didn't. I was there yesterday. What are you talking about?

Carter immediately hung up the phone. He thought it was his friend and fellow Bajan/Canadian Kevin Weekes who played a trick on him. The phone soon rang again, and Carter picked up.

Weeksy, enough! Quit calling me. Enough. Are we playing street hockey today? What are we doing today? Quit playing games.

Carter hung up again. A third call came, and Carter was told to check that day's newspaper. Carter called to his dad, who had the *Toronto Sun*'s back page in their family basement. It included a full list of names from the draft. Sure enough, Carter found his name and the Quebec Nordiques, taken in the 10th round, 220th overall.

"I was shocked. And I was pissed," Carter said. "Because I'm not a 10th round [draft pick]. I'm a first-round draft pick."

That snub added "fuel to the fire" once Carter enrolled at Michigan State University to play hockey ahead of his freshman season. At 6'1", 157 pounds, Carter felt his game would translate better at the collegiate level versus playing at the major junior level in Canada where they'd prefer heavier players. Carter's parents also insisted he get his education.

"They didn't want me to go to the [Ontario Hockey League]," Carter said. "There's tons of fighting back then. Players are dropping out of high school in ninth grade to try to pursue their dreams. I was like, 'I'm not going to go and live in some Canadian small city.' Which, yes, they're passionate about hockey. But if it doesn't work out, then what am I going to do? No education. What am I going to do exactly with my life?"

In Carter's first season, he was named the Central Collegiate Hockey Association's Rookie of the Year after a 19-goal, 30-point season in 36 games. Carter was a Hobey Baker Award finalist and an All-American in 1995, his junior season, after a 34-goal, 51-point campaign.

"Anson Carter was just a superstar on those teams,"The Athletic's Craig Custance said. "He was just so dominant at that level. I was convinced, at that point, this guy is going to be an absolute superstar in the NHL."

Carter never played for the Nordiques—they became the Colorado Avalanche and won the Cup in their inaugural season in 1996—when he arrived on the professional circuit. He was instead traded to the Washington Capitals in 1996 in exchange for a fourth-round pick (which the Avs used to select defenseman Ben Storey). But his Washington tenure was short-lived, lasting all of 19 games before he was flipped to the Boston Bruins alongside Jim Carey, Jason Allison, and the Capitals' 1997 third-round draft pick for Bill Ranford, Adam Oates, and future NHL on TNT panelmate Rick Tocchet.

Carter spent parts of four seasons as a Bruin, scoring 70 goals and 143 points in 211 games. A high point for the Scarborough native came during the 1999 playoffs, when he scored a double-overtime game-winning goal in Game 5 of the Bruins' Eastern Conference Quarterfinal series against the Carolina Hurricanes. Boston won the series in six games.

Another enduring memory of Carter's time in Boston revolves around his jersey numbers. He wore 11 and 33. He had wanted No. 22, a number that followed him from his collegiate days as an homage to Bossy. But when he approached the Bruins' front office about changing his number, there was no negotiation to be had.

"The manager looks at me says, 'Don't worry about it, kid. Just focus on playing hockey,'" Carter said.

Carter was unaware of any history that followed the No. 22 or much of the Bruins' history in general. It was not like his days at Michigan State when players were given a program guide that allowed them to learn about the players that came before him. The walls of Boston's Fleet Center—now known as the TD Garden—were "sterile, gray, and cold" to Carter, in contrast to the present day where you'll find many photos, jerseys and related paraphernalia that honors the Bruins greats of the past and present.

Carter was once intrigued about an elderly gentlemen working for the Bruins solely to hand out per diem and itineraries to players. The forward had no idea who the man was until he went to teammate Ray Bourque. Turns out, the man was Bruins legend Johnny Bucyk.

"If I had that guide, I would know all this stuff," Carter said. "And I wouldn't be walking around ignoring not having a clue what's going on."

Case in point, Carter was given the opportunity to meet hockey legend Willie O'Ree before a Bruins game. The Bruins planned to honor O'Ree with a pregame ceremony and to give him a Bruins jersey marked with his name and number on it. O'Ree made his name as the first-ever Black player to step on NHL ice, accomplishing the feat on January 18, 1958, against the Montreal Canadiens as a member of the Bruins.

It was only when Carter stood alongside O'Ree that he realized the latter's number was the famed No. 22 Carter himself wanted.

"I tried my best to not be mad in that picture," Carter said.

After those four seasons in Boston, Carter spent three seasons with the Edmonton Oilers. Carter was traded alongside first- and a second-round draft picks for Bill Guerin and future considerations. Carter was one of five Black players in Oilers colors during the 2000–01 season, joining goaltender Joaquin Gage, defenseman Sean

Brown, and forwards Georges Laraque and Mike Grier. The NHL had 16 Black players in the league that season, according to the *Globe & Mail*—and 30 percent of them were with the Oilers.

"There will always be some race tension, and you can't save the world," Carter told the *Washington Post* in a feature about the five Black Oilers written in April 2001. "But this is an example where you can show your kids, hey, there's a black player, and black kids and white kids look up to him, which hasn't happened a lot in this sport.

"Who's to say that some guys on this team even ever had a black person over to their house before? Obviously through sports, a lot of barriers get broken down. Kids grow up and see that, and their beliefs are different than if you were never here."

Carter spent almost three full seasons in Edmonton. He was traded to the New York Rangers in 2003 with Aleš Píša in exchange for Radek Dvořák and Cory Cross. When the Rangers failed to make the playoffs, Carter was an ideal candidate to play for Canada at the World Hockey Championship in Finland. And he would prove his worth in the gold medal game for Canada against the Swedes.

Carter's journey featured more stops after his tenure with the Rangers ended in January 2004. He was flipped back to the Capitals in exchange for future Hall of Famer Jaromír Jágr. His stay in Washington lasted less than two months before he was traded to the Los Angeles Kings for forward Jared Aulin.

Following the 2004–05 NHL lockout, Carter resurfaced with the Vancouver Canucks to begin the 2005–06 campaign on a one-year contract. He joined a team that was upset by the Calgary Flames in the opening round of the 2004 playoffs, but still featured talents like Markus Näslund, Todd Bertuzzi, Brendan Morrison, and a pair of Swedish twins Daniel and Henrik Sedin.

"I had offers to sign other places multiple years," Carter said. "I turned them down because I thought we'd have a real chance to win in Vancouver. And that's what I wanted that late in my career. I wanted to win."

Carter rode shotgun with the Sedin twins and likened his role as a mentor to the two budding stars. However, it didn't mean their line always got the same treatment as the West Coast Express (a combination featuring Näslund, Bertuzzi, and Morrison) from head coach Marc Crawford, according to Carter.

"We get on the ice our first practice," Carter remembered. "We go down three on to make a sweet play, but we hit the post. He's yelling, 'I can't believe you three p—ies, like you guys. Hit the net, whatever, whatever'. He was always all over [the Sedins]. I remember them looking over at me like, 'Ace, this guy's all over us.'

"And I'd watched the West Coast Express go down. They'd miss the net by like 10 feet and there'd be crickets. We go down, same thing, not score, hit the crossbar, and he's all over us."

Carter took the young players aside and enforced that they should pay more attention to Crawford's message than the coach himself. The trio ended up building chemistry and trust alongside one another, with Carter scoring a career-high 33 goals in the process. The forward added 55 points in 81 games played with the Canucks, achieving success with the Swedish twins. In an article written for the Players Tribune, the Sedin twins acknowledged that Carter helped them find their game in Vancouver.

"When we started playing with Anson, it was an eye-opener for me," Daniel Sedin wrote in the article. "That's when I realized that we really can play in this league, and we can be really good. Before that season, every time we would go back to Sweden in the summer, a part of me would think, Can we really do this? Should we just stay here? Everything clicked for us because of Anson. He's probably why we're still here at 36 years old."

"He knew how to be successful in the league," Henrik added in the article. "He helped us work on our cycle game down low because he gave us that confidence to get in those gritty areas and be physical. He was sort of the opposite of us."

When the Sedins were inducted into the Hockey Hall of Fame, they made sure to mention Carter in their speech.

"Anson Carter, you taught us to take ownership of our play. I still remember you dragging us in to watch video of our power play, or things we needed to do better as a line, you wanted us to be go-to guys. An attitude we took with us the rest of our careers. Don't leave it up to someone else, take the initiative. Great lessons for life. Great lessons for us, too," Daniel Sedin said.

Despite Carter finding success with the Canucks, his stay only lasted that one season in Vancouver. Carter told Sportsnet 590 The Fan in a 2020 interview that he believed race played a role in him not staying with the Canucks for a longer period of time, saying that if he was a "different color hockey player" he'd be "looked at a lot differently."

Carter said he would've been willing to stay in Vancouver on a three-year deal worth $2 million annually. The forward even expected teams on the free-agent market would want to sign him for $3 to $4 million per year. But while the Canucks signed the Sedins to three-year deals of their own worth $10.75 million, Vancouver's front office wasn't willing to sign Carter to a similar deal. Carter says that he was given a one-year deal worth $2 million. The Canucks were potentially willing to raise their offer by $100,000, but the damage had already been done.

"I got too much pride," Carter said. "This is not going to happen. This happens my whole career, whenever my deal was up. Obviously, people kept moving the goalposts.

"People in Vancouver were saying that 'Oh, Carter's greedy.' He priced himself out of the market," Carter said. "And nobody knew that they weren't offering me a raise in my deal."

Instead, Carter signed a one-year contract with the Columbus Blue Jackets. He laments not signing a longer term deal while also not being in the right frame of mind after departing Vancouver. He experienced a drop off in production, scoring 10 goals and 27 points in 54 games with the Blue Jackets in 2006–07. Carter was then traded to Carolina in February 2007 in exchange for a fifth-round pick. The forward joined the Edmonton Oilers on a professional tryout agreement ahead of the 2007 season, but he ultimately signed with Switzerland-based Lugano HC for the 2007–08, his final professional hockey season. He scored three goals and eight points in 15 games.

Despite the numerous stops at his career's end, Carter still ended his NHL playing days with more than respectable numbers. Through 674 career games played, the Scarborough native scored 202 goals and 421 points for eight NHL teams.

In the present day, Carter can be found on television as a hockey analyst. He is a part of TNT's NHL coverage, working alongside host Liam McHugh and fellow analysts Paul Bissonnette, Henrik Lundqvist, and Wayne Gretzky. Carter has also worked for NBC Sports and has made appearances on Sportsnet.

Longtime play-by-play man Gord Miller remembered working with Carter when he first joined NBC to cover Notre Dame hockey games. Miller said he knew pretty early on why Carter was going to be a "good broadcaster."

Miller remembered "his ability to explain things to the audience in an entertaining and non-jargony way."

Carter is also the co-chair of the NHL's Player Inclusion Coalition and is helping to make the sport more accessible to minority groups. The forward was also inducted into the Michigan State Athletics Hall of Fame in September 2024.

Finally, Carter is leading the charge for NHL hockey to return to Atlanta for a third time while also serving as minority owner of the

ECHL's Atlanta Gladiators. In March 2024, Carter and his group made a request to the NHL for them to add Atlanta as an expansion franchise to their current list of teams.

"I have no doubt that the best league in the world will thrive in its return to Metro Atlanta," Carter said, according to the Associated Press. "I have been in dialogue with Commissioner [Gary] Bettman since 2019 about an expansion team returning to the Fulton County Metro Atlanta market, knowing that NHL franchise decisions are exclusively decided by the NHL Board of Governors."

Not bad for a Scarborough kid who once upon a time had to convince his parents to pay $3,000 for his gear at a local Canadian Tire.

THE INTERNATIONAL ICE HOCKEY Federation says the review actually took 10 minutes for referee Vladimír Šindler to look over Anson Carter's potential gold-medal-winning goal against Sweden at the 2003 World Hockey Championship in Finland. When the goal judge gave him enough confirmation over the phone, Šindler pointed to center ice and the Canadians resumed their celebration. The IIHF says it's the first gold-medal goal to ever be confirmed by video replay.

"He endured the longest replay review in history at the World Championship," Miller said.

When the goal was confirmed, Carter raised his arms and stick, skating up ice in triumph. He wasn't thinking about his throbbing knee, still in pain from the premature celebration.

"It was clear as day to me. There was no doubt in my mind. It was in," Carter said. "I just didn't know if they had the technology to show it during the game."

"The Anson Carter goal is just legendary," former teammate Steve Staios said.

But what made Carter's happiness even more special was his look while celebrating. His black dreadlocks flowing behind the back of his jersey, forever remembered as an iconic, winning hockey hairstyle. The forward might not have ever considered adding twists in his hair if it wasn't for a suggestion from his sister, Michelle. But that suggestion came after the urging of teammates to consider another idea.

In 1997, when he was still a Bruin, Carter's teammates wanted him to grow an afro. Teammates even convinced Carter to take a $10,000 bet to grow it out. But he went bald, shaving his hair off in homage to Michael Jordan. It was a departure from the high-top fade days at Michigan State University.

Once Carter grew his hair, his fellow Bruins comrades tried to convince him to keep it. Instead, Michelle suggested for her brother to add twists in his hair. Carter eventually visited a salon in Dorchester, a Boston neighborhood, and was tended to much longer than anticipated during the afternoon of a game day.

"I didn't know it was going to take two hours to sit in that chair to get all locked up and ready to go," Carter said.

When Carter made his way to the rink for that day's game, he ran into his head coach Pat Burns. The bench boss was immediately taken aback by his forward's new hairstyle.

"I tried to sneak into the room," Carter said. "I got there early and [Burns] sees me and he's like 'Oh, you're starting tonight for sure.' His eyes are as big as saucers."

Sure enough, Carter stood on the blue line that night during the anthem with Bruins coaches and front office staring at his hair. The forward usually stood on the far end, away from the benches, moments before the game. Carter did the exact opposite that night, trying to be as close to the Bruins bench so fewer people would notice his new hair.

Despite not wanting to command attention, the irony is that Carter kept that look for the remainder of his playing career and we now remember it as one of hockey's most iconic hair styles.

"It's no different than having any other kind of hairstyle really," Carter said. "It's just that your hair takes a lot longer to dry. You've got to really be on top of it. When you have dreads your hair is so thick, and it takes hours and hours and hours to dry."

The hockey world has seen its fair share of "flow" or "lettuce"—appropriate hockey terms for hairdos. Jaromír Jágr's mullets are recognized among the sport's most memorable hair styles. Mika Zibanejad, Duncan Keith, and Erik Karlsson have rocked long hair under their helmets.

But as more Black players enter the league, we've seen more twists, afros, and dreadlocks become the norm. During a preseason rookie game in September 2025, Ottawa Senators prospect Djibril Touré rocked a durag underneath his helmet to protect his braids. Unfortunately, not every team has been as welcoming. When Anthony Duclair cut his dreads and shaved his face after joining the New York Islanders during the summer of 2024—then-GM Lou Lamoriello had a rule that required players to be clean-shaven—it led to social media outrage. For what it's worth, Duclair says he wasn't aware of any reactions online and was fully aware of the rule before he signed.

During Carter's playing career, he remembers being told by an unnamed general manager to shave his dreadlocks. But he pushed back and kept his locs.

"How come I don't see Jágr or Gretzky, or Joe Thornton, all these guys around the league cutting their hair?" Carter said. "What's so different about my hair? And he couldn't answer that question. And as you can see, I never cut my hair. I always had locs the whole time in my career.

"You're not going to tell me what to do with my hair if I'm being a decent citizen here. Like, why is my hair triggering you?"

Since Carter's pushback, the forward feels he's played a role in the diversity of hair styles that have sprung thanks to players past and present. Georges Laraque has rocked dreads during his playing career. J.T. Brown has grown out his hair and dyed it blond or had blond tips on his own dreads. P.K. Subban and Mathieu Joseph have also played with an afro under their helmet.

And that list won't stop growing any time soon.

"A lot of boys and girls are playing the game now with locs and feel comfortable because they saw Anson Carter do it," Carter said. "And if Anson Carter can do it, then they could do it. So that, to me, is probably the most satisfying thing knowing that I can help people feel comfortable, just being their authentic selves when they're on the ice because that's what we want a hockey game to be about."

7

Fred Brathwaite

Trivia time!

Without looking, can you guess which NHL goaltender started the first game of the 1998–99 Calgary Flames season? He started for the Flames against former Flame Mike Vernon and the San Jose Sharks, securing a 3–3 tie in their season debut. Through that point in his career, he had played for three teams, with more than 500 NHL games and a Stanley Cup on his resume.

The answer? Ken Wregget. How long did his Flames tenure last? Twenty-seven games. (I'm so sorry to have to make you revisit the Young Guns era, Calgary fans. I pray you'll forgive me.) He was supposed to be a veteran presence on a young squad working toward being a playoff team. Instead, Wregget battled back spasms among other injuries, limiting his time in goal with the Flames.

During an early November game, Wregget gave way to a young Tyler Moss four minutes into the second period because of those spasms. Five years earlier, Moss was a second-round pick of the Tampa Bay Lightning who bounced around the minor leagues before making his NHL debut for the Flames during the 1997–98 season.

Moss played 10 full games during the 1998–99 season with Calgary. Before Game 11, a date against the Tampa Bay Lightning, Moss sat in the trainer's room debating whether to wrap his groin to preserve it from further wear and tear. His trainer advised him to do so and if it felt good after a few minutes, he'd be in the clear.

Moss lasted all of six minutes and 11 seconds. He made a save on a breakaway chance before he felt the pain.

"I snapped my groin off the bone," Moss remembered.

"It just looked like I got shot. Snapped off the bone. Couldn't even move my leg after. I had to get carried off."

Jean-Sébastien Giguère came on in relief of Moss and helped the Flames win over the Lightning, making 21 saves on 22 shots. Giguère was the third goalie to make an appearance for the Flames that season. Andrei Trefilov and Tyrone Garner also played games for the Flames that season.

That Christmas, the Flames' eventual sixth goaltender was representing Team Canada at the Spengler Cup. Though he didn't know he'd be suiting up for the Flames in due time.

Journeyman goaltender Fred Brathwaite spent time with the Canadian national team awaiting a chance to return to the NHL. He played 40 games across three seasons with the Edmonton Oilers before bouncing around the American Hockey League and the International Hockey League. Brathwaite helped Canada win their fourth consecutive Spengler Cup with a 35-save performance in a 5–2 win over Switzerland's HC Davos and was later named to the tournament's All-Star Team.

When Brathwaite wasn't donning the red and white for Canada, he spent time as Moss' roommate in his downtown Calgary condo. The two were both Ottawa natives, attended the same high school briefly and lived in nearby neighborhoods. Moss even bought a pair of Heaton goalie pads off Brathwaite for around $500. Both men grew to be best friends, which made him the ideal roommate for Moss.

"I was like, 'Fred, why don't you just move in with me?'" Moss remembered. "'I got a two-bedroom condo downtown and you're going to be traveling all the time. We're always away. It's perfect.'"

With injuries stockpiling for the Flames goaltenders, Brathwaite eventually received a call in January 1999 with the intention of playing for Calgary's minor league affiliate in Saint John, New Brunswick.

"I would love to go play in Saint John's," Brathwaite said.

Brathwaite was in Ottawa when he received the call, but he would need to go back to Calgary to retrieve his gear before making another trek out east.

"[The Flames were] like is Freddie staying with you?" Moss said. "I'm like, yeah. They're like, 'Can you bring him tomorrow?'"

Days before the Flames were supposed to play against the Dallas Stars, Giguère aggravated his hamstring, according to Moss.

"They said, 'We don't actually have a goalie for tomorrow's game,'" Brathwaite said. "So, can you play against Dallas tomorrow? And I think well, obviously I could do that. I don't know how well I'll do, but I can do it."

And that is how Brathwaite became the Flames' sixth netminder to appear in a game that season when he stood between the pipes against the Dallas Stars. Brathwaite was another failsafe option for the Flames, who might as well have been cursed at the goaltending position that year.

But whatever voodoo hovered over them didn't affect Brathwaite that night.

He made 21 saves in a 1–0 victory over the Stars. Brathwaite ended the season playing 28 games with an 11–9–7 record to go along with a 2.45 goals-against average and a .915 save percentage.

"And then I ended up signing and then playing [in Calgary] for three years, which was awesome," Brathwaite said. "The city, the fans, the organization was awesome."

"Next thing you know, it was 'Freddie!' chants from the Saddledome for the rest of the year, and it was well deserved," Moss said. "He ended up playing great and he ended up resurrecting his career."

It was the beginning of Brathwaite's short yet memorable tenure with the Flames and his days as a Calgary flame favorite. Despite being an undersized goaltender—something that would be absolutely unheard of in the modern game—Brathwaite found success as an athletic goaltender who still found ways to make key saves.

"I think of how crazy quick he was laterally," Calgary broadcaster Pat Steinberg said. "And how he used his pads to make stops that you didn't think he was going to get to. How he was able to kick his left or right pad out to stop a shot."

"He was an unbelievable athlete," former Flames GM Craig Button said. "Just an unbelievable athlete. You think about it. Five foot nine? [The NHL has Brathwaite listed at 5'7"]. I mean, that might be stretching it, right? He never gave up on a play.

"I always said he would have been a great tap dancer if he didn't want to be a goalie. Because his feet were so fast, and his agility was phenomenal. His footwork was just so beautiful."

THIS CHAPTER COULD HAVE easily been about Rod Brathwaite. There's a reason why you haven't heard nearly as much about him compared with his brother.

Rod grew up in the neighborhood of Briargreen, nestled in the suburb of Nepean, Ontario, in Ottawa. Just like NHL goaltenders who've come before him like Grant Fuhr, Rod took up the position of masked man in goal.

His younger brother, Fred, wanted to be just like his big brother. He'd watch him play goalie and tried to mimic him—without any real knowledge if his brother was actually good, or dedicated, enough to play the position full-time.

Sure enough, Rod never pursued the sport past the age of 15. Fred, however, still wanted to be like his brother. But with equipment being so expensive, the younger Brathwaite was forced to play with hand-me-downs and rented equipment through the Nepean Minor Hockey Association in Ottawa.

"You'd probably get gloves. A chest protector. Pads," Brathwaite said, trying to remember the old days. "I think you'd have to supply your own pants and helmet and your own stick.

"I remember back then goalie sticks were probably twenty dollars. My dad was, 'Whew, you better hold on to this for quite some time.' Twenty dollars was pretty expensive for a hockey stick."

Fred had other goalie heroes beyond his big brother, including Fuhr, who has been acknowledged as the NHL's first Black superstar. Brathwaite even had posters of Fuhr hung up in his childhood bedroom. A photo of Fuhr dressed in Maple Leafs garb hangs in front of his trophy case.

"He was just an athlete," Brathwaite said. "I mean, he was in the net making saves where you thought the puck was going to go in, and somehow he'd come across with a glove save or a kick save or something of that sort.

"He could play the game and leave the game behind. Just so mentally strong. He could let in five goals, but he'd come up with that big save at the end. Where a lot of us, a lot of goalies, can't put those goals behind them and can't win the game. And that was something he did do."

Another goaltender Fred looked up to was Darren Pang. Both men were small goaltenders who both grew up in Nepean and attended the same high school, Sir Robert Borden High School. Both became NHLers despite their smaller statures.

"There is something to our resilience," Pang told the *Ottawa Sun* in November 2021. "I remember when I saw Freddy play for the first time. I always thought he played bigger than he was. When you're our size, you have to be more patient. You couldn't afford to go down too early."

Despite Brathwaite's size, he still rose up the junior hockey ranks, playing for Junior A level teams before surfacing with the Oshawa Generals of the Ontario Hockey League. In Brathwaite's first season, he played the role of backup behind fellow netminder Kevin Butt. The Generals ended the regular season as division champions before winning the OHL playoffs over the Kitchener Rangers, entering the Memorial Cup as a favorite.

"Oshawa was a really good team, and the expectations for Oshawa were to be competitive and to win," Craig Button said, who was then a scout for the Minnesota North Stars.

But when the Generals found themselves in a 1990 Memorial Cup final against the Rangers, already down 2–1, Brathwaite sprung into action. Starting goaltender Kevin Butt left partway through the championship game with an ankle injury, forcing the team to play Brathwaite.

"They ended up clearing a shot off Kevin Butt's leg and he's going down," Brathwaite told The Hockey News in a 2015 interview with Ken Campbell. "And I'm like, 'Well, he better get up.' And all of a sudden, he's going past me, and now I have to get in the net. I didn't have any time to think about it. I could just go out there, and after I got out there, I could just play the game again and do whatever I can, thinking, 'Hopefully I don't screw up.'"

Brathwaite made 22 saves on 23 shots, helping the Generals win the Memorial Cup in double overtime.

"He basically won them that game," play-by-play man Gord Miller said. "He didn't help them. He won it for them. He was unbelievable."

By the end of his OHL days, Brathwaite spent parts of five seasons with the Generals, London Knights, and Detroit Junior Red Wings. Brathwaite even scored a goal in his final junior season in 1992–93. Despite his major junior success, Brathwaite wasn't drafted by an NHL team.

Following the end of his major junior career, Brathwaite was set to join the Las Vegas Thunder of the International Hockey League. But with their training camp not open just yet, he was added to the Edmonton Oilers' rookie camp roster.

"So I was like, 'Yeah, I'll go to camp. I'll kill some time before I go to Las Vegas,'" Brathwaite said.

A chance invitation gave Brathwaite an opportunity to impress the Oilers, playing well enough to join their main roster that fall. As a 20-year-old, he backed up Bill Ranford and made 19 appearances during the 1993–94 campaign. He finished the year with a 3–10–3 record with a 3.54 goals-against average and an .889 save percentage. The Ottawa native stayed in Edmonton through 1996 before joining the Manitoba Moose ahead of the 1996–97 season in the IHL and eventually latching on to the Canadian National team in 1998 and winning the Spengler Cup by the end of the calendar year.

When Brathwaite joined the Flames in 1999, they were going through a dark point in their history. The Flames endured back-to-back losing seasons while ushering in a new era, long distanced from their championship-winning squad in 1989. Calgary reached the playoffs for four consecutive seasons between 1993 and 1996 but only advanced out of the first round once.

As those Flames teams failed, pieces like Joe Nieuwendyk, Gary Roberts, and Doug Gilmour were eventually shipped elsewhere. Theoren Fleury, another holdover from that 1989 team, remained a Flame for one more month after Brathwaite joined before being flipped to the Colorado Avalanche.

"It was just absolutely just disheartening," Calgary broadcaster Ryan Pinder said about the exodus of Flames players. "They're not going to be good anymore."

The Flames had young talents in Cory Stillman, Valeri Bure, and Jarome Iginla at the forefront on their 1998–99 team. A young Martin St. Louis also made his NHL debut for the Flames that season. But once Brathwaite entered the fold in Calgary, he made an instant impact.

"He was a really exciting goalie," Steinberg said. "When you watched him play, it was really fun to watch. He was kind of unorthodox in his style. His first game, he made three or four highlight reel stops. And then, during a relatively short period of time when he was a member of the Flames, the actual highlight reel moments you saw from him were off the charts. And we probably saw like 10 or 11 just in the back half of the season when he came in and played."

Steinberg says that Brathwaite being a visible minority played a role in his newfound Flames fandom.

"He had this massive swarm of human beings around him as he's trying to get off the ice," Steinberg said. "There was probably about 900 people just crowding around him trying to get Freddie's autograph as he's trying to get off the ice. He was as good-natured as he possibly could be. But because it wasn't super well organized at the time, people were pushing and shoving and shoving things in his face. I was probably 15, 16 at the time, and I was sitting there like, this guy is handling this with way too much grace."

Brathwaite's first season already endeared him to fans as well as to ownership. When the Flames began a marketing campaign in the late 1990s in the hopes of retaining fans after some tough playoff-less seasons, known as "Flames Forever," Brathwaite was a focal point thanks to the fandom surrounding him and community impact.

But it was in Brathwaite's second season with the Flames that he produced a moment that is still discussed by fans to this very day.

RED WINGS BROADCASTER KEN Daniels was sure that puck went in. You can hear it in his voice when he makes the call alongside partner Mickey Redmond after Detroit forward Kirk Maltby wired a shot on goal.

Here's Maltby racing in! Left wing! The shot! Brathwaite! Rebound! Scores!

Yes...No!

No?!

Oh my! I'll tell ya something!

How did that not go in? They'll have to look at that!

He got it with the goal stick!

Maltby blew past a Flames defenseman before shooting from the faceoff circle to Fred Brathwaite's right. It looked like a sure goal once the puck trickled past the Flames goalie. There was no chance the netminder would be able to save the puck from going in. The tens of thousands at Joe Louis Arena in Detroit were convinced of it, too. Many of them had their arms up in the air, ready to celebrate. The goal would've tied the game at two goals apiece in the Calgary Flames' opening game of the 2000–01 season.

"I thought for sure it was going to still cross over the line," Maltby said.

But the joy was short lived.

Brathwaite desperately turned his body and hoped to scoop the puck out of the net with his stick. He succeeded, with the puck rolling off the edge of his goalie paddle and out of harm's way, denying Maltby and the Red Wings.

"I thought it was in when it was going up in the air," Daniels said. "I reacted too quickly. That's what I remember most about that play. I was pissed off. I called it [a] goal. Not even 50-goal junior scorer Maltby could get it past Freddie who, by the way, I was happy for."

"I guess TSN plays it probably once every six months or every year," Brathwaite said. "So when that happens, usually I have buddies will write or call. They're like, 'Freddy, I just saw you on TSN.' There people are still talking about it. I just found it kind of funny. Because there's so many great goalies out there and there's a lot of great saves. But people still bring that up.

"I mean, it was a nice save. But I didn't think it was that good of a save. But obviously people still like it. And I paid enough people to keep it going on TSN as well."

Now, why would Brathwaite not be as impressed with his own save?

"Well, to be honest with you, I should have made the first save [to] start it off," Brathwaite said. "I think he just came down the wing and took a normal shot that ended up going through me. But yes, me turning around and being able to get it with my stick and then somehow lifting it up—which, I don't know how that happened. That was obviously pretty cool, but I think the original save should've been made off the bat."

Sure enough, Brathwaite's highlight-reel save has made many an appearance on a SportsCenter Top 10 in Canada. It has remained in the hearts of many a Flames fan and is still remembered by hockey personalities and journalists alike.

Most are still dumbfounded at how the puck rolled off Brathwaite's stick.

"What I remember is Freddie scooping it and I actually thought it was going in after he scooped it," Daniels said. "With goal judges now so far away, I've learned to look at the referee first. But sure enough, upon video review, the ref on the play then waved it off in a pretty good spot. So, he didn't think it was in. Can't recall if there was a red light on or not."

"Not only how did he get there? Not only how did he have the presence of mind to look back and make that stop. And to even try it?" Steinberg said. "The way his stick was angled. You're like, is he going to deflect it into the net? But I kind of almost think he was thinking as it was going in, he's got to have that angle on his stick, and it's got to be 100 percent proper so it doesn't flip up or he doesn't scoop it in.

"He kind of knifes it, doesn't he? As he's going back, he knows the angle of his body—which is as ridiculous as it is at the time—he kind of has to knife the puck so it doesn't go in."

"I love it," Pinder said. "It's full extension. It's literally touching the goal line. And it somehow flips up off his blade. I don't know how the physics work on this thing. That's unbelievable."

"It was an unbelievable play," Maltby said. "You probably could never do it again."

"It's probably one of the more athletic scenes you're ever going to see no matter what era," journalist Avry Lewis-McDougall said. "No matter if it's in the nineties, the 2000s. That is a save. It's a once in a lifetime save where Fred was in the right place at the right time to keep that puck out. Any other time, that's going in. That's a Detroit goal. The fact that Fred Brathwaite made that save is going to go down, to me personally, as probably a top-10 save of all-time."

It has been a while since Brathwaite has heard Daniels' call, but he remembers the Red Wings announcers being excited. Brathwaite was also curious about something else.

"What did the game end up?" Brathwaite asked. "Did we win or lose? Did we lose 7–1? What was the score in that game?"

When Brathwaite made the save, the Flames held a 2–1 advantage on the Red Wings. Calgary even added a third goal to give themselves a two-goal lead. However, the Red Wings stormed back with three unanswered goals including the eventual game-winning goal from Maltby in the third period.

"I'll just leave it at we made a good save and that was that," Brathwaite said jokingly.

Brathwaite played 61 games during the 1999–2000 season, going 25–25–7 with a .905 save percentage, five shutouts, and a 2.75 goals-against average. Save for seven games played by Jean-Sébastien Giguère, Brathwaite was backed up by one of his early heroes in Grant Fuhr.

Fuhr was acquired by the Flames from the St. Louis Blues in September 1999 in exchange for a third-round pick in the following year's draft. The Blues wanted to get younger in goal and found a willing taker in the Flames, allowing Fuhr to play closer to home to end his career. The then-future Hall of Famer played 23 games, posting a 5–13–2 record with a 3.83 goals-against average and an .856 save percentage.

"Spending the year with Freddie was awesome," Fuhr said. "One, it was a lot of fun. Two, Freddie's a great guy."

"I learned a lot from him," Brathwaite said. "Just the way he carries himself. It was a pretty cool thing to have two Black goaltenders for pretty much a whole season in Calgary. I was lucky to be a part of that with Grant."

The Flames failed to reach the 2000 Stanley Cup playoffs, however. They sat at home while the New Jersey Devils and Dallas Stars squared off in the final. Jason Arnott was the double overtime hero for New Jersey, giving the Devils their second championship at the expense of the reigning Cup champions.

Two days after the loss, Stars director of player personnel Craig Button left the organization and began his duties as the Flames general manager. His very first order of business was trying to decide between keeping Brathwaite and Giguère. While it was not the specific reason for keeping Brathwaite, his impact on the team's fan base did play a role in Button opting to keep the Ottawa native over Giguère. The Anaheim Mighty Ducks eventually acquired Giguère in exchange for a 2000 second-round draft choice.

"The community mattered to the [Flames] owners," Button said. "This is not a criticism of Giguère. They felt that Freddie represented all the values that they represented.

"His impact on the community, the values that the owners saw in him. It's not just about the hockey. And for them, it mattered. And that mattered to me."

Brathwaite's time in Calgary lasted one more season, however. He finished the 2000–01 campaign with a 15–17–10 record to go with a .910 save percentage and a 2.32 goals-against average. Brathwaite shared the net with Flames legend Mike Vernon, who returned to the organization to finish his Hall of Fame career. Following another season without playoffs, the Flames wanted more draft picks and an upgrade at the goaltending position.

"I had a long history with Roman Turek in Dallas," Button said. "He'd done very well with the St. Louis Blues after we traded him after the Stanley Cup in 1999. But they were looking to move on from him. So, an opportunity arose where we felt we were improving the goaltending. And that's what ended up leading to the Fred Brathwaite trade. He was fine for us that year in Calgary. It was more the thinking of how can we upgrade certain conditions and certain areas of our team. And we felt Roman was that upgrade. But that wasn't one of those [trades] were you trying to move Fred Brathwaite."

The deal was made in June 2001. Brathwaite, alongside Daniel Tkaczuk, Sergei Varlamov, and a 2001 ninth-round draft pick, would go to St. Louis in exchange for Turek and a 2001 fourth-round pick.

Thus ended the love affair between the Flames and Brathwaite. And that love and appreciation wasn't one-sided.

"I enjoyed Calgary," Brathwaite said. "I really didn't want to leave at the time. Even though I went to St. Louis where it was great. But I didn't want to leave Calgary. That's where I had my most success. The city and the fans and their organization was great to me from the time I got there."

Button remembers receiving some direct feedback from the people who mattered most to him after making the trade: his two daughters.

"My daughters were ready to disown me. My daughters' friends were ready to disown me," Button said. "I remember going to a youth soccer game and all the questions were from all the kids on my older daughter's team. 'What are you doing? Why are you trading Freddie?'"

As the Flames moved on with Turek, Brathwaite spent two seasons with the Blues. The Ottawa native played 55 games, posting a record of 21–20–8 in that span of time. One enduring symbol of his time in St. Louis has nothing to do with his on-ice play.

The Ottawa netminder famously made an appearance in a music video from superstar producer/rapper icon Jermaine Dupri. The song was called "Welcome to Atlanta," but the video featured three other locations including St. Louis. The goaltender wore sunglasses and a Blues jersey while hanging out with members of the St. Lunatics and St. Louis Cardinals second baseman Fernando Viña at Busch Stadium.

"I think I got in trouble from the Blues because of that," Brathwaite said. "I didn't ask to have the Blues jersey in it."

Brathwaite's final NHL season was spent with the Columbus Blue Jackets in 2003–04. He played 21 games and posted a 4–11–1 record to go with an .897 save percentage and a 3.37 goals-against average. Brathwaite would then have stints in the American Hockey League with Syracuse and Chicago.

The goaltender also spent time in Russia with Ak Bars Kazan—where he won Goalie of the Year honors in 2006—and Avangard Omsk before surfacing with Adler Mannheim in Germany to start the 2008–09 season. Brathwaite finished his inaugural season with Adler Mannheim as league MVP after recording 20 wins, 17 losses, a .925 save percentage, and a 2.37 goals-against average. He spent four seasons in Germany with his last game being played in 2012.

"I was at the end of my career," Brathwaite said. "Still thought I could play and had that opportunity to be over there and play. I didn't expect much of the league and realized now what a great league that German league was.

"The only thing that didn't happen was I never won a championship over there which was probably the biggest thing—I wouldn't say I regret—it's the biggest thing that never really happened. But I was able to play, make some good friends, and win goalie of the year and MVP of the league which was an awesome way to cap off my career."

Brathwaite has since plied his trade as a goaltending coach. He has worked with Team Canada's U18 and U20 teams as a goalie coach and consultant and also spent a season with the New York Islanders. Brathwaite currently works for the AHL's Henderson Silver Knights, the minor league affiliate of the Vegas Golden Knights. He's had a hand in the development of goaltenders like Logan Thompson, Jiri Patera, Thomas Greiss, and Eric Comrie from his time at the IIHF World Junior Hockey Championship, among others.

While Brathwaite's work is mainly with goaltenders during practices, Brathwaite once donned his gear as an emergency backup during a 2021 game once Thompson was made unavailable. Anything to help the team win in his eyes. But Brathwaite clearly still loves the sport and wants to be around it any way he can.

"I've been very fortunate, I've been very lucky," Brathwaite said. "I've played for however long I've played and then able to work with Hockey Canada which is awesome. Being able to work for your country. And then coming to an organization like Vegas, winning a Stanley Cup six years in.

"I was very fortunate, very lucky to play 19 years of pro hockey. Considering I wasn't drafted, people said I was undersized. I was able to do that and be able to see all parts of the world, play for Team Canada.... It's been a pretty good ride, and hopefully I can do it just a little bit longer."

8

Georges Laraque

Georges Laraque stared down his next opponent as he took his place along the boards. Most men wouldn't have bothered asking for permission. They'd already be knee-deep in chirps against their next combatant before hurling haymakers. But most men aren't Laraque, then playing for the Phoenix Coyotes, who opted for a more gentlemanly approach with Los Angeles Kings forward Raitis Ivanans.

"You want to?" Laraque said to the equally hulking left winger.

Ivanans obliged.

"OK. Square up?" Laraque asked again. Ivanans agreed, again, to fight Laraque once the faceoff was won.

"OK. Good luck, man," Laraque said before calmly dropping his stick and gloves and raising his fists.

It's a humorous yet revealing moment between two enforcers. Hockey fans and media usually resort to reading lips in the hopes of figuring out what was said between players. Oftentimes in the heat of battle, players just lean into their instincts and start fighting. So, seeing—and hearing—Laraque ask to fight as if he was asking a neighbor to borrow some sugar was very different from the norm. Laraque wore a microphone for the Coyotes broadcast, so the mic caught every word of that exchange.

"I love the Ivanans [fight]," Dan Gallant of Hockeyfights.com said. "Because you get to see that peek behind the curtain. You see the documentaries like *Ice Guardians* speaking about it afterward, talking about how Georges was a guy that just approached the fight in a different way, asking and agreeing to it. And wishing the other guy good luck. It's those mind games that he's almost playing with these guys that you just love to see. But we don't get to see that peek behind the curtain too often."

Once the politeness ended, it was time to fight. Both men spun around, patiently looking for an opening to swing or grab the other's jersey. Laraque reached for Ivanans' collar, but the Latvian forward leaned back just enough for him to be out of reach. The waiting game resumed. No man wanted to be exposed first and neither wanted to be the second to grab hold of one another.

Eventually, Ivanans reached for the Quebecois enforcer and tried to throw punches while keeping himself balanced. Laraque ducked, trying to weather the oncoming barrage before raising his head and swinging his left hand. He soon became the aggressor, throwing punches as the duo continued their brawl. Both men swung wildly, spinning and holding on to each other. Ivanans slipped and fell to a knee as he took on Laraque's punches. The Latvian even lost his helmet after Laraque threw two more lefts.

It never truly felt like Laraque ever lost control of the bout, which spoke to his pedigree and quality as a fighter.

"He's the heavyweight champion of the league, no question about it," Darren Pang said on the Phoenix Coyotes broadcast.

Ivanans eventually tried to pin Laraque to the boards. But Laraque grappled and brought Ivanans down to the ice, securing another win for his fight card. His teammates tapped sticks along the boards, their way of cheering on their teammate for doing the dirty work once again.

Laraque is defined by many as one of the premier NHL enforcers of the 2000s. Hockeyfights.com, a website that tracks fights and allows fans to rate how good they were, says he's participated in 159 career fights—including preseason games. At the time of this writing, Laraque received 59 percent of the votes on Hockeyfights.com when voters were asked who won that particular contest against the Kings forward.

The list of opponents is long. Ivanans, Bob Probert, Stu Grimson, Jody Shelley, Shawn Thornton, Brad May, Andrew Peters, Wade Belak, and dozens more have thrown shots and taken their fair share of fists to the face from Laraque.

"When I think of heavyweights I think of a few guys, and you're at the top of the list," former NHL enforcer John Scott told Laraque on an episode of his podcast *Pound for Pound with John Scott*. "I see you around on the circuits and you're always this likeable, loveable, big teddy bear. But when I played against you, I was terrified."

Even young aspiring hockey stars remember Laraque for his pugilism, whether they watched his fights on television or spent hours using him as a playable character in the EA Sports NHL franchise.

"I do remember me and my brothers always playing as him in NHL video games because he was a fighter," hockey star Sarah Nurse said. "He was the guy that was always on our team when we made a team on NHL."

"He's like the gentle giant, and one of the most feared fighters of his era," reporter Chris Johnston said. "[He] was such a big, strong guy that doesn't eat meat. He's a tough guy to put in a box, and I say that as compliment. Because there's a lot of layers to Georges."

Laraque has used his platform to advocate for animal rights, even recording a "vegetarian testimonial" for PETA in 2011. The forward even represented the Green Party of Canada as a deputy leader from February 2010 to October 2013, until he was forced to step down due to fraud allegations from a former business partner. The forward maintained his innocence and the allegations were later retracted.

Laraque has also donated time and money to help his parents' birth country of Haiti through charitable work and contributions. He and P.K. Subban once visited a children's hospital in Haiti together as part of Laraque's efforts with World Vision Canada and the NHLPA to raise money in support of the hospital.

Here is something else you should know about Laraque. Contrary to what he's shown throughout his career, he doesn't always like being known as an NHL enforcer. Though he's certainly leaned into it at times. Whether it's through his T-shirt collaboration with Snoop Dogg's Death Row Records featuring him fighting or teaching New York Rangers enforcer Matt Rempe how to fight in the offseason, Laraque will never escape his fighting past. *Sports Illustrated* and *The Hockey News* have each recognized him as the best enforcer and fighter, respectively, through different parts of the 2000s.

But sometimes, Laraque would rather push against that persona whenever asked by fans.

"I didn't like fighting," Laraque said. "But [even] if I didn't like it, I have to be the best at it, so I don't have to do it as much. Because people will fear me. That was my attitude. Because if I don't like it and I suck at it, well Georges, I'm sorry, but you're going to have to do it a lot. Because people won't fear you. They're going to want to fight you all the time. That was my thinking about it.

"What am I going to say about fighting? Am I proud that I beat people up? No. There's nothing to be proud of. The goal of hockey is to put the puck in the net. But that's the job. This is what I had to do to make the NHL. So, that's why anything outside of it: playing in the playoffs, scoring in the playoffs, 13 goals one year, 29 points one year. All that stuff. I'm way more proud of all that stuff than any fighting that I've ever done in the NHL."

Fighting an opponent clearly paled in comparison to the joy and jubilation he felt on the night of February 21, 2000. One specific moment saw his physicality overshadowed by his finesse—a spin move—that led to him flying up the ice at Skyreach Centre after scoring his third goal of the night.

Read that again: *his third goal of the night.*

"Nobody's asking about it because nobody thinks that I've ever done one," Laraque said. "When somebody asks me what is my proudest moment in the NHL and I say I scored a hat trick, they're like, 'What? You scored an NHL hat trick?'"

Laraque beat Los Angeles Kings defenseman Aki Berg with that move before scoring past goaltender Stéphane Fiset, sending the big enforcer and the Oilers' fanbase into pandemonium. The Skyreach Centre goal siren in Edmonton blared as the Oiler skated in celebration, arms pointed to the sky. Not long after, the catchphrase of wrestling legend Dwayne "The Rock" Johnson echoed throughout the arena.

If you smell what the Rock is cooking?

"I skated faster than McDavid ever did," Laraque said. "I was screaming; I was going nuts. I was yelling so much. I couldn't believe it."

It is the only hat trick Laraque has ever scored in his 12-year career. Laraque scored eight goals that season and only 53 throughout his time in the NHL. Despite the hundreds of fights he's won, that February night serves as a pinnacle of Laraque's career.

Of course, it couldn't fully be Laraque's moment without him adding his own flair. And even on a night where his scoring prowess was on display, he still had to fight.

"I've decided to baptize something," Laraque said. "A Georges Laraque hat trick is actually a fight and three goals."

LIKE MOST CHILDREN ASPIRING to play hockey, Laraque looked up to the NHL's best. There was Edmonton Oilers superstar Wayne Gretzky and even Pittsburgh Penguins icon Mario Lemieux, a fellow Quebecer. Laraque wanted to be a goal scorer just like his hockey heroes.

"I was scoring tons of goals when I was a kid and I wanted to be like them," Laraque said.

Laraque played youth hockey in Sorel-Tracy, a city a little over an hour east of Montreal. He was originally born in Montreal to Haitian parents before moving to Sorel-Tracy at the age of five. The town has produced a handful of NHLers past and present such as goaltender Marc-André Fleury, defenseman François Beauchemin, and forward Anthony Beauvillier.

Laraque grew up playing football, soccer, and hockey. Hockey was his third favorite sport, and he was subjected to consistent racial abuse, often confronted with the word "nigger" by other hockey parents. While some may view Laraque's perseverance as a positive, and Laraque himself mentions that he used the racism he faced to fuel him through his developing career, racism shouldn't merely be an obstacle one must face to live their everyday life.

The racism Laraque faced was so unbearable that his own parents stopped attending his games and wanted their son to stop playing hockey altogether. Undeterred, Laraque rode his bike to the local rink on his own and kept playing. As Laraque remembers, it didn't stop opposing parents from being racist toward him.

"Listen, if you went to see me play in my youth in minor hockey," Laraque said. "You'd hear the n-word so much that you would think it was my name. Everybody was calling me like that. But I couldn't do anything. Because I was alone. I was a kid. And I didn't want to show people that they were affecting me."

Laraque would return home from games and cry silently under his pillow. If his parents saw that the racial abuse he endured was affecting him, they'd pull him out of hockey. In Laraque's autobiography *Georges Laraque: The NHL's Unlikeliest Tough Guy*, his former youth football coach—future CFL head coach and executive Danny Maciocia—tried to convince Laraque to play football instead of hockey.

"I remember the coach telling me, 'You won't go anywhere in hockey, Georges. No black players in the NHL. And I don't see one in the near future,'" Laraque said in his autobiography. "'You should stay with me and become a professional football player. That's where your future lies. And it'll be a bright one, trust me.'

"He couldn't have known that his words only made me want more than ever to make my mark on the ice. I smiled at him and said, 'I'm sorry, Danny, but I'll stick to hockey. I belong there. There are lots of black players in football. If I succeed in that field, I'll just be another black guy playing football. Hockey is different.'"

Laraque was afforded future opportunities in football and soccer. But when he was drafted into the Quebec Major Junior Hockey League, Laraque chose to fight back against those who didn't want to see him succeed in the sport.

"I had a lesson to prove to everybody that called me the n-word," Laraque said. "I didn't want to quit because hockey needs more minorities. They need more people of color making it to show everyone that hockey is for everyone."

The doubters and racism powered Laraque, as did learning about the perseverance of a Black sports legend when confronted with racial hatred. Jackie Robinson is a major reason why Laraque insisted on playing despite the ignorance he faced. Laraque read the French-language Jackie Robinson book, titled *Un Bon Exemple de Courage: Jackie Robinson Raconté aux Enfants*. (The title translates to *An Example of Courage: Jackie Robinson as Told to Children*.) His sister received a collection of children's books detailing the lives of famous celebrities, innovators, and athletes. He saw himself in Robinson, who broke Major League Baseball's color barrier in April 1947.

"I never cried after that for any racism. I was like, 'Yes, give it to me. You will see,'" Laraque said. "Oh yes, I'm going to use that as motivation.

"I became a machine after I read that book. And that was my mission, to make it like just like Jackie did."

Laraque continued to play as he progressed into his teens. At the age of 16, Laraque was drafted by the QMJHL's St. Jean Lynx. By his late teens, he grew in size.

It was in the QMJHL where his newfound size pushed him to become an enforcer. Laraque recorded 142 penalty minutes in his first season. That number grew to 259 minutes in his second season.

"I was like 240 [pounds] and I was a monster," Laraque said. "I wasn't the fastest player anymore. No one needed to tell me what I had to do to make sure I was going to play in the NHL. I could have had a junior career without fighting. But that's it. If I wanted to be drafted, I had to add fighting to my game, which I did."

Following that 259-penalty minute season, the Edmonton Oilers selected Laraque 31st overall in the 1995 NHL Entry Draft. Laraque spent his major junior career with four teams, suiting up for the Lynx, Laval Titan College Français, and the St. Hyacinthe Lasers before winning a Memorial Cup with the Granby Prédateurs in 1996.

Once Laraque joined the Oilers organization in 1997–98, there was no doubt he was there to fight. The young Laraque even fought Donald Brashear during his first-ever preseason with the Oilers. Laraque eventually made his NHL debut during a heated contest against the rival Calgary Flames on November 15, 1997. The forward wasted no time imposing himself physically, barreling into defenseman Jamie Allison during the game's opening period.

Flames captain Todd Simpson didn't appreciate the Oilers rookie throwing his body around, and he engaged in a scrap with Laraque at center ice. Laraque pumped Simpson with his left hand, eventually dropping the Flames captain to the ice. Partway through the brawl, Laraque grabbed the defenseman by his neck before punching him again.

Once the referees stepped in, local broadcasters were already enamored with Laraque's fighting ability.

...But I'll tell you what, Laraque almost murdered Simpson in the early stages. He was unrelenting with that left hand.

"It's crazy because after that fight he needed shoulder surgery," Laraque said. "I did pretty good on that fight and he got hurt."

The fights, willing combatants, and Laraque's legend grew. He remains a fan favorite in Edmonton to this day. But three years after his NHL debut, Laraque gave fans something else to cheer about.

BEFORE ANY GAME, GEORGES Laraque looked through the opposing team's roster and searched for their enforcer. It was usually the man who fought the most, racked up the most penalty minutes, or their biggest guy. On February 21, 2000, Steve McKenna, an undrafted, 6'8" left-shot defenseman fit that bill.

"I wasn't thinking about a hat trick before the game. I was thinking about Steve McKenna knowing that there was a chance [a fight] could happen," Laraque said.

The Oilers were coming off back-to-back losses against the rival Calgary Flames when the Kings came to town that February night. Laraque spent the game on the fourth line with center Jim Dowd and fellow forward Boyd Devereaux. The enforcer's fists were needed in the opening period, but not to fight McKenna.

Dowd unleashed a shot from near the blue line after taking a pass from Devereaux. Kings goaltender Stéphane Fiset made the initial save. But Laraque, parked in front of the net, whacked at the puck with his backhand and scored his fourth goal of the year. Minutes later, McKenna dropped the gloves for his first fight of the game. But it came against Edmonton Oilers defenseman Sean Brown.

After Kings forward Luc Robitaille tied the game in the second period, Laraque sprung into action again. Defenseman Roman Hamrlík found the puck from the slot after it was lost in a pair of skates unbeknownst to a Kings defenseman. Hamrlík spun around and fired the puck on net, hitting Laraque before beating Fiset. The Kings goalie fell on his back, reaching for the puck as it crept over the line. As the goal siren blared, Fiset laid down on the ice in frustration.

"Then I started to think about the impossible, something I would never thought I could achieve in the NHL: a hat trick," Laraque wrote in his autobiography. "I wanted that third goal, and so did my teammates. The crowd started chanting my name."

But before Laraque could get to that hat trick, he had to fight McKenna. Laraque dished out a hit on an opposing Kings player—he thinks it was defenseman Aki Berg. McKenna responded in retaliation and both men squared off.

"I don't like to say that I beat the guy up because I have so much respect for everyone. I'd rather people look at it online and make their own decision about it," Laraque said. "But anyway, I did a pretty good fight against him."

With every passing minute, anticipation grew from the tens of thousands at the Skyreach Centre. But the Oilers still had a game to win, too. A goal from Kings forward Craig Johnson cut his team's deficit to one goal, only down 3–2 minutes into the third period. But the Oilers gave themselves some breathing room with a goal from Doug Weight. But Kings defenseman Garry Galley drew back with one of his own with under 90 seconds to play.

The Kings pulled Fiset from their net in favor of an extra attacker. There was the moment for Laraque to ice the game and complete his hat-trick. But Oilers head coach Kevin Lowe opted for more defensive-minded players to preserve the team's lead. Then, with 29 seconds to go, Oilers defenseman Janne Niinimaa seemingly iced the game with an empty net goal. It should have ended Laraque's chances of earning his third goal of the night.

"And then [Lowe] puts the fourth line back out there," Laraque said.

With seconds to go in the game, the Oilers entered the offensive zone against the Kings. Fiset had already returned to his cage. Devereaux fished the puck from the boards and found Laraque who captured the puck on his stick before spinning around Berg.

"I don't know why I did that," Laraque said. "I did a Denis Savard spin-o-rama in front of Aki Berg. And I'm alone in front of Stéphane Fiset. In my mind, I'm like, 'Oh my God. How did I do that?'"

Laraque momentarily composed himself and stickhandled past Fiset, finishing with his backhand before raising his arms in the air to celebrate.

"I've tried many times to do that after and I would fall on my ass," Laraque said.

It served as the exclamation point in a 6–3 Oilers victory over the Kings. It was a night Laraque would never forget.

It was the exact opposite reaction for the Kings.

"I think maybe when Georges Laraque is freewheeling, we're not doing something right," Kings head coach Andy Murray said after the game, according to the *Edmonton Journal*. "It's a credit to him. I mean he made a great move on that last goal. Aki Berg is six-foot-four and 225 pounds and Georges just manhandled him."

"When I started making it to the NHL," Laraque said. "I found it really cool that we're getting all the NHL games for PlayStation where I was in it. Playing video games as a kid [to] now you're part of the video game. Well, let me tell you, it's only playing video games that Georges Laraque would get a hat trick. Not the real NHL."

As Laraque continued his celebration with teammates, hats flooded the ice to commemorate an unlikely hat trick from a man self-described as the league's unlikeliest tough guy. The moment was so unexpected, Wayne Gretzky called Laraque to congratulate him.

"He said I need 49 more to break his record," Laraque said. "I'll never forget that night. It was unreal."

There is one error Laraque made following his big accomplishment. The hats thrown on the ice by fans in attendance were collected in four garbage bags for Laraque to take home. Laraque's intention was to donate them to charity.

Until he forgot about them.

Time passed from Laraque's big night. Three years after the game, Laraque was preparing himself for a move into a new home he had built in Edmonton. It was then the Quebecois man rediscovered the bags. When he opened them up, the foul stench left him in disgust.

"I almost passed out," Laraque said. "Can you imagine thousands of hats closed in a garbage bag for three years with all the sweat from [everyone's] head? [A bag] that's closed and then you open that up? Oh my God.

"I had to throw it away. It stunk. The humidity and everything. They smelled in a different room. I totally forgot about them in my closet. It was the funniest thing."

Fortunately for Laraque, there is nothing to hold his nose over about his on-ice play from that fateful February 2000 night. It is a night that has forever left him filled with pride. Laraque has come a long way from biking in the snow to practices and games or convincing his parents that hockey was the way to go and not football or soccer. He hoped to emulate Jackie Robinson who played through racial abuse to become a Major League Baseball star and Hall of Famer.

Many will forever remember Laraque as a fighter, even if his relationship with fighting is complex. But Laraque would rather fans remember the night he scored a hat trick.

"I couldn't believe it. I'll never forget that night," Laraque said.

9

Quinton Byfield

It was off to the races when the faceoff was won.

The Columbus Blue Jackets won the faceoff. But it was Los Angeles Kings forward Quinton Byfield who got to the puck first. The Kings forward burst through the neutral zone like a freight train, handling the puck while moving toward the left wing in open space.

Byfield had one defenseman in front of him, Zach Werenski, as he entered the offensive zone. He slipped past the defender and found the puck at his feet. Byfield then kicked the puck to his stick blade, just as he lost balance, and fell to a knee. Byfield then put the puck on his backhand before lifting the puck past Blue Jackets goalie Elvis Merzlikins with a highlight-reel goal.

Byfield got up from the ice surface and stood in the corner to Merzļikins' left, waiting to celebrate with teammates. The young forward stretched out his arms and looked to the rafters, almost in disbelief at what he had done. His smile stretched wide once his teammates finally joined him.

An undeniable goal of the year candidate from one of the league's most promising talents.

"I was just kind of picking up the puck off the faceoff. I saw I had a lot of speed," Byfield told CBS Los Angeles. "I thought I was going to take Werenski on the outside and he tried to cut me off there. So, I just tried to take it to the middle. Saw the puck sitting there and just tried to do what I could to get the net and ended up working out."

"A sick, individual effort," teammate Phillip Danault said. "I think it just shows his skill and the quickness he has in his game. He's got that edge too."

"It's a nice dangle," fellow Kings teammate Drew Doughty remembered.

"I could have held a camera and filmed it," then-teammate Pierre-Luc Dubois, who was on the ice for the goal, told CBS Los Angeles. "It was a beautiful goal."

Byfield's goal went viral across the internet and on highlight-reel shows. But that moment, more importantly, certified that Byfield finally had reason to feel confident in his game after years of scratching the surface as an NHLer.

"I feel good with the puck right now," Byfield said after the Kings game against the Blue Jackets according to the Associated Press. "The confidence is definitely there knowing that I can make plays and trusting my shot. If I shoot it, I have a good chance of scoring."

The young forward's development in the NHL at the time of the goal he scored in Columbus had been a slow burn. It can take time for young aspiring centers, not to mention the additional pressure that accompanies being the second overall draft pick. Byfield certainly isn't the first young center to require more seasoning before becoming an impact player at his position, even if he's needed more time than most. And even then, he's still in his early twenties.

Leon Draisaitl, now considered a top five player in the NHL after being taken third overall in 2014, split his first season in the NHL and with the Kelowna Rockets of the Western Hockey League. Draisaitl even played six AHL games in his second pro season in 2015, before being fully ready for the NHL. Joe Thornton, the first overall pick of the 1997 NHL Entry Draft, had seven points in his first 55 NHL games with the Boston Bruins. New Jersey Devils forward Jack

Hughes scored a combined 52 points in his first two seasons before scoring 56 in year three and jumped to 99 points in his fourth year.

Those examples only scratch the surface.

Byfield flopped between the Kings and their AHL affiliate in Ontario to learn how to play at the professional level through his first three NHL seasons. At the NHL level, the Kings were patient and played Byfield at center and wing. Byfield battled injuries and illnesses on top of the pressure that comes with someone drafted at his position.

"There's definitely pressure that you put yourself in, but I feel like everybody in the NHL has pressure on them," Byfield said. "It's what you can do with the opportunity. I think there's a lot more going into it. A lot of it was opportunity in the beginning. I dealt with a lot of injuries, sicknesses. So, there wasn't much consistency for me when I came in. And I feel like that affected me. On top of being a high pick, you've got to perform. It was super tough for me at that point."

"People kind of want instant results," Byfield's former AHL teammate Devante Smith-Pelly said. "He's playing in the NHL [at] 19 and 20. You're not going to see it right away, especially with bigger players. I think he was just growing into his body. He was huge. But he was just a kid."

Despite experiencing growing pains in the first 99 games of his NHL career, Byfield showed tangible progress during the 2023–24 campaign. Byfield reached the 20-goal mark for the first time in his career and scored 55 points in 80 games, including that goal against the Blue Jackets. Byfield scored 23 goals and 54 points in 81 games the following season, before adding three goals and an assist in six playoff games in 2025. And his progression hasn't gone unnoticed by the Kings' veterans.

"He plays a two-way game. He cares about defense. He works hard for a young guy," Doughty said. "Young, high picks like him, they come in, 'Oh, I got to get 90 points.' All they're worried about is selfishly getting their points.

"He cares about the team winning and that is honestly his main thing. He wants more minutes. He just plays so well. He's one of the best forecheckers in the league. And now his confidence has grown. So he's making plays and scoring goals."

"He's a good guy," former Kings pro scout Blake Bolden said. "He's young, but he's so talented. I mean, with his size, like, if you've ever watched him in person, the way he goes from zero to 60 is just impressive."

Byfield isn't just any ordinary high pick with high promise and talent. He's the highest-drafted Black player in league history, selected second overall by the Los Angeles Kings during the 2020 NHL Entry Draft.

"It means a lot to me, it's something special," Byfield told the *Los Angeles Times* after being drafted in 2020. "Being in the record books for anything is something special, but that especially. My dad and mom didn't play hockey, didn't have too much knowledge about it. It just shows that there's a lot of opportunity in the world and you can play every sport and be successful in it."

QUINTON BYFIELD IS A native of Newmarket, a Southern Ontario town approximately 40 minutes away from downtown Toronto. Byfield was born in August 2002 to a white mother, Nicole Kasper, and a Black Jamaican father, Clinton Byfield. According to The Athletic, both parents were athletes growing up. Clinton participated in track and field, soccer, and cricket, while Nicole was a gymnast, a soccer player, a basketball player, and even played field hockey.

Young Quinton played a handful of different sports growing up including basketball, football, lacrosse, and volleyball. The youngster ultimately chose between soccer and hockey before committing full time to the ice.

"I think I was pretty good at soccer. But the possibilities are next to none when it comes to making it and you are from Canada," Byfield told Ryan S. Clark of The Athletic in October 2020. "I liked hockey a lot more and most of my buddies were hockey fans. My family always supported me and let's say they supported me a little more with hockey because they loved it, too. I am glad it went that way."

In his youth hockey days, Byfield took inspiration from forwards like Auston Matthews and Hockey Hall of Famer Martin St. Louis while admiring players like Sidney Crosby and Evgeni Malkin. But Byfield's hockey beginnings include some time at defense, which helped him understand the game at both ends of the ice. He modeled his game after longtime NHL defender and former Penguin Sergei Gonchar. Byfield even wore Gonchar's No. 55 in homage to his "biggest idol" while thinking of the number as "lucky," according to *The Sudbury Star*.

"He was the catalyst on those Pittsburgh teams on the back end. He really did not get too much publicity with Crosby and Malkin, but still got attention and for me, he was the backbone," Byfield told The Athletic about Gonchar.

Byfield eventually transitioned to center and was good enough to be taken first overall in the Ontario Hockey League priority selection draft in April 2018 by the Sudbury Wolves. The Wolves immediately committed themselves to fine-tuning his defensive play.

"We worked hard on his defensive coverage," then-Wolves head coach Cory Stillman told Elite Prospects back in 2019. "As a young guy playing midget, they can just fly around and he's now learning to come back in his own zone. Now that he does that, he also kills penalties. His learning degree, curve, is continuing to grow and he's only going to get better."

"My development, my defensive game, learning to play on both sides of the puck, I think they really helped me with that," Byfield told the *Sudbury Star* in October 2020. "Coming to Sudbury two years ago as a 16-year-old kid, moving away from home for the first time, that was something new to me, but I was able to stay with the greatest billets ever and they really made me feel at home. It was just a great place in Sudbury for me."

Through Byfield's first OHL season as a 16-year-old in 2018–19, he was a near point-per-game player with 29 goals and 61 points in 64 games for Sudbury. Byfield even added three goals and eight points in eight OHL playoff games that spring, helping the Wolves reach the OHL Eastern Conference semifinals. For Byfield's efforts, his debut season was enough to earn Rookie of the Year honors from both the OHL and CHL.

Gord Miller remembers seeing Byfield for the first time at the 2019 Hlinka Gretzky Cup for under-18 players in Czechia (then known as the Czech Republic), representing Team Canada. The Canadians were practicing at a Břeclav rink in the middle of summer, as mist and steam surrounded the ice.

"I just saw this freight train come out of the steam, going 100 miles an hour," Miller said.

According to Elite Prospects, Byfield scored three goals and five points in five games during the tournament. Byfield scored in the gold-medal game against Russia, but the Canadians settled for silver following a 3–2 loss.

While Byfield had room to grow in his late teens, he already possessed NHL size at 6'4", according to Elite Prospects. He would only improve in his second OHL season, scoring 32 goals and 82 points in 45 games. Byfield also joined Team Canada as a 17-year-old in their quest for World Junior Championship gold at the 2020 event in Czechia. He was Canada's youngest player at the tournament, posting one assist in seven games.

"From the time I spent with him, we were roommates early in the tournament, he's a pretty laid-back dude, loves to have fun," Team

Canada teammate Jacob Bernard-Docker said. "Obviously, is very talented and good at what he does. It's fun to watch when guys have that calm demeanor away from the rink and then they get on the ice and they can really show up every night. He's so skilled and so fun to watch.

"The maturity for a 17-year-old was impressive. I just remember his ability to take guys on 1-on-1. He was a big part of our team, for sure."

The Canadians won their 18th championship, defeating the Russians in the gold medal game. Byfield's future Los Angeles Kings and Ontario Reign teammate Akil Thomas scored the game-winning goal in the victory, breaking a 3–3 deadlock with under four minutes to play.

As is the case with most prospects who play in major junior or collegiate who are draft eligible, Byfield should have had his moment with his family at the upcoming NHL Draft's host city. He should have been in the building, hearing NHL commissioner Gary Bettman announce his name before walking up to the stage to accept his jersey and meet his new team's front office staffers for the first time.

Instead, a worldwide pandemic changed Byfield's—and many others'—plans and affected his developmental trajectory. Not only was he unable to finish the 2019–20 OHL season, but he was left to experience joy—and history—from his family basement remotely.

THE COVID-19 PANDEMIC ROCKED an entire planet's day-to-day routine. The sporting world was no exception.

By March 12, 2020, the National Hockey League announced it would pause the remainder of the 2019–20 season. Before the end of the month, the NHL announced the cancellation of that year's scouting combines, awards, and in-person draft, which was originally to be held in Montreal. Major junior leagues like the OHL were also forced to abandon the remainder of their regular seasons and postseasons before the Memorial Cup was cancelled.

The 2020 NHL postseason was delayed all the way to August of that year, with teams playing in Canadian bubbles set in Edmonton and Toronto. Teams would participate in a qualifying round before the winning teams ascended to the Stanley Cup playoffs.

That year's draft order was determined by a special lottery featuring the teams that failed to qualify for the 2020 postseason, as well as eight positions reserved for teams that would be eliminated from that year's qualifying round—a one-off change from the NHL's usual playoff format that pits the league's 16 best teams against one another. Following the first phase of the NHL's draft lottery in June 2020, it was determined that the No. 1 overall selection would go to one of those eight teams eliminated from that play-in round.

At the conclusion of the lottery's second phase, the New York Rangers were given the first overall selection. The Blueshirts were more than likely to select Quebec Major Junior Hockey League phenom Alexis Lafrenière at that spot. The Kings fell to second while the Ottawa Senators were given the third overall draft choice.

The NHL draft was held remotely, with teams announcing selections from their respective headquarters. Players like Byfield stayed home, celebrating their success with their families while being filmed for onlookers to see. Byfield sat in his living room with his family, wearing an all-white suit and dress shirt topped with a black, subtly patterned bowtie.

One thing you should know about Byfield: bowties are his thing. When asked by a fan in a video interview after being drafted how many he owned, Byfield said he had bought 30 or 40 bowties. This number may very well have grown years after the fact.

"Growing up I used to just hate wearing ties and those kind of bothered me, so I just switched it up with a bowtie," Byfield said in the interview. "I think it was just cool being just a little bit different.

Just a little bit out there wearing something different. I kind of started that trend early on in my life."

Some wondered if the Kings would take German center Tim Stützle second overall after he showed promise in the Deutsche Eisehockey Liga as a young teenager. Stützle scored seven goals and 34 points in 41 games in his age-17 year with the Mannheim Eagles prior to being drafted. But the Kings instead opted for the bigger center prospect in Byfield, whose resumé was stacked thanks to his OHL, CHL, and IIHF World Junior accomplishments.

"For the good of the direction of our franchise, we know a guy like Quinton Byfield will really help us," L.A. Kings president Luc Robitaille said after Byfield was drafted. "The way he plays. A full 200-foot game. He's got great hands. A ton of speed. We really feel that's going to help us in the future. Having a guy like Anže Kopitar to mentor him, we really feel that's going to help him."

Two weeks after being drafted, Byfield signed a three-year entry-level deal with the Kings. With CHL leagues still unable to play because of COVID-19, Byfield played pro hockey with the Ontario Reign—the Kings' minor league affiliate in Ontario, California. In normal circumstances, Byfield would've had to wait until his age-20 season before ascending to the pros.

"Q, at least, was thrown into pro hockey," AHL teammate Devante Smith-Pelly said. "He probably should've been back in the OHL that year."

COVID-19 parameters still kept professional leagues from playing out the 2020–21 season until the new year, resulting in Byfield sitting for months before he played a professional game. Byfield, however, played for Canada at the 2021 World Junior Championship before the season began. Unlike his first time at the annual Christmastime tournament, Byfield only emerged with a silver medal after losing to the Americans in the gold medal game.

Byfield only made his professional debut in February 2021, picking up an assist in his AHL debut in a 5–2 loss against the Henderson Silver Knights. The 2021 campaign was also the same season where Byfield momentarily shared a line with Thomas and Smith-Pelly, forming an all-Black line. It has been regarded as the first line of its kind since the 1940s, when Herb and Ossie Carnegie played alongside Manny McIntryre while suiting up for teams across Ontario and Quebec.

"It was cool to play with [Byfield] and [Smith-Pelly]," Thomas told John Hoven of the Mayor's Manor Kings blog in 2021. "We're all teammates. It doesn't really matter what color we are, it's just cool that we have an opportunity to inspire other people and hopefully grow the game a little bit at the same time."

Byfield ended his first pro season with eight goals and 20 points in 32 AHL games for the Reign. The young forward even played six NHL games with the Kings before season's end, only mustering one assist. But as a young player, it didn't take much for Byfield's potential to flash in front of his teammates.

"I saw right away at 18 that he was going to be a force," Smith-Pelly said.

Despite his talent, Byfield's development at the pro level was slowed by oncoming hurdles and challenges. The young forward split the 2021–22 campaign between the NHL and AHL but was slowed by a significant injury. During a preseason game against the Arizona Coyotes in October 2021, Byfield was pushed into the boards by Yotes forward Christian Fischer and fell awkwardly. The collision led to a fractured ankle that sidelined him for about two months.

"It wasn't that painful or anything like that," Byfield said in a short documentary produced by the Kings in February 2022. "I knew something was off when I was kind of just laying there and my foot was just throbbing. I was like, 'It can't be good.'"

Byfield was on the verge of making his season debut in December 2021 after a four-game conditioning stint in the American Hockey League. That was the case until he was added to the Kings' COVID-19/non-roster list just days before Christmas. Byfield eventually returned to the Reign in time for their game on New Year's Eve 2021, staying in the AHL until mid-January 2022. He played 40 NHL games that season, just picking up five goals and 10 points.

His numbers only slightly improved in a 53-game set with the Kings during the 2022–23 campaign, in which he scored three goals and 22 points. Once again, Byfield split his time between the NHL and AHL as well as playing on the wing and at center. But Byfield was hampered by an illness that caused him to lose 25 pounds, according to The Athletic's Eric Stephens. The Hockey News also reported that Byfield played through much of the season with two sprained wrists.

Finally, things clicked for Byfield during the 2023–24 season. His year was defined by his iconic goal against Columbus and career-high numbers in goals, assists, and points. It was aided by his overall health and offseason improvements.

Stephens reported that Byfield spent the prior offseason working with former NHLer turned personal trainer Gary Roberts to improve his core. Byfield also worked with coach Barb Underhill, a former world champion figure skater, to improve his own skating. Of course, Byfield leaned on advice from teammates like his captain Anže Kopitar, who commented on the youngster's improving ability of using his size to his advantage.

"There's not very many guys that are 6'4" or 6'5" and 225 [pounds] that can skate like Q," Kopitar told The Athletic. "And maybe he was guilty at first [of] just trying to play a skill game when he got here. The skill game doesn't necessarily get you the consistency that you're looking at. Yeah, there's going to be games where you dominate completely with skill.

"But now he's using his frame. He's using his speed. He's using his body to protect pucks. Now, you can tell he's a lot more consistent making plays. Holding onto the puck versus trying to toe-drag it around guys and do all that stuff, which I know he's got in his bag. We saw it the other way, obviously. But the consistency of holding onto pucks and wearing people down with the frame that he has, it's going to help him in the long run."

Despite the developmental challenges presented and mounting expectations from the year to year, Byfield can still say he's an NHLer and can still grow as a young center in the league. And perhaps certain labels that were thrust upon him were a bit premature.

"I remember people saying he was a bust," journalist and podcaster Omar White said. "Immediately, 'Oh, bust, he can't do it. Waste of a second overall pick. We should've picked someone else.' And seeing him now. It's only getting better. It's just so impactful for me."

"He's an athletic phenomenon and he's going to excel in this game," former Kings scout Blake Bolden said. "He just needs the time and the space to be able to grow into his body, and now you see him producing.

"Have you seen him play on the penalty kill and create chances? Have you seen him just do all the things that a dynamic center is supposed to do? Learning from [Anže Kopitar] and learning from [Phillip] Danault and learning from all of our veterans on the Kings team. I think he's in good hands."

Those abilities have helped the Kings in the regular season and in the playoffs. It has also led to a significant investment in his future in Silver and Black.

IT WAS SUPPOSED TO be an icing call.

Kings defenseman Mikey Anderson sent the puck up ice in overtime of Game 2 of his team's 2024 first-round playoff series against the Edmonton Oilers. Giving up an icing would have been dangerous for a team trailing against a high-octane, offensive machine like the Oilers, led by Connor McDavid, Leon Draisaitl, and other talents.

But Byfield was there to tip the puck when Anderson's pass shot up the wing. It's not uncommon for hockey players to tip long stretch passes in the neutral zone to avoid icing being called.

"I'll try and take credit for that," Byfield said after the game. "I saw Mikey, the puck bounced on him. Got a little high. So, I was just thinking, 'No icing here' and just trying to get a stick on it."

Byfield's tip, however, redirected toward open space in the middle of the ice. Kopitar was the first to the puck, even catching Oilers defenseman Darnell Nurse by surprise, and he sped toward the goal. Nurse dove to stop the shot attempt, but Kopitar roofed it past Oilers goaltender Stuart Skinner.

What could have been a simple tip, saving his team from having tired legs on the ice for an ensuing faceoff, turned into a savvy offensive play that led to a game-winning goal the Kings needed.

"I knew it was going in," Byfield said. "He's lights out on breakaways. So, I was confident about it."

The Kings tied the series at one game apiece thanks to that goal. Game 1 went differently with the Oilers emerging superior in a 7–4 win and many thinking this series wouldn't last long. Kopitar's ensuing goal swung the momentum back L.A.'s way, but where would the Kings be if it weren't for Byfield's tip pass? It ended up being another significant moment in Byfield's young career, cementing his arrival as an NHLer after years of building himself up.

Later that summer, the Kings furthered their commitment to their 2020 No. 2 overall draft choice. The Kings re-signed Byfield to a five-year contract extension worth $31.25 million through 2029 with an annual average value of $6.25 million in July 2024. While the contract allows him to become an unrestricted free agent once he reaches his prime, that didn't appear to be top of mind for Byfield, who only knows the Kings as his NHL home.

"When that time comes, hopefully, that time comes, I want to be an L.A. King for the rest of my life," Byfield said.

Maybe one day, Byfield could be a potential successor to Kopitar, a future Hall of Fame center who has won Cups and holds records for most games played and assists. All of them in a Kings uniform.

But Byfield knows there's ways to go before he reaches that plateau.

"He's had an unbelievable career," Byfield said. "It's very hard to replace a guy like that. I think the franchise knows that. He's well respected every year. If I can just follow along those footsteps as much as I can, I think we're going to be heading down the right track."

10

Sarah Nurse

It was a winter's night in February 2002 when Sarah Nurse was at her grandparents' home. Her grandmother and *pépère*—both French Canadian and from Nurse's mother's side of the family—invited Nurse and her family to watch the Olympic women's hockey gold-medal final. Nurse had turned seven one month earlier and was about two years into her hockey journey.

Sarah is one of three siblings, growing up with her fellow hockey-playing brothers Elijah and Isaac. She is the daughter of a white mother, Michelle, and Black Trinidadian father, Roger. Their family has since been known as one of the most decorated sporting families in North America. Sarah's cousin, Darnell, is an NHL defenseman for the Edmonton Oilers. Another cousin, Kia, is a WNBA star, Canadian Olympian, and two-time NCAA champion from her days at the University of Connecticut. Sarah's aunt, Raquel, was a basketball star at Syracuse University, where she met, and eventually married, football star Donovan McNabb. Not to be outdone, another uncle, Richard, played a few seasons for the Canadian Football League's Hamilton Tiger-Cats.

As young as three years old, Sarah took up figure skating. She wanted to learn how to skate, and the sport became her entry point. Her father would take her to Gage Park in her hometown of

Hamilton, Ontario, and teach her as she wore double-bladed skates. Sarah eventually transitioned from figure skating to hockey, thanks in part to her father. After coming to Canada, Roger became a fan of the Toronto Maple Leafs and watched games at the Maple Leaf Gardens. Sarah eventually took after her father and embraced Leafs fandom, watching team legends like Tie Domi, Tomáš Kaberle, and Curtis Joseph. Of course, Mats Sundin was her favorite.

"He's the captain," Nurse said. "Iconic. He's always scoring goals."

Jarome Iginla and Georges Laraque were two Black hockey stars Nurse enjoyed seeing during her youth. Iginla made his Olympic debut in 2002 as a member of Team Canada's men's team. But Nurse didn't visit her grandparents' house to watch the men's squad play that night. Nurse wasn't fully aware at the time, but the team she'd watch compete for an Olympic gold medal would change her hockey life forever.

Before the Canadian men squared off against the Americans, Team Canada's women's hockey team had a gold medal date of their own against the United States in Salt Lake City that year. It was all about revenge. The United States one-upped Canada at the 1998 Olympic Games in Nagano, Japan. It was the first year women were part of ice hockey competition at the Olympics.

The Canadians featured a handful of players who won multiple gold medals at the Women's World Hockey Championship throughout the 1990s, which made them a favorite against the United States. But it was the Americans who took the Canadians by surprise in 1998, scoring the game's first two goals. Canada's Danielle Goyette cut the lead in half partway through the third period, but once Sandra Whyte scored in an empty net with eight seconds remaining, it cemented the United States as the first country to win a gold medal in women's ice hockey.

"I know for me, personally, I really felt that I let down that traditional of group of France St-Louis, Stacey Wilson, the women who played in 1990 that this was going to be their only chance potentially at the Olympic level just simply because of their age," Cassie Campbell-Pascall told the CBC in a 2023 interview.

Four years later, a rematch was needed. A tense, back-and-forth tilt ensued. After Canada took an early 1–0 lead, the Americans opened the second period with an equalizer from Kathryn King. Canadian legend Hayley Wickenheiser then gave the lead back to Canada moments later. It looked like the Canadians would enter the second intermission just up one goal. But Jayna Hefford's breakaway finish, cutting to her backhand before the puck dribbled past American goalie Sara DeCosta added to their lead. The United States would get one more goal from Karyn Bye in the third period, but it was as close as they would get.

Canada finally exacted their revenge with a 3–2 gold-medal victory and reveled in beating their cross-border rival. Wickenheiser even alleged that the Americans stomped on the Canadian flag in their own dressing room and defiantly told the media afterward that she'd want the flag signed. The comments led to investigations by both USA Hockey and the Canadian Hockey Association (now known as Hockey Canada), which later revealed that the Americans hadn't engaged in such civil disrespect.

Nurse was inspired by the Canadian women's national team, as were many other young Canadian women that day. Nurse played hockey on a boys' house-league team with a female teammate, but she had no idea of any women's teams playing hockey at any level.

"I remember thinking we're the only two who are doing this, there are no other girls who play hockey," Nurse said. "When I got to my grandparents' house that night, I was just blown away that there wasn't one team of girls, there was two teams of girls and they're playing on TV. I couldn't believe it. I was like, 'Oh my gosh.' Like, 'I have to be on this team one day.'"

Wanting to be like the women on the ice, Nurse ran into her grandmother's craft nook during a break in the game. She grabbed a pair of scissors and some construction paper and got to work. The final product was a handful of homemade Olympic medals. Nurse gave one to each of her family members once she finished. Sarah's own was colored yellow for gold, held up by a blue ribbon. As the paper heirlooms were passed along to relatives, Sarah spoke her dream out into the universe with one line that resonated with family.

When I play for Team Canada one day.

"From that moment on when I talked about playing at the Olympics and playing for Team Canada," Nurse said. "It was like, 'when I make that team.' I never said 'if'. I never doubted it.

"That was a cool moment that really set the trajectory of my hockey career, I suppose."

Nurse then progressed in her youth hockey career and showed promise. As a 10-year-old, Nurse played for both a boys' and girls' team. She split time between both teams before joining a girls' team full-time as a teenager, playing in Ancaster as well as with the Stoney Creek Sabres of the Provincial Women's Hockey League. In 2012–13, her final year with the Sabres, Nurse scored 36 goals and 56 points in 35 games. According to the league's website, Nurse set a record that season for most goals scored in a season. Nurse was already on Hockey Canada's radar by then. She won gold in 2011 and bronze in 2012 as part of Team Ontario (Red) at the National Women's U18 Championship. Nurse eventually won gold with Team Canada at the 2013 IIHF World Women's U18 championship.

Nurse also caught the eye of a handful of American colleges thanks to her play. From as young as 14, college coaches from Ohio State to Mercyhurst and even Princeton expressed interest through phone calls and letters to the Nurse household. Nurse remembered the process as "overwhelming." But she did have an idea of what type of school she wanted to attend.

"At the time, I thought that Syracuse was the biggest school in the world," Nurse said. "There's a football team, there's a basketball team. It's this huge university. It's funny, because it's a big school. But it's not the biggest school. But I had that idea. I wanted to go to school and just be a number. My dad's family has eight kids. Growing up, I was always daughter of, niece of, cousin of. I never felt, like, anonymous. I want to go to school with 40,000 people, and I don't want anybody to know who I am. I don't even want them to know that I play hockey."

Despite the familial ties, Syracuse's hockey program "wasn't where it needed to be," according to Nurse, which ultimately eliminated the school from contention. Supplanting it was another large school with a high pedigree.

Nurse remembers preparing to leave her house one day with her father when the phone rang. The Nurses, however, let the call go to voicemail. The voice on the machine said the following:

Hey, it's Jackie Friesen from the University of Wisconsin. And we just want to let you know that we love the way you play. We're super interested in you. Want to wish you the best of luck throughout the season. And we'll be watching.

Sarah and Roger both froze. The University of Wisconsin wasn't just any school. The Badgers had won three out of four national titles between 2006 and 2009 at the time they contacted her. Nurse wouldn't know it quite yet, but the school would eventually boast prominent women's hockey alumni like Meghan Duggan, Hilary Knight, Laila Edwards, and Ann-Renée Desbiens in addition to older names like Meaghan Mikkelson, Jessie Vetter, and Sara Bauer.

"They're the best team in NCAA hockey and they're calling me at 14 years old," Sarah said.

When she eventually visited Wisconsin, the school had her sit in on a class filled with 400 people. Combined with the school's penchant for Frozen Four success, the Badgers were the perfect school for Nurse.

"I was obsessed," Nurse said. "It was between Ohio State and Wisconsin. They're both so similar. But at the end of the day, Wisconsin just had a better hockey program, a better hockey setup. I knew that I would be very happy there, even if I didn't play hockey. And so that was what I chose."

Nurse spent four seasons with the Badgers, beginning with her freshman year in 2013. She won a Western Collegiate Hockey Association's Final Faceoff conference title in her sophomore season, scoring twice in a 4–0 thumping of Bemidji State. It earned her Most Outstanding Player honors at tournament's end.

"I was just like, 'Oh my God,'" Nurse said. "'This is crazy. I am playing at Wisconsin. I'm on one of the best teams in the country and here I am winning a conference championship, and having a big hand in it.'"

That conference championship was the first of three for Nurse at Wisconsin. Nurse and her team also made the NCAA tournament in all four years she played as a Badger. But during her junior season, Nurse experienced a dark, painful moment in her collegiate career.

Following a collision with an opposing player during a 2016 Frozen Four matchup against Minnesota, Nurse fractured her wrist. She finished the game, but the wrist kept hurting.

"We did a bunch of imaging, a bunch of tests right after that," Nurse said. "It turned out it was broken pretty badly. I didn't know, obviously during the game, and kept playing. And [doctors] were like, 'We don't know how you played in that game.'"

Surgery soon followed, leaving her in a cast for approximately eight weeks. What made matters more dire was that her recovery timeline would nearly coincide with the start of Canada's under-22 development camp.

"I had to be at Team Canada camp the next month," Nurse said. "I haven't held a stick in three, four months at this point. That was terrifying, because that was the first time I'd really ever been badly injured to the point that I couldn't play through it.

"It's funny because, looking back at it, I've had a way more significant injury since then. So, thinking back to that moment and the timing of it, you think it's the end of the world, you really do. You get injured and you're like, 'My career is over. This is the worst possible thing that could ever happen to me.' And in the moment, it is. But in the grand scheme of your career and who you are as a person, it's really not."

Optimism returned when Nurse was cleared to play just two weeks before development camp. She was also healthy enough for her final season at Wisconsin later that fall, in which she was named an alternate captain. By season's end, she had her best statistical year as a Badger with 25 goals and 53 points in 39 games. During an 8–2 blowout at the expense of the University of Minnesota partway through the season, Nurse recorded her second hat trick of the season and the first-ever hat trick recorded by a Badger against the vaunted Golden Gophers.

Nurse was also named a second-team All-American and a second-team All-WCHA conference player. Nurse and the Badgers reached the 2017 tournament final, where they had a date against Clarkson. But Wisconsin failed to win a national championship, losing 3–0 to the Golden Knights.

Nurse did not make Team Canada's world championship roster for the 2017 tournament in Michigan. But once her time at Wisconsin ended, Canada invited Nurse to take part in its centralization camp to give her a chance at cracking the roster for the 2018 Winter Olympics in Pyeongchang, South Korea.

It was her first opportunity to prove her seven-year-old self correct. And if she made the roster, she would face immense pressure to uphold a national standard. The Canadian women sought their fifth consecutive gold medal at the Winter Games, a streak that began the night Nurse vocalized her Olympic dream to her family.

"I am moving out there at 21 years old," Nurse said. "I'm playing with Marie-Philip Poulin, Shannon Szabados, Meghan Agosta, Haley Irwin, women who've been on the team since 2006, 2010. And I'm so intimidated, and you have so many doubts creeping in, because there are so many girls who you think are better than you that you know you don't bring what they bring. I felt like I was just coming in fresh faced and new."

Nurse remembered feeling "lost" and wondered if she would even make the team out of centralization camp. But she felt reassurance after a video session with then assistant coach and future Canada and Toronto Sceptres head coach Troy Ryan, who showed her everything she was doing was right. Nurse even told the CBC in August 2022 that Ryan was "instrumental" in helping her make the Canadian team for Pyeongchang. But Nurse still admits feeling "overwhelmed" throughout her first Olympic experience.

"We had the chance to break an Olympic record for the longest [gold-medal-win] streak," Nurse said. "There was so much pressure on us. I was not prepared for the amount of distractions, media attention."

Nurse scored one goal through five games at the 2018 Games, a game-winning goal versus the United States in a 2–1 victory during round-robin play. The next time Nurse and Canada would see the Americans was in the gold medal final. The game is most remembered by a six-round shootout pitting the world's two best women's hockey programs in the world against one another. Both sides traded goals through regulation, with Monique Lamoureux scoring the game-tying goal with under seven minutes to go.

When both teams required a shootout, it was Monique's sister, Jocelyne, who got the better of Szabados in the sixth round to give the

Americans the advantage. Agosta was given the chance to tie but was stopped by Maddie Rooney. Rooney tracked Agosta as the forward tried to find an opening to shoot at, only for the netminder to make a pad save. Rooney then swiped the puck away from her crease and ran toward her teammates who stormed the ice in celebration after earning their first gold medal win since 1998.

The American celebrations meant Canadian disappointment. It meant Nurse would have to wait four more years to get a crack at her first Olympic gold medal.

"You feel like it's the end of the world, and you feel like you've disappointed your entire country," Nurse said about the 2018 Olympics ending in a silver medal performance. "But being able to bond with my teammates and come back and see just how proud of us everybody was and realizing that going to the Olympics is a huge accomplishment,

"Although we wanted a gold medal, we got a silver medal. It's not the color that we wanted. We still got there. We still played and we still made everybody proud. And so I really think that that fueled me to want to continue going and wanting to get back to another Olympics and wanting to win a gold medal."

NURSE KNEW EXACTLY WHAT she was going to say when the phone rang.

Hockey Canada was about to check in on the Olympic silver medalist ahead of the 2022 Olympics. Her childhood dream remained unfulfilled. It had been nearly four years since her last attempt. Nurse had experienced so much since then.

Months after the 2018 loss to the United States, Nurse was drafted second overall in the Canadian Women's Hockey League by the Toronto Furies. Despite a successful statistical season, she notched 14 goals and 26 points in 26 games during her rookie season, her experience with the Furies was a bit mixed. Nurse went from a positive experience with the University of Wisconsin, where she felt she and her teammates were "treated like absolute gold," to her year with the Furies, which she says was the "worst" she had ever been treated in her hockey career.

"[At Wisconsin], we had a beautiful locker room. I remember one time we got off the ice and there were iPads just waiting in our stalls for us just to have. We were treated like absolute gold. Then I went to Hockey Canada, where you're not treated as good as you are at Wisconsin, but you're still treated pretty well. You play on Team Canada, so you're still treated pretty well.

"I got to the CWHL and the Toronto Furies and we were kind of treated like crap. We practiced at 9:30 at night. We had a tiny little rinky-dink locker room. Our coaches didn't have a locker room. We had to buy our own tape, bring our own skate sharpening. We weren't treated with respect at all. I was like, this sucks. It wasn't even a true draft either. There were five teams, I believe. You put your name in for the city that you were going to live in. So, if I was going to live in Boston, I put Sarah Nurse, Boston. And that's who I was getting drafted by. It wasn't a true draft. I put Sarah Nurse, Toronto. Because I was going to live in Toronto, and so that's who I was drafted by."

That experience made Nurse want to join the Professional Women's Hockey Players Association as a player rep despite being, as she describes, an "annoying little rookie" who pushed herself onto the players association. It meant she was among the first players to know the league wouldn't have sufficient funding to continue for the 2019–20 season and that it would cease operations by May 1, 2019.

"We realized this model is no longer viable in the economics and the future of the CWHL," then CWHL chairwoman Laurel Walzak told the *New York Times* in March 2019.

Nurse later joined the PWHPA's board of directors in 2020. She grew uncomfortable with the sport's silence with the Black Lives Matter movement after the death of George Floyd. Former goaltender and member Liz Knox even resigned to open up a place for Nurse to join.

"It's a blind spot we've had in women's hockey," Knox told Emily Kaplan from ESPN. "Resources are important. Education is important. But I feel like we were missing a piece. If we want to set the standard for inclusion, there's a logical next step."

On the ice, Nurse finally made her World Championship debut in 2019, winning a bronze medal with Canada. Nurse notched two assists in victory over Russia. After the 2020 World Championship was cancelled due to COVID-19, Nurse returned to Team Canada for the 2021 Women's Worlds at WinSport Arena in Calgary, Alberta. The tournament was supposed to be held in Nova Scotia, but COVID-19 concerns led to the province cancelling the event. The IIHF eventually announced they'd hold the event in mid to late August 2021 behind closed doors in Calgary.

Nurse made the team but worked primarily as a fourth-line forward. She was called upon to be "defensively responsible and offensively responsible" in her role.

"She played that role and never complained," Canadian women's hockey legend Cassie Campbell-Pascall said. Campbell-Pascall worked as a management consultant for Canada at the tournament. "I know she didn't like it, because I know when you're the public face and the figure and you're seen as a fourth-line center, it doesn't always mesh. And that was one thing [she] and I kind of worked through together, is that it doesn't matter what the outside expectations are. It's what we need you to do in here."

"Sometimes it sucks to be on the fourth line," Nurse said. "But you have to put it in perspective. I'm literally on Team Canada. There are hundreds of thousands of girls who would kill to be on this team. And so that's kind of the way that I tried to frame it. And me and my linemates, my teammates, tried to frame it.

"And we ended up winning a gold medal."

Team Canada erased a 2–0 deficit against the Americans in the gold medal match, eventually winning the game with an overtime winner from Marie-Philip Poulin. The victory gave Canada its first World Championship gold since 2012.

The success was sweet for Nurse and Canada, but the forward still felt nervous about her chances at making the roster ahead of centralization camp later that year, largely because she played fourth-line minutes at the 2021 Worlds. Canada would need its best players ahead of the 2022 Olympic Games in Beijing, seeking revenge after losing in the gold medal game four years earlier. What made matters worse for Nurse was when she suffered a torn MCL, causing her to miss the remainder of the centralization period.

Which brings us back to that phone call. It came the day before Canada was supposed to formally announce its squad for the 2022 Olympics. It didn't matter that Nurse hadn't participated in the centralization camp leading up to the 2022 Games, about a month away. Nurse intended to join Team Canada when the women traveled to Beijing in February. When Hockey Canada called and asked if she'd be ready to play, Nurse answered in the affirmative.

Yes, I will be able to play at the Olympics.

"I think I convinced myself in that moment, because I didn't know if I could play at the Olympics," Nurse said. "I had no expectations going into the Olympics. I just wanted to do whatever the team needed me to do to be successful, whether that was being in the stands, being the biggest cheerleader, or whether that was playing a couple shifts a game, whatever it was."

Nurse began the tournament on a third line with Rebecca Johnston and Blayre Turnbull. Her time on that line lasted about two games until a COVID-19 scare involving teammate Emily Clark—her test was eventually deemed inconclusive—forced her to miss a game against the Russian Olympic Committee (ROC) and Canada to shuffle its lines. Nurse was bumped up from third-line duties to first-line duties.

"They needed someone to play with [Marie-Philip Poulin] and Brianne Jenner," Nurse said.

Two minutes into the game against the ROC, Nurse opened the scoring. She would later pick up a power-play assist en route to a 6–1 Canada victory. Three games into the tournament, Nurse had scored four goals and three assists.

"I was like, 'Oh, this is kind of fun,'" Nurse said. "And then from there, I just stayed with them and we kind of tore it up together which was a lot of fun."

The trio powered Canada through its matchups in the knockout round. Nurse picked up points throughout, including a four-assist game in a semifinal win over Switzerland. Nurse was within striking distance of two records held by Canadian legend Hayley Wickenheiser, both set during the 2006 Olympics in Turin, Italy.

"So, going into the gold medal game it's in the back of your head," Nurse said. "But having come off of so much defeat in major competition, the only thing that was driving me was winning a gold medal. To me, a record doesn't mean anything if you don't actually win. I know maybe that's a hot take. I don't know. But we need to come home with a gold medal. Because, at the end of the day, I'm not going to be in an interview talking about how I got this record if I have silver medal. That's not going to happen."

Of course, it was the Americans who stood in Nurse's way in Beijing. As was the case when Canada and the United States met in Pyeongchang during the 2018 Games.

The Canadians should've opened the scoring with a 1–0 goal from Natalie Spooner. But the goal was eventually disallowed because Nurse was offside on the zone entry that led to the goal.

"Spooner, I owe you one," Nurse remembered saying to her teammate afterward.

Minutes later, the Nurse–Jenner–Poulin line won a faceoff in the offensive zone. There was supposed to be a set play. Nurse thought she heard Poulin call out a play name. Defenceman Claire Thompson heard a different play call from Poulin, as did Jenner. But somehow, Nurse found herself in the right place to redirect Thompson's shot past U.S. goaltender Alex Cavallini to give Canada a 1–0 lead.

Poulin scored Canada's next two goals to extend the lead to three goals partway through the second. Thanks to an assist on Poulin's second goal, Nurse had broken Wickenheiser's record for assists and points in a single Olympics. The Americans mounted a comeback attempt and scored the next two goals in the game, including an Amanda Kessel goal with 13 seconds remaining in regulation. The United States couldn't find an equalizer after that.

When the final buzzer sounded, Canada had officially secured its gold medal. And in winning, Nurse became the first Black female hockey player to win an Olympic gold medal.

"There were so many women that I knew of who played for their national teams," Nurse said. "There was Angela James, who I knew didn't go to an Olympics, but I knew that she was such an impactful player and had such a big impact on Hockey Canada, in the Hall of Fame and [has] all of these incredible accolades. There's Blake Bolden who, again, you don't think about these women not going to the Olympics or not winning a gold medal."

Twenty years after making a gold medal out of paper and dreaming of winning it on the world's biggest stage, Nurse earned a real one and made history in the process.

NEARLY 21 YEARS AFTER that fateful day watching hockey at her grandparents' place, Sarah Nurse is among star-studded company on the ice at FLA Live Arena in Sunrise, Florida. It's the 2023 NHL All-Star Game skills competition, and despite not being an NHLer, she doesn't look out of place standing next some of the league's biggest stars on the ice.

Nurse is given the chance to go toe-to-toe with Vezina Trophy winner Igor Shesterkin during one of the night's events. She skates toward the goaltender and smoothly puts the puck in goal, besting him with the "Forsberg," the move made popular by Swedish Hockey Hall of Famer Peter Forsberg, in which the skater carries the puck and tries to beat the goaltender by holding the puck with one hand on their stick after going to their backhand.

As Nurse skates away from Shesterkin, she looks up, smiles, and covers her mouth, almost embarrassed at the fact that she successfully eluded one of the best NHL goaltenders in the game today.

"One of my friends, we were talking about this event, and they were like, 'You should try this,'" Nurse said, according to the Associated Press in February 2023. "I didn't even think about it until afterward. I was just like, attack the day. Seize the moment."

It's moments like those that have built Nurse's profile around the hockey world, making the women's hockey star one of the most marketable faces in the sport.

Nurse has had brand deals with a handful of companies including Adidas, CCM, Royal Bank of Canada, and Canadian Tire. She has graced the cover of EA Sports NHL, sharing the spotlight with American star Trevor Zegras. Tim Hortons and Barbie even collaborated to create Barbie dolls of Nurse and Marie-Philip Poulin.

"She's the face of women's hockey," TSN broadcaster Kenzie Lalonde said. "I wholeheartedly stand behind that statement.

"It sounds like she made a conscious decision of being a face in this sport, in this world. She's everywhere, and what an amazing person to be everywhere."

"If you would have asked 15-year-old me or 18-year-old me, or 22-year-old me, I would have never, ever imagined that. Or even really thought about having that," Nurse said.

Nurse has also made in-roads as a broadcaster, making appearances and providing analysis on Sportsnet and TNT.

"I think Sarah's going to be a big star on TV when she's done," hockey insider Elliotte Friedman said. "I think that she has a presence. And the limited amount of time that she's done TV, she's clearly not afraid to say what's on her mind. I think that one thing I've learned about Sarah, she's got a bit of a bite to her. In the sense that she's not afraid to deliver, not a scathing comment, but a sharp comment. I don't think there's a real fear of saying too much."

Nurse even appeared with Sportsnet's Caroline Cameron in 2020 as protests raged in light of the death of George Floyd, a death that led to pauses in sports action across various sports leagues, and even discussed personal stories of racism she suffered in her youth.

"With hockey, it's always been a little bit difficult," Nurse said to Cameron. "Because [in] my career and me growing up playing hockey, I've always been under the microscope and I've always been questioned on why I am a hockey player. Obviously, growing up, I was a female hockey player, and I was playing in a male-dominated sport. I played with the boys. And then, being a biracial child, they're wondering why I'm playing hockey.

"I've been told, 'You should really straighten your hair,' which is something I've been doing for a decade now because I wanted to fit in with my hockey community. I've been asked why I don't play basketball. Someone just came up to me and blatantly said, 'I will just never understand why people like you play hockey.' It's crazy because I look at Black kids and Indigenous kids and unless they're excelling at hockey, unless they're good at hockey, they're not afforded any respect."

Nurse's platform, visibility, and success have turned her into a natural role model for young women following her path.

"She's been a great role model," Team USA's and Wisconsin Badger Laila Edwards said. "I got to watch her play at Wisconsin.

That was great. She was a great player, and I got to watch her have great success with the Canada Women's National Team. It hasn't been fun for the U.S.A, but it's great to see for the BIPOC community in hockey."

Nurse has collaborated frequently with Black Girl Hockey Club, a nonprofit charity that gives scholarships to aspiring young women who want to play hockey, through 'Nursey Nights.' Young girls who attended select PWHL Toronto games got to hang out with Nurse post-game, and even took part in a private Zoom session with the Olympian and hockey star.

"She is an amazing community supporter," R. Renee Hess, the founder of Black Girl Hockey Club, said.

"Black girls from all over come and watch her play and meet her after the game. And just kind of make that connection right with somebody who looks like them, who's playing the game and playing it really well."

On the ice, Nurse's play remains at a high level. Nurse presently plays in the Professional Women's Hockey League and continues to be one of the sport's most prominent players.

"I'll tell you that Sarah Nurse is a glue player," Cassie Campbell-Pascall said. "She can play fourth line center or top line wing. She always has a smile on her face. She's always positive."

"Sarah has just been such a freaking force for the Canadian women's team," former defenseman Blake Bolden said. "She kind of just flips hockey upside down, just how she carries herself, the things that she's interested in, she's a great ambassador for our game."

Nurse juggles her off-ice responsibilities with her on-ice ones, making time for young aspiring players and taking her day-to-day life as a professional hockey star very seriously. Her schedule doesn't stop her from living her life as close to a set routine as possible: working in the gym at 8:00 AM, finishing all of her on-ice work by 1:00 PM, and listening to Beyoncé before games. (Nurse considers the Beyoncé ballad "I Was Here" one of the "greatest of all-time.")

Such is life when you're one of the most prominent hockey stars on the planet.

"I never dreamed of even being in this position, I never dreamed of being a professional athlete playing professional hockey," Nurse said. "I wanted to play at the Olympics, and that was it. There was no professional space. And so to be able to help kind of create a professional landscape for women's hockey, and now being able to actually play in it is amazing."

11

Angela James

It shouldn't be this difficult to find highlights of Angela James online.

A YouTube search for James will return clips that celebrate her legacy. You'll find her Hockey Hall of Fame speech from her induction in 2010 and even a video from the Hall displaying an old scoring trophy she won from her minor hockey days. James has been featured in numerous documentaries throughout her hockey life, and you can find them online too. You can even find videos of James teaching how to pass the puck.

But there's no highlight reel of James' exploits, torching opposing teams in the 1990 IIHF Women's World Championship. Her first game of the tournament, where she scored four goals against Team Sweden, wasn't even televised, a common problem for most games from that tournament.

"Basically just the gold medal game was televised. I did the 1997 Women's Worlds in Kitchener. I think we did Canada's last three games," broadcaster Gord Miller said.

There is no sizzle reel from her Central Ontario Women's Hockey League days either, where she perennially led the league in scoring. It's the unfortunate result of James' success coming at a time when the women's game was obscure.

Despite being recognized as the first female hockey superstar, drawing comparisons to Wayne Gretzky, and being inducted into the Hockey Hall of Fame, James' spotlight doesn't burn nearly as brightly as her contemporaries'.

"When I think about her contributions to the sport, I always think of them as being forgotten," hockey star Sarah Nurse said. "I never saw her play. I've seen clips. I've heard people talk about the way she plays, but the way that she's regarded and the way that she played the game with this tenacity.

"Man, had I known about Angela James when I was seven years old, I would have lost it."

"I actually was not even aware of Angela James until I got involved with the NHL female advisory board," NCAA hockey coach and former National Women's Hockey League star Kelsey Koelzer said. "That was really my first introduction to Angela James. I remember being at a meeting with her the first time and just being wowed. Even not fully knowing her background, just being familiar with it, you could tell that you were sitting in the room with hockey royalty.

"It was like one of those experiences where you just sat back and shut up and soaked in everything that she had to say."

For those unfamiliar with her résumé, James' career is more than deserving of Hall of Fame glory. James is four-time World Champion with Team Canada. James shares the record for most goals at a women's world championship with American Cindy Curley. James also has two gold medals from the formerly named 3 Nations Cup, and even a title from the Women's Pacific Rim Championship.

A two-time collegiate champion at Seneca College in Ontario, James won three collegiate scoring titles and three MVPs in the 1980s as a defender. When she joined the senior circuit, James reconverted to forward and dominated as a member of the COWHL, winning six MVP honors, eight scoring titles and six gold medals at the Hockey Canada Women's National Championship. When James joined the

Grant Fuhr was an integral part of the 1981 Victoria Cougars, helping his team win 60 games en route to a berth in that year's Memorial Cup. Fuhr was named a first-team All-Star in his two seasons—1979–80 and 1980–81—-with the Cougars. (Credit: WHL Archives)

(top) *Following his two seasons in the WHL with the Victoria Cougars, Grant Fuhr embarked on a 19-year Hall of Fame career, where he won five Stanley Cups with the Edmonton Oilers. Fuhr also played for the St. Louis Blues, Buffalo Sabres, Toronto Maple Leafs, Calgary Flames, and Los Angeles Kings.* (Credit: Bruce Bennett / Getty Images)

(left) *Jarome Iginla spent three seasons as a member of the WHL's Kamloops Blazers, winning two Memorial Cups. Iginla was also the 1996 WHL player of the Year after a 63-goal, 136-point season with the Blazers. The forward later joined the Calgary Flames for their 1996 postseason run, playing two Stanley Cup playoff games. It was the start of a 20-year Hall of Fame career that saw him win two Olympic gold medals with Team Canada.* (Credit: WHL Archives)

For a brief time during the 1999–2000 season, the Calgary Flames boasted three Black players: Fred Brathwaite (left), Jarome Iginla (middle), and Grant Fuhr. Other teams like the Edmonton Oilers and Atlanta Thrashers have also boasted multiple Black players on their rosters. (Credit: Calgary Flames)

Jarome Iginla won the first of two Maurice "Rocket" Richard trophies during the 2001–02 campaign where a league-leading 52 goals. Iginla also led the league in points (96), good enough to secure his first, and only, Art Ross Trophy win. (Credit: Calgary Flames)

Fred Brathwaite currently works as a goaltending coach for the Henderson Silver Knights, the AHL affiliate of the Vegas Golden Knights. Brathwaite played nine NHL seasons with the Edmonton Oilers, Calgary Flames, St. Louis Blues, and Columbus Blue Jackets. (Credit: Henderson Silver Knights)

Sarah Nurse wasn't aware of women's hockey before watching the gold medal game between Team Canada and Team USA at the 2002 Winter Olympics in Salt Lake City, Utah. Twenty years after making a gold medal at her grandparents' place, Nurse eventually won gold with Team Canada at the 2022 Olympics in Beijing. (Credit: Courtesy of Sarah Nurse)

Nurse is among many players who have skated in the PWHPA Dream Gap Tour. But she presently plays in the Professional Women's Hockey League. Nurse joined the expansion Vancouver franchise in June 2025. (Credit: Shanna Martin-Book)

Canada Post unveiled a stamp of Black hockey pioneer Willie O'Ree in late 2023, celebrating his legacy as the first Black player to break the NHL's color barrier. O'Ree made his NHL debut for the Boston Bruins in 1958. Hockey players past and present, including Sarah Nurse, Evander Kane, Grant Fuhr, Anson Carter, Georges Laraque, and Nazem Kadri, were on hand for the event. (Credit: Julian McKenzie)

Kevin Weekes played for several teams in his 11-year career, including the Carolina Hurricanes. Weekes played an integral role in the Hurricanes' Cup Final appearance in 2002 against the Detroit Red Wings. Weekes now works as a hockey broadcaster. (Credit: Courtesy Carolina Hurricanes)

To date, Quinton Byfield is the highest-drafted Black player in NHL history. Byfield was selected second overall by the Los Angeles Kings during the 2020 NHL Entry Draft. In July 2024, Byfield signed a five-year, $31.25 million contract extension. (Credit: L.A. Kings)

O'Ree's statue at the Smithsonian National Museum of African American History and Culture in Washington, D.C., is among a handful of hockey artifacts on display as part of the "Sports: Leveling the Playing Field" collection. There are also hockey cards featuring O'Ree, Tony McKegney, Bill Riley, Mike Marson, a Seth Jones Columbus Blue Jackets jersey, and an autographed stick from former NHLer Joel Ward. (Credit: Jason Mehta)

Herb Carnegie, along with his brother Ossie and Manny McIntyre, formed the Black Aces line, while playing for teams in Quebec including the Sherbrooke Randies. It is the first all-Black line in hockey outside of the Colored Hockey League of the Maritimes. (Credit: Courtesy of Bob Dawson)

Carnegie is often recognized as the best Black hockey player never to make it to the National Hockey League. He was infamously told by a coach that he could join the Toronto Maple Leafs if someone could turn him white. Carnegie also turned down numerous offers by the New York Rangers to play for their minor league affiliates. The offers featured salaries that paid less than what he made playing semi-professionally in Quebec. (Credit: Courtesy of Bob Dawson)

Angela James is a four-time World Champion with Team Canada and even represented Team Ontario at the first-ever Women's World Championship in 1987—an unsanctioned tournament in the eyes of the International Ice Hockey Federation. James, however, was snubbed from Canada's 1998 Olympic team and never got the chance to play for her country at the Games. James was named to the Hockey Hall of Fame in 2010. (Credit: AP Photo/The Canadian Press, Frank Gunn)

Willie O'Ree, Mike Marson, Bill Riley, and Tony McKegney are the first Black hockey players to reach the NHL. Marson and Riley made history as the first Black teammates when they played on the 1976–77 Washington Capitals. Both men spent parts of three seasons together on the Capitals. (Credit: Laurel Sandage)

Duante' Abercrombie's unique hockey journey had him coaching for school and youth teams in Washington, D.C. before spending time coaching with the Arizona Coyotes, Nashville Predators and Toronto Maple Leafs. In Fall 2026, Abercrombie will be the first head coach of a historically Black college or university men's hockey program. (Credit: Photo courtesy of Duante' Abercrombie and Nick Guerriero)

Kelsey Koelzer is the first Black hockey player to be picked first in a North American professional hockey league entry draft when the National Women's Hockey League's Metropolitan Riveters selected her in the 2016 draft. Koelzer is now the head coach at Arcadia University, the first Black female head coach in NCAA history. (Credit: Hunter Martin)

(top) *Tony McKegney (right) spent parts of the 1981–82 Buffalo Sabres season with teammate Val James (middle). While James was more known for his pugilism and fighting throughout his professional days, McKegney had two 30-plus goal seasons in a Sabres uniform and retired with more than 300 goals and more than 600 career points across seven NHL teams.* (Credit: Bill Wippert / Getty Images)

(right) *P.K. Subban played 13 seasons, spending seven of them with the Montreal Canadiens, with whom he won the Norris Trophy for best defenseman in 2013. Subban is the first Black player to win the honor. Subban eventually made a Cup Final appearance with Nashville in 2017 against the Pittsburgh Penguins.* (Credit: Tasos Katopodis / Getty Images)

Through Georges Laraque's 12-year NHL career, the Quebecois forward amassed 1,126 penalty minutes in 695 career games through four teams (Edmonton, Pittsburgh, Phoenix, and Montreal). Laraque scored 53 goals and 153 points in 695 career games. (Credit: Pittsburgh Penguins)

Anson Carter played four years at Michigan State University, earning notoriety as a goalscorer and an All-American, and was a finalist for the Hobey Baker Award. Carter followed up his collegiate success with a 10-year NHL career and two IIHF World Hockey Championship gold medals for Team Canada. Carter scored the game-winning goal for Canada at the 2003 World Championship. Carter was inducted into the MSU Hall of Fame in 2024. (Credit: Michigan State Athletics)

Blake Bolden is the first African American player to play in the now-defunct National Women's Hockey League and eventually won an Isobel Cup with the Boston Pride in 2016. Bolden now works as a broadcaster for Amazon Prime and once worked as a scout for the Los Angeles Kings. (Credit: Cintia Freitas)

National Women's Hockey League at the tail end of her career, she won an MVP and a championship.

James possessed a hard shot, played with speed, and intimidated opponents with her physical presence. Whenever opposing players ran into contact with James, it was like "hitting steel," as mentioned in her biography. As a woman, she drew comparison to the most imposing power forwards in NHL history.

"She played in the era of body checking," Canadian hockey legend Cassie Campbell-Pascall said. "And I think people don't realize just how dominant she was. You know, not many people have ever got to see her play live. I would say she had this cross between Eric Lindros and Mark Messier, she was sort of a combination between those two.

"She was mean. Like, on the ice she was mean. And yet, off the ice, she was one of the nicest people ever."

Cheryl Pounder remembered being intimidated the first time she ever met James when they were teammates on the Toronto Aeros in the 1990s. Pounder even played with James as part of Team Canada's gold-medal-winning squad from the 1994 World Championship in Lake Placid. Pounder, however, wasn't used in the gold medal game against the United States. Pounder celebrated with her teammates but eventually retreated to the showers to hide her disappointment after not playing a significant role in the championship game.

But James eventually consoled Pounder. The legendary forward put her arm around the young defender, providing some much-needed wisdom.

Kid. Rome wasn't built in a day. You know how much time you got?

"Those words live with me, really, forever," Pounder remembered. "She was intimidating. But over time, I realized, not as a teammate."

As a 16-year-old, Campbell-Pascall remembers meeting James after the latter played at the first ever Women's World Championship in 1987. Even in line, waiting for autographs, Campbell-Pascall felt "scared" before meeting James.

"She just kind of had that presence," Campbell-Pascall said. "When I got to know her, we were teammates with the Aeros, [she was] just such a class act and just so nice and calm. A great leader. She really kind of had that split personality."

Those accolades, player comparisons, and stories culminated in James being one of the first two women ever inducted into the Hockey Hall of Fame and the first openly gay woman to be entered into the Hall.

"She was gay in a time where you weren't as forthcoming to come out," Campbell-Pascall said. "I think that she brought some attention to that, and she was confident in who she was, who she loved and her family."

James' moment came in 2010 when she joined the Hall alongside U.S. Olympic gold medalist and former captain Cammi Granato.

"The burden she carried being not just one of the first prominent female players, but a prominent Black female player, had to be a lot to carry, and she did that with a dignity and a grace that is pretty admirable," Miller said. "She wasn't afraid to stand up to authority. She wasn't afraid to ruffle feathers. And people forget. Women's hockey is super popular now. It was not in the 1990s. There were lots of people in positions of authority who said that women should not be playing hockey.

"Women's hockey owes a ton to her. And I think Black hockey players owe a ton to her as well. That's a double burden to carry, and she did it very well," Miller said.

Before her speech began, James took the time to look at the wall behind her, finding her name alongside other deserving names of that year's inductions class: Granato, four-time NHL All-Star Dino Ciccarelli, longtime Detroit Red Wings executive Jim Devellano, and longtime Calgary Flames part-owner Daryl "Doc" Seaman. James looked up at the names and raised her arms in disbelief.

"I used to run hockey schools back in the days and would always arrange a visit here to the Hockey Hall of Fame with different groups," James said in 2010. "And would always be in amazement of the class of athletes and read all about the great legends inducted. And if you ever would ask me if I would be standing here today? Not in a lifetime."

ANGELA JAMES IS FEATURED in the NHL documentary *Ice Queens* by director Kwame Mason. There is a scene near the beginning of the documentary where James shows around her neighborhood of Flemingdon Park in Toronto, including a wall where she would fire slapshots and even play goalie when going against the boys.

"Cause you're a girl, you had to be the goalie," James said in *Ice Queens*. "You get the tennis ball marks on the forehead."

James grew up in the North Toronto neighborhood as the daughter of a white mother, Donna Barrato, and a Black father, Leo James. According to the book *Angela James: The First Superstar of Women's Hockey*, written by Tom Bartsiokas and Corey Long, Leo came to Canada from Mississippi to escape racial segregation in the United States. But James mostly lived with her mother and siblings and was faced with constant discrimination and slurs surrounding her biracial identity. In one instance detailed in the biography, Donna remembers seeing her daughter scrubbing their arm in the bathtub to scrub her blackness off her skin after fellow schoolchildren told her she was "dirty."

According to Kristina Rutherford's Sportsnet profile of James, she was surrounded by many in her neighborhood suffering from "unforgettable circumstances" such as addiction, drugs, and even suicide. James would have to fend off other classmates who engaged in fist fights against her. But in spite of those tough circumstances, Angela was active as a child. She played sports like baseball and synchronized swimming, but hockey emerged as her first love from a very young age.

James took up ball hockey from as young as kindergarten, as written in Scott Russell's *Ice Time: A Canadian Hockey Journey*, playing in the streets of Flemingdon with other neighborhood kids. James also played ice hockey against others from Flemingdon and learned to skate following a deaf gentleman around on the ice while following his strides. James also noticed that he grunted frequently as he skated, and she eventually did the same.

"I didn't realize it but later in life, as I was playing hockey, everybody knew that when I was coming they could hear me going 'ungh, ungh, ungh.'" James said in *Ice Queens*. "I didn't realize that I was making that sound. They started calling me 'The Train.'"

At the age of eight, James joined the Flemingdon Boys Hockey Association—an all-boys league. The league was hesitant to include James, but her mother threatened legal action and so Angela played alongside boys, even moving up from the atom division to peewee according to James' biography. By the end of her first year, James led her league in scoring. In James' second year in the league, she switched numbers from No. 11 to No. 8, a number that would follow her through to the end of her playing days.

"But as I started to get better, and better, and better, then it became a problem," James said in the *Ice Queens* documentary. "Because, in the '70s, 'you can't be better than my son.' And so, they asked me to leave."

Specifically, James couldn't be better than the league president's son. Their father took exception to James' skill, leading to a back-and-forth between him and James' mother, Donna. Angela was finally pulled out of the all-boys league in favor of an all-girls one. But she initially resisted when she discovered most girls in Annunciation, a Catholic church-led hockey league in North York, didn't wear hockey skates.

"I was a little disappointed because when I first went there, there were all these girls in figure skates," Angela said in her biography. "And I was like, 'What is this? You shouldn't be wearing figure skates in hockey.'"

That wasn't the only strange thing about the league. James joined at the age of 10. But most of her opponents were already teenagers. And in some cases, girls as young as seven years old participated. But even in all girls' league, just as it was with the boys, James faced racist, sexist, and homophobic slurs from opposing players. She tried to respond by being physical against her opponents through hits and cross-checks.

"It's really hard to prove when you're being discriminated against all on the ice. Because if the referee doesn't hear it, how do they know?" James said in *Ice Queens*.

James eventually joined the Central Ontario Women's Hockey League's Toronto Islanders, where she—as a teenager—played against much older women in a senior league. She later joined the Seneca College women's hockey team as a 16-year-old. James was already a star athlete for Seneca, helping the women's fastball team win a league championship during the 1981–82 season. James had spent most of her hockey life as a center until she joined the team, led by coach Lee Trempe. James was converted from forward to defense.

"With her talent and ability, it made sense to give her more ice to work with, as opposed to cutting it down on her," Trempe said in James' biography. "She was able to set up plays, get the puck out of our own end and incorporate the rest of the players into whatever system we were using."

Even as a defender, James remained prolific for Seneca College. James scored 15 goals and 25 points in eight games during her first season in 1982–83. The Scouts finished as runners-up at season's end, falling just short of an OCAA championship. But James' season was still good enough to win her first of three Ontario Colleges Athletic

Association MVP honors. James' second year on the team saw her match her goals output from her debut season, but she posted 30 points in 10 games en route to a second consecutive MVP trophy and her first league championship with the Scouts.

But it was James' third season that earned her the moniker of "the Wayne Gretzky of women's hockey" from local media, according to her biography. James scored 50 goals in 14 games as a defender, adding 23 assists for a 73-point season. Not only did James secure her third MVP as a result, but she also helped Seneca win a second straight OCAA title. James ended her time in the OCAA, which disbanded in 1989, as the league's all-time leading scorer.

With her collegiate days behind her, James added to her legacy in the COWHL. James won her first of many COWHL scoring titles in 1987 as a member of the Toronto Aeros where she worked with head coach Ken Dufton. In her book, James calls Dufton the "best coach" she had growing up.

"Ange was just one of the most intense competitors I've ever had the opportunity to work with," Dufton said. "At the time when I started coaching her, which would have been in the '80s, she was the most dominant forward in the world."

Two years before James joined the Aeros, she spent a season with the Brampton Canadettes where she played with an integral figure in women's hockey, Fran Rider.

"You always knew, in any game you were in, if Angela was on your hockey team, you had a solid chance to win," Rider said in James' biography. "Some days, when you were down a goal, or a couple of goals, you'd look down the bench and see that No. 8: 'Okay, now's the time, Angela.'"

Rider first joined the Canadettes as a teenager in 1967 according to Hockey Canada, after spotting an ad in a local newspaper about a women's hockey tournament. Rider had never played the sport for a team before, yet her passion for the sport stemmed from her childhood days when she played on a rink in her backyard. Rider eventually became an all-star player in the COWHL. But her impact resonates further in her off-ice achievements and it ultimately paved a road for players like James to succeed.

Following an executive career that led to her becoming the president of the Ontario Women's Hockey Association and part of Hockey Canada's Female Council, Rider helped organize the Canadian national championship for women in 1982. Five years later, Rider led the charge for the first Women's World Championship, unsanctioned in the eyes of the International Ice Hockey Federation but hosted by the OWHA.

There were some doubts about the tournament being played—West Germany withdrew from the event at the last second once they learned body-checking wouldn't be allowed. The Canadian Amateur Hockey Association had already began phasing out body checking in 1986. From James' biography, CAHA deduced it was "hazardous" for players who weren't trained in receiving and giving hits to engage in such physical contact.

But the tournament went on as planned with seven teams. Canada, Sweden, Japan, the Netherlands, Switzerland, the United States, and an Angela James–led Team Ontario. According to her biography, the Ontario squad was James' team at the time, the Mississauga Warriors. James began the season with the Warriors before joining the Hamilton Golden Hawks for women's nationals that year. But when the Warriors were named the Team Ontario representative, James returned to her old team.

Team Ontario made it to the final of the first-ever women's worlds, losing to a Canada squad consisting of all-stars from across the country. Canada upended Ontario in the championship final. But the tournament's success led to a European Women's Championship in 1989 and an IIHF-sanctioned Women's Worlds in 1990.

"I don't think both Hockey Canada or the IIHF thought that women's hockey was necessarily ready for it at that time," Dufton said. "But the tournament went off so well that they had to recognize that, yes, these players are playing at a much higher level, and they're much more serious about their sport than maybe we realized.

The success of 1987 set the table for the 1990 Worlds, allowing the hockey world to first open its eyes to James' talents. The 1990 Worlds featured one of James' best single-tournament performances of her international career.

WHEN TEAM CANADA PLAYED at the 1990 Women's World Championship in Ottawa, they struck many by surprise with their outfit choice.

While Canadian jerseys have occasionally strayed from their usual color palate, the best Canadian international hockey jerseys typically have some combination of red and white. Canada's 1990 jerseys, however, stood out with their usage of hot pink. The color dominated the body of one of their jerseys, while another had the pink adorn their shoulders with white serving as its main base.

James, like many of her teammates, hated them. In her biography, she likened the jerseys to being dressed as "pink flamingos." *Ottawa Sun* writer Jane O'Hara even called them "the wussiest uniforms you've ever seen."

"Real women don't wear pink," O'Hara said, according to James' biography. "Pink does not inspire fear. Pink does not spark aggression. When you think about battling it out in the corners, you do not think pink. As a team colour, pink stinks."

Despite the players and Hockey Canada—including future president Bob Nicholson—being less than thrilled with their colors, they acquiesced and accepted the style.

"We just wanted to play hockey and play for our country. And if they told us to wear polka dots, we'd wear polka dots," James said in her biography.

James was on a roster loaded with fellow stars who shone when given the chance at the 1987 tournament. Teammate Geraldine Heaney played with James on Team Ontario at the 1987 Worlds. France St-Louis was named the best forward at the 1987 Worlds. Defender Dawn McGuire was named tournament MVP. The tournament also brought back bodychecking, the only women's world championship to allow it, a benefit to James' play style.

The Canadians were unbeatable through the group stage as James racked up goals against opposing teams. In Canada's first game against Sweden, James scored four times including the first goal of the tournament. According to James' biography, Canadian television network TSN decided to air the remainder of Canada's World Championship games after that game. Canada then ended the round-robin portion with a 17–0 win over West Germany and an 18–0 win over Japan.

Canada rolled through the elimination rounds and set up a date with the United States in the championship. By the time James reached the final, she had already scored her tournament-best 11 goals.

Once Canada reached the final, it was matched up against the United States, the first of many championship finals against the team's southern border rival. The game is most remembered for Heaney's highlight-reel goal, in which the defenseman deked out an opposing player by putting the puck between her legs before scoring past the American goalie. As Heaney finished the move, she flew in the air after being tripped.

Heaney's heroics were one of five Canadian goals scored after being down 2-0. The Canadians went on to win the game and the tournament. James didn't score in the championship final but was still named to the tournament's all-star team.

The success of the women's tournament led to an increase in women's hockey participants, according to James' book. At the time, CAHA reported a 75 percent increase in registered female players.

"I had some fans, young girls who would look up to me. I realized that," James said in her biography. "I tried to, as best as I could, behave myself. But there were others as well, older people. I didn't really think of it much. But you are representing your country, and being as successful as we were, there was some popularity amongst different groups. You tried to be gracious about it, knowing very well that one day that will stop. You have to enjoy it while you can."

The 1990 World Championship was the first of four titles for James, as she'd go on to win in 1992, 1994, and 1997. James added two 3 Nations Cups and a Pacific Rim Championship to her name as well.

James' trophy case bursts at the seams with successes at the women's worlds and other international tournaments. An Olympic gold medal, or any opportunity to participate at the Olympic Games, is missing. It remains a point of controversy.

Women's hockey was first implemented as an Olympic sport during the 1998 Olympic Games in Nagano, Japan. The International Olympic Committee made the decision to add both women's hockey and curling six years earlier, according to the Associated Press.

As Canada ran through a decade of hockey dominance in the 1990s, many expected James to be on Canada's roster for their inaugural Olympic run. But when James arrived to centralization camp in Calgary ahead of the 1998 Games, her role had been reduced. According to her biography, Canadian head coach Shannon Miller decided to put James on the team's fourth line and wouldn't have her on the team's power play or penalty killing units.

"It was a month into camp, and I knew something had gone wrong," James told Scott Russell in his book *Ice Time: A Canadian Hockey Journey*. "I knew they wanted to release me."

In December 1997, two months before the Nagano Games, James was told she wouldn't make the Olympic roster. In a press conference after the decision, Miller told the media that James was a "defensive liability."

"The game has changed," Miller said, as said in James' biography. "It's a lot faster. More team play is necessary. Angela has been very strong for us in the individual type of play. She was struggling with the execution of team play. At the same time, we had different players who could produce offensively. I don't think she was totally surprised."

But when James learned of Miller's comments, she claimed she was "set up and cheated."

"They did everything in their power to keep me down. I don't know what their agenda was," James told Joe Warmington of the *Toronto Sun*. "Maybe they thought I was an old hag and shouldn't be around or maybe it was because I received too much attention."

Unbeknownst to James at the time, however, the forward was suffering from Graves' disease, an autoimmune disease that affects the thyroid gland. James wasn't feeling 100 percent during camp and notified Team Canada's medical staff, according to her biography, but the reason wasn't immediately spotted. Meanwhile, James was much lighter than normal. She was playing 20 pounds under her regular playing weight because of her condition. Despite health challenges, James still led her team in goals during exhibition games as written in Bartsiokas and Long's book about James.

The forward only discovered she had the disease after she was released from camp. But even with having to recover from an unexpected disease, some still see James' exclusion from the 1998 Games as a mistake. Canada lost to the Americans 3–1 in the 1998 gold medal final in Nagano, giving the United States the first gold medal in Olympic women's hockey history.

"I still think she should have made that team, but she wasn't the Angela James that we all knew," Campbell-Pascall said.

"It's disappointing to me," Dufton said. "She should have got that opportunity. She had earned it."

"How do you take your best player off the team?" American Hockey Hall of Famer Cammi Granato said in James' biography. "Your most clutch player off the team? It was really shocking. She brought a lot to Canada in big games."

Once James was properly treated for Graves' disease, she returned to Canada for one final international tournament: the 1999 3 Nations Cup in Quebec. Before the end of the championship final—once again pitting Canada and the United States against each other—James told her teammates she'd be retiring from international play so she could spend more time with her wife, Ange, and their infant son, Christian. When both teams were tied at the end of regulation and overtime, a shootout was necessary. James and teammate Jayna Hefford both scored—James' shootout goal was the winner—and the Canadians edged the United States in a 3–2 victory.

James' final year of competitive hockey came in 2000, with the NWHL's Beatrice Aeros. She captained the team to an NWHL championship after scoring 44 points in 27 regular season games. A fitting end to a successful career that saw her as the best women's player in the world at her peak.

CHERYL POUNDER HAS GONE from a women's hockey winner at the international level to color commentator and broadcaster, with her work frequently seen on TSN. Pounder has even made appearances on TradeCentre, the network's annual frenzy and near nonstop broadcast detailing every trade that occurs before the NHL's trade deadline.

Pounder took part in a 2022 segment called "The Tradey Bunch" in which host James Duthie asks panelists, insiders, and other in-studio personalities fun questions to pass the time. Each panelist involved was asked which hockey sweater they'd love to have from a player past or present. Pounder selected Angela James, her former teammate from the 1994 IIHF Women's Worlds in Lake Placid, New York. Pounder lauded James' abilities and physical presence, particularly her dominant showing of the 1990 Women's Worlds, briefly mentioned the pink jerseys James and her teammates wore in 1990, and even mentioned how terrified she was meeting the superstar for the first time.

Moments later, James emerged onto set with a Team Canada sweater as a surprise for Pounder. It genuinely was a surprise as TSN staffers did everything they could to hide the Canadian hockey legend from Pounder all day. When James emerged on set, she held a red and black Team Canada jersey with her name and the No. 8 on the back. Pounder ran to her former teammate and gave her a big hug.

"You're a legacy, you are everything, and you're just such an awesome human being and I'm going to cry now. And you did straight-arm me at practice when I got by once and said 'Don't ever do that again, kid,'" Pounder told James, prompting laughter.

James' impact on the sport of hockey endures. She has been a certified referee since 1980, attaining certification through Hockey Canada, and even served as the OWHA's Referee-in-Chief. James was once a director and owner of her own hockey school, the Breakaway Adult Hockey School.

In addition to being a Hockey Hall of Famer, James was named to the Order of Canada as an officer and is also a member of the IIHF Hall of Fame and Canada's Sports Hall of Fame.

James was also a part-owner, general manager and coach of the Toronto Six, a professional women's hockey team in the Premier Hockey Federation. In the PHF's final season, 2023, the Six won the Isobel Cup as league champions.

"This is my take," journalist Erica Ayala said. "She wanted for the players, for that team and throughout the league, to feel how she did at her height, her best memories of hockey. I think she brought a lot of joy to the role."

James' résumé is stacked with hardware at the international level, the senior women's club level, and even the managerial level. But while the hockey world has commemorated her success with her induction into the ultimate pantheon of hockey success, many people in hockey still think her story should be more widespread.

"I think she's very underrepresented," former Toronto Six team president Digit Murphy said. "I know she's in the Hall of Fame and everything. But I think her story could be told more in the U.S. I think the NHL could do a better job exposing someone like her and what she did for the game, and what she did for, you know, hundreds of thousands of people of color."

12

Blake Bolden

Blake Bolden's days as a child growing up in Cleveland, Ohio, usually began at two in the morning. Forget the sun not being up. Even the most dedicated of hockey children would be fast asleep after spending hours and hours on their local backyard rink. Bolden, however, wasn't waking up early to skate on a public square or in her yard where her family could see. Instead, she had to go help her mother at work. The Boldens hopped out of bed and into their car, an old Toyota Tercel, and drive off in the middle of the night.

Bolden was raised by a single mom, LaTanya, who had her at the age of 21. To make ends meet, LaTanya worked three jobs. She worked as a nanny, at the local hospital, and on early mornings, she'd take her daughter to the local newspaper depot. They'd stuff bags with copies of the *Plain Dealer* newspaper, Cleveland's longtime local daily, before starting their newspaper route. LaTanya's mother delivered newspapers, so she took after her. Blake followed her mom, and sometimes her grandmother too, on their morning delivery shifts.

"We would just whip around in my mom's stick shift," Blake said. "I would be in the backseat. I would fall asleep on papers sometimes. They're super slippery because they're covered in plastic, and it would just fill the entire car."

Many Clevelanders had a particular way they wanted their papers delivered. Some would rather have it by their side doors instead of the front, or maybe by the garage at the end of their driveway. Eventually, the Boldens would come to know many of the people they delivered newspapers to, and some of them would leave generous tips around Christmas. By 8:30 or 9:00 AM, their daily route would end. The Boldens found breakfast, and Blake would fall asleep again.

One morning while bagging papers, LaTanya met Leslie Dean—a police officer from Warrensville Heights. When he wasn't doing police work, he worked as a handler for the local hockey team, the Cleveland Lumberjacks. If players needed help getting around the city or staying out of trouble, Dean was their guy. Dean's brother even worked as a billet for one of their players.

LaTanya and Leslie took a liking to each other and eventually started dating. Dean would take Blake to local Lumberjacks games at Gund Arena. She'd watch games, roam around the locker room and make the arena her second home.

"I remember standing in the tunnel at Gund Arena for the first time," Bolden wrote for The Players' Tribune in 2021. "Picture a small, six-year-old Black girl with braids, standing awestruck as these hulking giants wearing razor-sharp metal on their feet, boxing gloves on their hands and the coolest looking uniforms I'd ever seen saunter past me. Fully outfitted for battle, I remember thinking as they passed me, smiling and giving me knucks, the only thing they were missing was a full set of teeth.

"As a kid, you're not really seeing so much as experiencing it. The sounds, the smells, the anticipation and excitement. As soon as that first puck hit the ice, I was hooked. It was amazing, it was magic."

As Bolden watched games, she found heroes in players like Jock Callander, a former NHLer turned International Hockey League star with the Lumberjacks. Bolden was also inspired by an undersized yet "fearless and fast" winger who spent part of a season with the Lumberjacks. The player eventually jumped to the NHL the next year and began a 16-year NHL career, winning a Stanley Cup, an Olympic gold medal, and a list of individual honors before being inducted into the Hockey Hall of Fame in 2018.

Martin St. Louis was his name.

"He was out there to prove to the world that like he was in it no matter what," Bolden said. "I think he inspired me. Because it almost seemed like he was an underdog, but he wasn't. Because he just willed his way through games. And that's kind of who I wanted to be."

Dean eventually asked Bolden if she wanted to take up hockey and give herself a chance at emulating her Cleveland Lumberjack heroes. Bolden immediately said yes.

"I didn't even ask my mom if it was okay," Bolden said.

Once Bolden got her equipment, at the age of six, she learned to skate at a local Kent State University rink. She was hooked immediately. Even though she couldn't make stops on her left side, Bolden still joined a co-ed team. Bolden then attended power skating clinics to improve her abilities every Sunday. Within two years of first learning how to skate, she progressed to triple-A level before joining a boys' league. Bolden and future American hockey Olympian Megan Bozek were the only women in the league. Not to mention that Bolden was one of the few players of color.

And opposing players noticed, as Bolden once recounted to *USA Hockey Magazine*.

"People were cruel," Bolden told Jessi Pierce of *USA Hockey Magazine* in 2020. "I would beat their sons, and they would stare me down in the lobby, or I would walk in and people would wonder what the heck I was even doing at a rink."

"Once they realized I could play, it seemed like I gained their respect," Bolden added. "And to me, that was huge. I wanted that more than anything. From then on, I was just a part of the team and every one of the guys on the team from the coach down had my back.

"I remember being in front of the net and a kid cursing me out, calling me [a slur], saying something nasty toward me, and one of my other teammates immediately stepped in to defend me. It just felt really good."

As Bolden fended off detractors and continued to play well, interest in her grew. One school in particular, Northwood School in Lake Placid, New York, wanted her to play for its team.

"My mom was like, 'What is prep school?'" Bolden said. "I thought that was just a place that you send, you know, a place where rich people send their kids."

Bolden spent her teenage years attending the predominantly white school filled with athletic alumni and future Olympians. Even NHLers like Mike Richter, Craig Conroy, and Tony Granato once graced those hallways. Bolden played on the school's women's team and eventually served as captain. Bolden even earned the opportunity to play for the Americans on two occasions for the Under-18 Women's World Hockey Championship, winning gold in 2008 and 2009.

It was at Northwood that Bolden laid eyes on her future school, Boston College. Bolden watched a game at the Herb Brooks Arena, the site of Team USA's "Miracle on Ice" at the 1980 Olympic Games, between the Eagles and the University of Minnesota–Duluth during the 2007 Frozen Four tournament. The Eagles traded goals with the Bulldogs but fell in double overtime.

"I just told myself I wanted to go to that school, to change the school and be like a big fish in a smaller pond," Bolden said. "University of Minnesota was good. Wisconsin was good. All these Midwestern schools were good, and I really liked Boston. I loved going to the Beanpot tournament. I loved going to the Chowder Cup."

Sure enough, head coach Katie King and associate head coach Courtney Kennedy showed interest in the young Bolden and conducted a home visit as part of their recruitment process, trying to entice Bolden to play for their school.

Blake, we want you to come to BC.

It didn't take much for Bolden to say yes, leading to her making the move from Lake Placid to Boston.

In four years with the Eagles, the young defender once again rose up the ranks. Bolden led all first-year defenders in scoring before increasing her scoring totals and leading her team in power-play goals the next year. By her third year, Bolden was very much on Team USA's radar for its senior women's team. Bolden was invited to the U.S. camp ahead of the 2012 Women's World Championship.

Even if Bolden didn't make the team, her junior year was one to remember.

Bolden was shortlisted as a nominee for the Patty Kazmaier Memorial Award as women's college hockey player of the year. Bolden was also a First Team Hockey East All-Star. Bolden was then named captain for her senior year and ended her time at BC as the school's second-highest defender in goals, assists, and points. She won a handful of accolades including Hockey East Defender of the Year and was even named a Second-Team All-American.

The defender's career looked destined for appearances with the United States' women's senior national team and skating alongside star teammates at the Women's World Championship and at the Olympics.

But that trajectory was never guaranteed, nor fulfilled.

WHEN BOLDEN WAS 12 years old, years after learning how to skate and watching Cleveland Lumberjacks games at the local Gund Arena, she told her mother about her Olympic aspirations.

"I told my mom I was going to give my all," Bolden said.

Her dreams doubled as personal affirmations. Bolden told herself she would be the first Black female hockey player to represent Team

USA at the senior level, whether at the World Championships or the Olympics. Following her years at the under-18 level, winning gold twice for the United States, Bolden was first invited to try out for the American senior women's team in December 2010. Bolden was also given the opportunity to try for the U.S. squad ahead of the 2012 IIHF Women's World Championship while she was a junior at Boston College and, most notably, thought she could accomplish her Olympic dream by joining the United States' women's team for the 2014 Olympic Games in Sochi, Russia.

Bolden remembers her tryouts for the American national team as eye-opening experiences. She drew on her confidence from her collegiate career, helping Boston College by reaching numerous Frozen Fours. She wrestled with the pressure of trying to be better than other players competing for spots, trying to outwork them on and off the ice.

On the ice, she flanked American superstars she grew up watching and admiring. Hilary Knight, Meghan Duggan, and Natalie Darwitz were among those superstars. Bolden even remembers skating alongside Angela Ruggiero, who won a gold medal in 1998 with the United States and four Women's Worlds.

"I had her book [*Breaking the Ice: My Journey to Olympic Hockey, The Ivy League & Beyond*]. She was my idol," Bolden said. "Just being able to be on the same ice as them, compete with them, learn how they train their bodies and their minds and fueled themselves, it was overwhelming. I'm not going to lie.

"You don't want to mess up. You want to be great, but you're also like a kid, and you're trying to get your schoolwork done and you're trying to perform, and you're trying not to psych yourself out. So, it was hard."

Bolden also struggled with Team USA head coach Katey Stone ahead of the 2014 Olympics, claiming that Stone called her "uncoachable." It's been more than a decade since Bolden tried out for the 2014 team, but that experience still hurt the young defender.

"I don't even say her name anymore," Bolden said.

"She was not uncoachable," former Canadian Women's Hockey League and National Women's Hockey League coach Digit Murphy said. "Not uncoachable. It's completely false."

"That was really crappy," Bolden said. "I felt personally that I was kind of getting pushed and pulled and tugged. And they would always say, 'Hey, you're an offensive defenseman. We need you to basically change your entire game and play the way that we want you to play.'

"It was kind of challenging for me [as] an offensive power-play quarterback. Rushing pucks. Playing my game to being contained. So, that was really a mental challenge for me. I just wasn't doing it the way that they wanted me to. I guess I was just not the person that they wanted, and I was always a bubble player. So, that really sucked."

After a grueling camp, a phone call ended Bolden's Olympic dream.

"The way that they would do it was either a phone call or if it was like a camp leading up to World Championship, they listed off audibly while you guys were all in the room," Bolden said. "So, I always knew that once you got past C's—because my last name is B—if you skip over my name and you get to C, then I didn't make the team. So, I found out always pretty early. But in this instance, they just called me.

"Not only [did they say] I wasn't going to make the team, but that I was pretty much cut completely from the program."

"Blake was training for a national team, an Olympic team, which she never made," Murphy said. "Which was, in my opinion, bulls—t. Because she…was just ahead of her time. She was like a [P.K.] Subban kind of player. The kind of player that just joined the rush. She was just an incredible D, she had a shot. It's just a rocket. She deserved to be on Team USA and she didn't get the opportunity. And that kind of used to piss me off.

"I think they made a big mistake. Had Blake been on the team in 2014 when they lost that game to Canada, we would have been having a gold medal instead of a silver that year."

With her time at Boston College at an end, Bolden returned to Cleveland without a contingency plan. Bolden was in a "funk" after spending eight years away from home. She had her university degree, but she still felt like she had failed. Then one day, the phone rang again.

It was Murphy, the head coach of the CWHL's Boston Blades.

I'm going to draft you for in the first round, stop crying and get your butt back to Boston.

You're good. You're going to play, I'm going to play the crap out of you. Let's go. Let's make you the best you can be.

THE CANADIAN WOMEN'S HOCKEY League, or CWHL, was founded in 2007, a successor to many women's leagues, including the Central Ontario Women's Hockey League and the original National Women's Hockey League. The CWHL began in Canadian markets like Montreal, Toronto, Mississauga, and Brampton. But it eventually expanded to American markets. Boston was granted a franchise in 2010 that would be named the Blades. One of the first players who joined the Blades was Angela Ruggiero. The defender played one season, 2010–11, before retiring. In August 2013, the CWHL held its draft. The Blades held the fifth overall selection and took Bolden, who became the first Black player selected in the first round of the CWHL Draft.

Bolden made the move back to Boston, finding a roommate from her BC days. She found a job as a social worker for a nonprofit, helping people find jobs and affordable housing in Boston. When Bolden's workday ended, she'd practice as late as 10:00 PM with her Blades teammates. On the ice, Bolden tried her best to make an impact. In her first year with the Blades in 2013–14, she scored five goals and 19 points in 23 games.

"I'll say that it was a grind," Bolden said. "I wasn't getting paid to play, but we would always say we're playing for the love of the game, and that was exactly what it was like. I was playing just because I knew I was still good. That was the only thing I knew how to do, pretty much. And we had fun. I had fun with my teammates."

That season is also when Bolden experienced an epiphany. Following a game during her 2014 rookie season, Bolden was at a low point. She still felt crushed after missing out on the 2014 Olympic team while several of her American compatriots, including teammates Knight and Duggan, got the opportunity. A young fan approached Bolden after the game with a glitter-laden poster featuring Bolden's name and her No. 5 and told her inspiring and heartwarming words.

You were the reason why I played hockey."

"I feel like in that moment, my perspective of why and my purpose of playing kind of shifted," Bolden said. "You don't need to be this crazy Olympic gold medalist, or even just medalist or Olympian at all. You just have to be a good person that younger kids want to look up to and aspire to be."

Bolden was inspired from that interaction to begin a mentorship program called "emBolden Her," organizing weekly meetings with young women based in North America aspiring to play hockey.

"A lot of young girls and young athletes are just trying to figure out how to be their best selves on and off the ice," Bolden told The Athletic in 2021. "I really wanted to develop a program for these individuals to set goals, and not only set them but achieve them. Everybody should have a path. Everybody should have a marker that they want to reach. And it's not necessarily to say that if you don't make that marker, you fail. But you're learning along the way.

"I've been through a lot of ups and downs in my career as a professional athlete. I've been cut numerous times. I've been told I wasn't good enough. I've won championships. I've been MVP. I've captained my teams. Life is a roller coaster, and I wish when I was younger that I had someone that I could just use as a resource to say, 'This is what's going on in my mind and help me unpack it all so we can make a plan.'"

On the ice, Bolden focused on her play with the Blades. In her second season—the 2014–15 campaign season—Bolden scored three goals and 13 points in 22 regular season games. Bolden was named a CWHL All-Star that year and helped the Blades reach the CWHL postseason.

"No one wanted to mess around with Blake," Murphy said. "She would just chop you down, like she would chop trees down in the front. No one wanted to get in front of the net with her. But the other piece of her game that was so awesome was her ability to take the puck and go end to end at will. And she had incredible stamina.

"I sometimes only play four D. Sometimes, I would play three D. I didn't care. But Blake was always on the ice for me. Always, always, always, always."

The Blades won the Clarkson Cup that year with an overtime win over the Montreal Stars, making Bolden the first Black player to win the CWHL's top prize.

But despite her success, playing in a league for no pay while adjusting to life post-university was taking a toll. It's what made the thought of bolting to the National Women's Hockey League all the more enticing.

The NWHL was founded by Dani Rylan, a former hockey player turned entrepreneur. According to Yahoo Sports, Rylan drew inspiration from the 2014 Olympic Games when Canada and the United States squared off in women's hockey. Rylan initially wanted to bring a hockey franchise to New York City as part of the CWHL. But she eventually discussed the idea further with former U.S. Olympian Angela Ruggiero. The NWHL was then set to launch in 2015. The league had operating costs of approximately $2.5 million, according to ESPN, and each team would have a salary cap of $270,000. The league would start in four markets, Connecticut, New York, Buffalo, and Boston. It caught the attention of many women's players, including Bolden.

"There were just these whispers that this new league was coming about," Bolden said. "And they were going to pay players, and we were just going to all make this big jump. I wasn't someone who was in those conversations, but I was just ready for the next big thing. When I was playing in the CWHL, you just always felt, 'Is this what I'm doing? I'm just playing. I'm not getting paid. I'm using a lot of time and energy.' You just don't know what's happening. You're playing to win games and for the fun of it."

And so, Bolden made the jump to the National Women's Hockey League during the 2015–16 season as a member of the Boston Pride. Teammates Knight, Brianna Decker, Jillian Dempsey, and Brittany Ott were among those who made the transition to their new team. And as expected, the players were paid. According to the Ice Garden, Bolden's salary was listed at $15,000.00 for her debut season. But the defender remembers her salary being closer to $17,000.00.

Bolden's joining the NWHL, however, was much more significant than her adding more income. Her inclusion drew a rather large comparison. Major League Baseball legend Jackie Robinson broke the color barrier in 1947 when he suited up for the Brooklyn Dodgers. Sixty-eight years later, Bolden was recognized as the NWHL's first Black player and the first female Black hockey player to play in a professional league.

"When I became the first [Black] woman to play in the NWHL, I also didn't even realize that when it happened," Bolden said. "Because I was always one of the only, if not the only person of color on my team. When I was playing in AAA boys hockey. When I was playing in college, until Kaliya Johnson started playing with me.

"So when that happened I was like, 'Oh, crap. This is, this is a big deal.' I was also really young, and that's when I realized that being a mentor and being a good role model was a little bit more important than just playing for my own benefit."

Bolden's debut NWHL season was marked by some standout moments, a year where she scored a goal and nine points in 18 games. The defenseman was named an All-Star as part of the league's first-ever All-Star weekend. The defender also participated in the first ever outdoor game featuring women's teams, the 2016 Outdoor Women's Classic at Gillette Stadium in Foxborough, Massachusetts. The Boston Pride hosted Les Canadiennes, Montreal's successor to the CWHL's Stars, on New Year's Eve 2015. The next day, the NHL would hold its own Winter Classic game, which also featured Boston and Montreal.

The Pride and Canadiennes played two periods outdoors. Les Canadiennes struck first with a goal from Kim Deschenes in the first period. But late in the game, it was Bolden who scored a game-tying goal by deflecting a Rachel Llanes pass into goal. The game ended tied 1–1.

"I had butterflies," Bolden told the media after the game. "I didn't even know it went into the net until my teammates raised their arms.

"I just passed it over to Rachel to the right and sprinted to the net. She made a beautiful thread through the defenseman right on my tape and it just kind of deflected into the net."

While the game was considered a success, it was marred by a career-ending injury to one of Bolden's teammates. Denna Laing, who won a Clarkson Cup with Bolden in Boston, crashed head-first into the boards during the game's first period and suffered a spinal cord injury that left her paralyzed from the chest down.

The Pride soldiered on without Laing but still ended the regular season as the league's best team and made it to the Isobel Cup Final against the Buffalo Beauts. The Pride won the best-of-three final in a two-game sweep, with their injured teammate in mind.

"After that game, we kind of all corralled around her and won the championship in her honor," Bolden said.

The championship capped off a banner year for Bolden. An All-Star nod, a goal in an outdoor game, and becoming the first Black player to win an Isobel Cup.

IT WAS HOURS BEFORE Bolden worked her first game with Amazon Prime as a broadcaster, and she wanted to catch up with a Cleveland Lumberjacks icon.

In 2024, Amazon Prime began Monday night broadcasts of NHL games exclusively through its streaming platform and focused on its game of the week. The Bell Centre played host to Amazon's first game of the 2024–25 NHL season, between the Montreal Canadiens and the Pittsburgh Penguins.

Before games, broadcast rightsholders usually get to speak privately with a team's head coach after they've addressed most of the media contingent. That meant Bolden got to catch up with Canadiens head coach Martin St. Louis, who Bolden watched during his lone season as a member of the Lumberjacks. It was St. Louis' first year as a professional hockey player.

"I don't think he thought it was that as cool as I thought it was," Bolden laughed.

Following Bolden's championship success with the Pride, she played two more seasons in the NWHL. She remained in Boston until 2017 before playing a season in Switzerland. Bolden returned to the Buffalo Beauts in time for the 2018–19 campaign before playing with the Professional Women's Hockey Players Association as part of its Dream Gap Tour.

In 2020, Bolden joined the Los Angeles Kings' front office and became the NHL's first female Black pro scout. During her time with the Kings, Bolden also worked with ESPN as a reporter and analyst. But when Amazon came calling in 2024, Bolden consulted Kings president Luc Robitaille about what her next steps should be.

Blake, you have to take this job. This is a tremendous opportunity. You know, even just look down into the future of where Amazon could potentially be and or you will be.

In August of that year, Bolden jumped ship and joined Amazon. Now, she's part of its weekly broadcast, working with talents like Andi Petrillo, Mark Messier, and Adnan Virk.

"I've had the pleasure of working with many former athletes over the years but never someone like Blake Bolden," Amazon Prime Monday Night Hockey teammate Adnan Virk said. "She's been a trailblazer at every level as a player, as a scout with the LA Kings, and with all of us now at Prime Monday Night Hockey. She's passionate about the sport of hockey and is someone who uses her experience on the ice to her advantage off the ice as a broadcaster.

"An effervescent personality, I've been fortunate to call Blakey a colleague and a friend."

As Bolden's hockey life continues off the ice in the media, other young Black women have picked up where she left off. There is one heir apparent that stands above the rest.

Wisconsin Badger Laila Edwards became the first Black female hockey player to play for the United States at the senior level when she played at the 2024 Women's World Championship in Utica. Despite Canada toppling the United States in the final, Edwards emerged as tournament MVP after scoring six goals and eight points in seven games. Edwards was also named tournament MVP and the best forward at the 2022 U18 World Championship. Both times, the Americans emerged as silver medalists.

"It took me a long time to be able to take a step back and reflect on that, because it was all so much at such a fast time, so many different emotions," Edwards said about being the first Black female player to suit up for the Americans at the senior women's level. "But I was able to, eventually.

"But I don't want to get stuck here. I want to keep going. I don't want to get caught admiring the thing I've accomplished."

The hockey world has taken notice of Edwards' size and skill—the University of Wisconsin has her listed at 6'1". The Athletic has described her as "one of the most unique and exciting prospects in the game."

"She's giving IQ," journalist Erica Ayala said. "She can set up plays. She can create for herself. She is strong on the puck. I think she plays a game that the United States has on the women's side, has played since the beginning of time and been very good at, which is down your throat. It is absolutely fast, it is relentless, and you attack, and that's what I see in her."

Edwards was even shouted out by fellow Cleveland Heights natives and NFL stars Travis and Jason Kelce on their podcast, *New Heights*.

"Just being from the city, you've got my love and support. Go out there and hold it down for USA, baby!" Travis said on the podcast's October 18, 2023 episode.

And, unsurprisingly, the Cleveland Heights native has a fan in Bolden.

"And her sister, [Chayla]," Bolden said. "They're Cleveland girlies. I remember being one of their OG role models back in the day, coming back from BC and talking to both of them. Now, to see Laila be so successful and dominant with her size and her power. It just makes me really proud."

Bolden's impact on the game remains in retirement, whether it's working on broadcasts talking hockey or players and coaches reminiscing about her legacy. Her career is befitting of the 'trail-blazer' moniker bestowed upon her.

"I want my daughter to be like Blake Bolden. Everyone should want their daughter to be like Blake Bolden," said Bolden's former coach, Digit Murphy.

13

Kevin Weekes

Kevin Weekes was at a crossroads as he contemplated his career while sitting in a catamaran on blue Bajan waters during the summer of 2009. The Canadian goalie spent 11 years in the NHL, a veteran of nearly 400 games. But playing opportunities and job prospects were dwindling.

The most games Weekes had ever played in a season was 66. That came during the 2003–04 season as a member of the Carolina Hurricanes. After the NHL lockout wiped out the following year, Weekes joined the New York Rangers ahead of the 2005–06 season. Weekes' number of games fell from 66 to 32. Then, he only played 14 games with the Rangers the next year.

"When Henrik Lundqvist is Henrik Lundqvist, you're not playing," Weekes said.

In 2007, the New Jersey Devils came calling. Weekes was given the backup role behind Martin Brodeur, another workhorse and legend of the game. Weekes made 25 appearances in his two seasons with the team.

"Same thing," Weekes said. "You're not going to get to play that often either."

Weekes was already contemplating the end before his second year in New Jersey came to a close, considering a common career transition for athletes: broadcasting. He sought advice from analysts and personalities like Chico Resch, Ken Daneyko, and even play-by-play voice Doc Emrick. He also consulted family, friends, and even strangers. Particularly, a dreadlocked man in Barbados outside of his hotel one night.

"I literally talked to a dread on the beach explaining my situation," Weekes said. "I talked to a dread on the beach at the Fairmount Royal Pavilion in Barbados. He said, 'You've got to take the TV opportunity, man! You've got to do that.'"

Those conversations helped Weekes make his career change official. Fortunately for Weekes, it didn't take long for him to find work.

Hockey Night in Canada producer Sherali Najak says his introduction to Weekes came during a drive home from work later that summer. He was listening to sports radio, and Weekes came on to talk hockey. Najak was intrigued by his voice, which was a "different kind of voice than normal." A voice that oozed "style" and "swagger," and was distinctly unique from other voices who would normally talk hockey. Najak figured it wouldn't hurt to reach out to Weekes, just to get to know him.

"That was part of the job," Najak said. "Just to meet different people in hockey and kind of expand a little bit of the mindset of what we think hockey should be. And the only way to do that is by having different voices inside your head instead of your own. So, I called him up and remember talking to him. He was a really humble guy and sweet, and you could tell that there was this sense of style."

Not long after, Weekes was in a voiceover recording booth in downtown Toronto alongside a play-by-play broadcaster. This was Weekes' chance to audition for *Hockey Night in Canada*. Najak, however, kept his expectations low. Weekes had never called a game before and anticipated it would be "rough." This was all about seeing if Weekes had enough "raw potential," but the goaltender surprised Najak.

"You could have put him on the air the next day," Najak said. "He was that good in terms of his presence and command of the game. He definitely had an understanding of the game.

"I remember looking at one of my producers and I said to him, 'Man, this guy's good,'"

Weekes joined *Hockey Night in Canada* that fall of 2009, making history as the first Black hockey analyst. Growing up, he enjoyed ESPN/ABC and Canadian media personality John Saunders, who worked for City TV in the 1980s in Toronto before covering sports like hockey and football south of the border. This was Weekes' opportunity to emulate him.

"I watched John [on] City News and City Pulse," Weekes said. "That was our news channel that our family watched. I grew up on City TV. I grew up on that. I watched it all the time.

"He was a great host, he had different roles."

Weekes didn't ease into the rigors of broadcast television at the start of his career, working double duty for HNIC and the NHL Network during his first year away from the crease. Weekes said he was on television five to six nights a week, traveling from Toronto to wherever he needed to be to broadcast games.

"I wanted to be as good as possible, as quickly as possible," Weekes said.

In the present day, Weekes handles being on multiple platforms just fine, including trade deadline and NHL draft coverage. Weekes was also live on NHL Network when the league announced it was forced to shut down due to COVID-19 concerns in March 2020, a distinct moment Weekes thinks back to in his media career.

"Those are things that you would have seen in movies, but you don't really see those in real life," Weekes said. "That was as real life as it got. That was a massive moment."

In recent years, Weekes has also added newsbreaker to his arsenal of skills. In his words, a blade to his broadcasting Swiss Army knife.

As he continued to make forays into the media world, he received intel from people in the know. But it was Kevin's wife, Megan, who urged him to report news as he got it.

"We were just at a local spot here getting a massage before I ended up driving up to Bristol to go to ESPN for the trade deadline," Weekes remembered. "I had news, info coming in. I had the hot intel. And, in certain instances, I knew that I was able to report it. So she's like, 'What are you waiting for?' I'm like, 'Well, we're in the middle of the street.' She's like, 'And?'"

That led to some humorous news reveals from Weekes on social media, typically in the style of a vertical video that shows a portion of his head as he breaks news. Some videos, including one where he wears a recycling bin over his head, don't show his face at all. The setting doesn't matter either; Weekes even reported on a story while on site at the annual Kentucky Derby horse race at Churchill Downs.

"Kevin is clearly grabbing this part of his career by the horns," The Athletic's Craig Custance said. "He's taking risks and saying, 'This is how I'm going to do it. I'm going to do it my way.' And I think that just attracts people."

Since Weekes became the first dedicated Black hockey analyst in 2009, dozens of Black hockey reporters and analysts have followed in his path.

"It's not only about you getting there or you being there," Weekes said. "It's also about how you can kind of empower the people on their path and try to share some of your knowledge and your experience, and your expertise with others to help them on their path."

Weekes has now made a name for himself as one of hockey's most recognizable personalities, working as an analyst and hockey insider, alongside compatriots Chris Johnston, Elliotte Friedman, Pierre LeBrun, Emily Kaplan, and more.

"He's become a trustworthy representative of hockey, and you can tell he cares about the game still," Najak said.

"You talk about a guy who had a great career as a goalie and an even better career as a broadcaster," play-by-play man Gord Miller said. "He's one of the most versatile broadcasters there is. As an insider in the studio, doing live games. He really does do it all."

And unlike his colleagues, he possesses a background that few of them have.

"If you look at all the other insiders, there's not, in any major league sport, another insider that's a former player," Weekes said.

KEVIN WEEKES' HOCKEY JOURNEY begins with a goalie net that wasn't even his own.

Like many Canadians, Weekes played road hockey while growing up in the Toronto suburb of Scarborough. A neighbor moved from Greece and bought a hockey net that the children in the neighborhood used frequently. But when the neighbor moved back to Greece, the net didn't make the trip. It meant Weekes and his friends could continue to play. When they needed a goalie, a very young Weekes volunteered himself.

"Yeah, that's exactly what I want to do," Weekes said. "That's exactly where I want to be."

Weekes remembers being quite young, as young as five or six, when he first played hockey. When he first stepped on the ice at a local rink, it wasn't in a pair of skates. Before owning a pair, Weekes slid around the ice in black winter boots. As Weekes became more enamored with playing goalie, he soon found inspiration in goaltending legend Grant Fuhr, who burst onto the scene with the Edmonton Oilers in the 1980s.

"He played a style that nobody else fully really played at the time," Weekes said. "Delivering huge for Canada, internationally, with the Oilers, all the Stanley Cups. The big saves. The clutch saves at clutch times."

Weekes wanted to play hockey in an organized league. He followed his cousin, who also joined a local house league, leading Weekes to beg his parents to sign him up. They relented, paying the $65 registration fee to join. When registration was completed, he received his jersey. He was a member of the "green team." When interviewed by the *Globe & Mail* in March 2024, he named that jersey as his most prized possession.

"I saw that [jersey] at my parents' house in the hockey room when we were home at Christmas," Weekes said in the interview. "And you know, that almost makes me emotional even thinking about it now. Just because you start off with a huge dream at six, and there was kind of a direct correlation to that dream of wanting to play in the NHL. So from then to here and everything in between, that was the start of it."

From youth, Weekes knew how pricey becoming a hockey player would be. His parents, Carl and Vadney, immigrated from Barbados to Scarborough and worked full-time jobs while supporting their son and his hockey dreams as well as his younger sister, Renee. If Kevin's parents weren't driving him around Toronto to games, they ensured Weekes could participate in big events like the Quebec International Pee-Wee Hockey Team in his youth. That tournament was the same one, as Weekes remembers, where his father was approached by an NHL scout and told him his son was on the "right track."

"Not everybody had that two-parent household where both parents were working," Weekes said. "And then my parents were always trying to work overtime on top of working, right?"

Their efforts propelled Weekes through his minor league journey, joining the Owen Sound Platers of the Ontario Hockey League ahead of the 1992–93 season. Weekes split the year with future NHLer Jamie Storr in net, ending the season with a 9–12–15 record and an .868 save percentage. But he still attracted attention from NHL teams ahead of the 1993 NHL Entry Draft in Quebec City.

That draft day is seen as a "special time" in Weekes' life.

The goaltender hoped his name would be called at the Colisée de Quebec that day. Weekes was interviewed by many NHL executives and scouting directors leading up to the draft. He was also followed by a local news crew, from documenting him answering questions about his skill set to seeing him iron his tie on his hotel bed ahead of his big day.

"For all the sacrifices that my parents made and all the sacrifices that I made," Weekes said. "A lot of things just really came together. A lot of things really crystallized with getting drafted. And then buddies of mine, childhood friends or guys that I played with in junior or that I played against that were getting drafted in that year, too.

"It was me that got drafted. But it felt like there were a lot of people, certain people, behind me that helped me get there."

Weekes was drafted 41st overall by the Florida Panthers. Though he'd have to wait years before his NHL debut during the 1997–98 season with the Panthers. Weekes spent two more seasons in the OHL, including one year with the Ottawa 67's, before spending time in the American Hockey League with the Carolina Monarchs and the Fort Wayne Komets of the International Hockey League. Weekes was also loaned to the Rochester Americans, the first-ever professional hockey team from North America to be included in the Spengler Cup, an international tournament regarded as the oldest in the sport.

His journeyman days began almost immediately at the start of his NHL career. Weekes only played 11 games as a Panther before he was traded to Vancouver on January 17, 1999, as part of a trade that sent Russian dynamo Pavel Bure to Florida. Weekes spent part of two seasons with the Canucks before his tenure met an unceremonious end following a knee injury that was met with skepticism by the team's coaching and training staff. Weekes was then traded to the New York Islanders partway through the 1999–2000 season.

The following year, he joined the Tampa Bay Lightning. He was the Lightning's starting goalie during its 2000-01 season, playing 61 games with a 20–33–3 record, a 3.14 goals-against average and an .898 save percentage. Tampa Bay was Weekes' home until March 2002, when he was traded to Carolina in exchange for Shane Willis and Chris Dingman.

Weekes credits much of his success in Carolina to long-time head coach Paul Maurice, who had coached the franchise since they were in Hartford.

"Sometimes you go to work and you're like, 'Oh, God, I gotta see this person,'" Weekes said. "They've got power. They're in a power position. They're upset even just when I walk in, you never had that [with Maurice]. So, you walk in [the arena], you feel nice. You walk in the dressing room, you feel hyped. You get to the rink, you're excited to get there. No head games, no foolishness, no racism, no undercutting. No anything. Just like 'Yo, I'm here and I feel light and I'm ready to rock.'"

Weekes played two regular-season games nearly a month apart for the Canes entering the 2002 playoffs, both victories over his former team, the Florida Panthers. His third appearance with the Canes came during the third game of their Eastern Conference quarter-final series against the New Jersey Devils, his first-ever Stanley Cup playoff appearance. Starting netminder Arturs Irbe allowed three goals on 12 shots through 20:58 of play. Weekes relieved him, allowing one goal in a game the Canes lost 4–0.

After Weekes relieved Irbe again, after Game 4, Weekes was given the reins for the rest of the series. Weekes won Game 6 with a 40-save performance before winning a 1–0 shutout in Game 7 to clinch the first-round series.

"All great goaltenders have always had a certain calm about them," Maurice said about Weekes after Game 7, according to UPI. "There are points in the game when he is down and he slides across and he passes that calmness to everyone else because everybody is pretty relaxed on the bench."

Following his opening-round success, the Canes leaned on Weekes for the first three games of their second-round series against the Montreal Canadiens. Weekes shut out the Canadiens in Game 1, his second consecutive shutout victory of the postseason. This time, the Scarborough native recorded 25 saves in the win. However, Weekes would drop the next two games in the series and was pulled after the first period of Game 4. To make matters worse, a fan threw a banana on the ice—a heinous, racist act—in Montreal after the Canes came back to defeat the Canadiens in overtime.

"I know it's 2002, but I fully understand that there's always a couple of idiots everywhere you go and I won't let it mar my experience of being here," Weekes said, via the Associated Press. "I love playing in this building and playing against the Canadiens. I won't let that dim my experience at all. There were 20,000 people, and I'm sure 99 out of 100 are good-natured people compared to one percent of fools."

The Canes won their second-round series before defeating the Toronto Maple Leafs in the third round and earning a Stanley Cup Final berth. Carolina lost its Cup Final series in five games to the Detroit Red Wings.

Weekes was given the lion's share of starts for Carolina over the next two seasons, playing 51 and 66 games respectively. However, Weekes wouldn't suit up in another playoff game until 2006, when he joined the New York Rangers. After the 2003–04 season, the Hurricanes declined to sign Weekes to a qualifying offer worth $2.35 million U.S. for one season, according to the Associated Press.

Weekes became a free agent and then signed with the Rangers before the 2005–06 season. He began the season as their starter, but an injury led to him losing his starting spot to future star Henrik Lundqvist. Weekes played 32 regular-season games that season and started Game 2 of the Rangers' first-round series against the Devils during the 2006 playoffs. Unfortunately, Weekes allowed four goals on 25 shots in a 4–1 loss. The Rangers were swept by Weekes' future team, the Devils.

Three years after that playoff loss, and a tenure in New Jersey later, Weekes' broadcasting career began in earnest. But his time in hockey isn't just limited to playing on the ice and speaking in front of cameras.

IF YOU WERE A young, Black aspiring hockey player in Scarborough, there was a strong chance you were likely enrolled at some point in the Skillz Hockey School.

The school was founded by Kirk Brooks, the father of Utah Mammoth skills development coach Nathaniel Brooks, and Cayos Levy. It opened its doors in 1992 and was known as the Black Hockey Federation. According to its website, the school had special guest instructors from NHLers past and present, including Tony McKegney and Fred Brathwaite.

Weekes was among a handful of future NHLers who participated in the camp, including Wayne Simmonds and Joel Ward.

"Going to camp like that and seeing a guy like Tony, it gave you incentive," Weekes told Mike Zeisberger of NHL.com in February 2022. "By the time I was a pro, I was underwriting the costs for the camp."

Weekes contributed financially and also became an instructor at the camp, working with a handful of future NHLers, including a young "snotty-nosed" P.K. Subban. Weekes said Skillz Hockey School offered clinics, fundraisers, golf tournaments and charity galas to bring awareness and raise funds for an initiative that allowed Black children, or any children from diverse racial backgrounds, to feel like they could have a place in a mainly white sport.

"You don't want to walk into the rink and see that the music stops, the puck stops, the play stops, and everybody looks at you," Weekes said. "Because you're an anomaly in a sport that's not easy for people to process. And quite frankly, a lot of people didn't want to play, or started playing and quit playing and pursued other sports because of those experiences."

Weekes has also contributed to the Herbert Carnegie Future Aces program, helping people establish core values like attitude, courage, example and service in their day-to-day lives.

"Kevin wanted to do something similar to what my father did by helping community," Bernice Carnegie, Herb's daughter and former executive director of the program, said, "His family's from Barbados, so he hired me and my education team to go to Barbados for a couple of years to do a conference. Kids from all over the island came to a resort and we trained them on future aces values, strengthening yourself and being the best you can be. We did hear that, you know, some of those kids went on to [become] leaders and feeling different about themselves because of that initiative."

Decades earlier, Weekes expressed gratitude for his parents and family members doing everything possible to help him become a professional hockey player. He has paid it forward in his life post-career. Weekes is currently a broadcaster and analyst, but he's considered other avenues. The former goaltender interviewed for the San Jose Sharks GM position when it was vacant in 2022 before it went to Mike Grier. Weekes was also bitten by the acting bug, appearing on television soap operas *All My Children* and *One Life to Live* and the comedy sitcom *Everybody Hates Chris*, even making appearances on daytime television shows like *Good Morning America*.

It has been quite the journey for a Black hockey goaltender turned broadcaster and analyst.

"I didn't choose the easiest path," Weekes said. "I never chose a sport that was easy for people that looked like you and I. That wasn't my choice. I chose to play in the National Hockey League, and I chose to become a broadcaster in the National Hockey League. It hasn't always been easy. What's upsetting sometimes is you love the game, you love the sport, you love it so much, and it doesn't necessarily love you back the same way for a reason that you can't control, which is the presentation of your skin.

"But ultimately, you know, I'm always indebted. My family and I are always grateful to the game, always grateful for everything that I've been able to experience and accomplish in the game as well. It hasn't been the easiest role. But it's certainly, in many ways, very gratifying although very challenging. But very gratifying at the same time."

14

Duante' Abercrombie

It was 2014 when Graeme Townshend readied himself for a near-11-hour drive to Maine. He couldn't wait to be home.

The Jamaican-born Townshend spent the previous weekend in Etobicoke, Ontario, running an identification camp for potential players. Dozens of hockey players, from as far out as Sweden, have tried out for Townshend's camp. The former NHLer went from journeyman pro player to hockey coach, becoming a skills coach to help his stepson as he ventured into the sport. Townshend eventually graduated from the world of training youth hockey players, even working as a development coach for the San Jose Sharks. Townshend even spent a few seasons with the Toronto Maple Leafs as a skating coach. Townshend had now turned to a more ambitious venture, putting together an ice hockey team for Team Jamaica so that they could one day compete in the Winter Olympics.

As Townshend was ready to leave, he was asked for a favor. One of the camp's participants needed a ride to a train that would've taken them to Whitby, an Ontario town east of Toronto. Townshend was originally going to drive through Buffalo, New York, to get back to Maine. But he could easily drive through Montreal to get home, and Whitby was on the way. Plus, he could even stop for breakfast. Those factors played into why Townshend decided to drive the young participant, a man named Duante' Abercrombie, home.

Townshend and his guest found a breakfast spot partway through their travels. As they sat down, Townshend wanted to know more about his mystery passenger. While there were random stragglers from other parts of the world, most of the participants were from Canada. Townshend was taken aback when he learned Abercrombie had traveled all the way from Washington, D.C., to attend the camp. He was just as surprised when he learned Abercrombie was also training in nearby Oakville at a hockey camp. Townshend knew the person who ran that camp and was aware of the quality of players who would be there.

"Wait a second. You train up there?" Townshend exclaimed. "That's where [Connor] McDavid and those guys train."

"Yeah, I know," Abercrombie responded. "That's why I want to train there."

"Well, that doesn't explain why you're living all the way out in Whitby," Townshend responded. "What are you doing going out there?"

Abercrombie found a billet family willing to house him as he trained toward his dream of making the NHL. Every day, Abercrombie would take a train from Whitby to Oakville, a near-90-minute commute, to train with other hockey hopefuls. Abercrombie even started a GoFundMe page to raise funds for training, hockey equipment, travel, food, lodging, and more. Abercrombie also documented his path for a YouTube channel with the hashtag #NHLBound, sharing an open desire to play at the sport's highest possible level. Years earlier, Abercrombie played with a professional hockey team in New Zealand to further his professional aspirations. He was dead serious.

Townshend noticed Abercrombie's ambition because it was similar to his own. Even if it was brief, he accomplished his dream of being an NHL player. Townshend wasn't directly behind the bench, but he worked as part of an NHL team's coaching staff. He could still say he was in the league. Townshend eventually offered Abercrombie a coaching opportunity. Maybe it could help Abercrombie reach the NHL, too. The former NHLer started a camp in Maine and thought Abercrombie would work perfectly alongside him, teaching young players the necessary skills to improve.

"We can train you for free and, in return, you can help me coach the kids," Townshend said.

Abercrombie agreed and began teaching at Townshend's camp. Within two years, Abercrombie was Townshend's best instructor. Whenever Townshend would get mad at hockey-crazed parents who acted like bullies, Abercrombie—also known as Mr. Calm—stepped in.

"From now on, he handles all the parent issues," Townshend said. "And so there's no more yelling and screaming. He takes care of it all. He handles it and he diffuses the situation. He's really, really good.

"He's very calm, very firm, he's no pushover. It's amazing how he operates. He's amazing. He's incredible. He's such a great leader."

Two years after meeting Townshend, Abercrombie became an assistant coach for Georgetown Prep back home in Washington. Abercrombie then coached a U-16 squad, the Washington Little Capitals for four seasons. He even picked up an assistant coaching gig for Stevenson University, an NCAA Division III in Maryland. Abercrombie's opportunities soon snowballed into NHL ones. Abercrombie was a coaching intern with the Arizona Coyotes during their fall development camp in 2021. His time with the team was documented through a series titled *NHL Bound* that was shown on Sportsnet and the NHL Network. It can now be watched on YouTube. Abercrombie spent a season with the Toronto Maple Leafs as a player development coach, the same team that gave Townshend a chance as its skating coach once upon a time. The Nashville Predators also invited Townshend as a guest coach during their development camp in July 2024.

"Duante' never says I want this, I want that," Townshend said. "Duante' says, 'I'm going to do this; I'm going to do that,' like it's already a foregone conclusion."

Abercrombie's next coaching venture is a unique one. He's been actively scouting players across the hockey landscape to see it through. He's made history in the process. Abercrombie is now the head coach of Tennessee State University's men's hockey program, a historically Black college/university.

"I think the sky's the limit for Duante'," reporter Chris Johnston said. "He's just left a good impression everywhere he went. I know that the Leafs were really impressed by everything he did during his year with them. And obviously, that's opened some doors for him.

"I think he's just getting started on a trajectory that's going to go up into the right."

The Tigers will hit the ice for the first time in Fall 2026 as a Division I school, running as an independent. TSU will be the first HBCU to play ice hockey and Abercrombie is the first head coach of an HBCU hockey program.

"Growing up, Duante' Abercrombie as a coach, Duante' Abercrombie, most recently with the Maple Leafs, had always dreamt that this day would come," Abercrombie said. "That there would be an HBCU that stuck its neck out and said, 'We want to offer ice hockey at our school.' It's something I wanted when I was growing up. But then my mind got going even further. Because this is a Division I school. And my dream was always to have it at the Division I NCAA level. Not, 'Hey, we offer hockey here.' But we offer hockey here at the highest level. We are one of 65 teams in the country that offers ice hockey at this level. And that, to me, was massive.

"I also never imagined myself being a collegiate head coach, I had always wanted to be a professional coach and still have aspirations of being a professional coach, way down the line once what is supposed to happen here, happens. I wanted to make sure that this was built the right way."

IF YOU'RE WONDERING, YES. The apostrophe is part of his name. No, Duante' doesn't know why he has it. But he knows his mother, Devara, gave it to him when he was born. Abercrombie hasn't asked her why his name has that apostrophe, but he anticipates the reason not being overly significant.

"She probably is going to tell me just like this: 'Duante', I don't know. I was 19 years old and thought it was a good idea.' There you go."

Abercrombie was born in Washington, D.C., in February 1987 and was raised primarily by his mom. He knows of his father, Michael Armstead. But he wasn't a main figure during Abercrombie's upbringing. They've since developed a relationship. Abercrombie knows his father was arrested for something drug-related but doesn't know the specifics. It coincided with a dark time in Washington's history as the city turned into a hub for crack cocaine during the United States' "crack epidemic." The American capital also had the highest homicide rate in the nation in the late 1980s and 1990s, according to the *Washington Post*.

"They called it Chocolate City back then. They also called it the murder capital back then," Abercrombie said.

Because of his father's exposure to the drug scene, Devara wanted to ensure her son would remain out of trouble. Fortunately for Duante', there were other role models for him to follow. His grandfather, Jimmie, worked his way up from an entry-level mail clerk position for *National Geographic* before becoming an editor for the publication. Duante', meanwhile, grew up playing many sports and other activities to keep him shielded from street life. Swimming, gymnastics, poetry, soccer, basketball, football, and even skating lessons were part of his weekly routine. Traveling to skating lessons was made easy by living close to the nearby Fort Dupont Ice Arena in D.C.

After finishing a skating lesson when he was "roughly five or six years old," Abercrombie watched a nearby hockey game and quickly fell in love with the sport. Devara then signed up her son for hockey lessons.

"I had never seen that," Abercrombie remembered. "I've seen basketball. I've seen football. I've probably seen soccer at that point.

"But there was just something about [it]. This is different. And no one around me does it. It's just mine. I doubt I was having those actual thoughts at that age. But it's possible that I could have been thinking that way. This is something that my mom just had me try and I fell in love with it."

Hockey soon became Abercrombie's thing. The hometown team, the Washington Capitals, soon became his team. At a school book fair, Abercrombie bought himself a Wayne Gretzky poster despite not watching many of his games. He just knew the name.

At Fort Dupont, Abercrombie learned the game from coach Neal Henderson. According to the Washington City Paper, Henderson discovered the sport in his youth when he visited his father living in Canada. By 1978, he founded the Fort Dupont Ice Hockey Cannons. The club has been recognized by the National Hockey League as the "oldest minority hockey program in North America." Unfortunately, due to "insufficient response to registration" according to its website, the club did not ice a squad for the 2024–25 season. Henderson was named a finalist for the Willie O'Ree Community Hero Award in 2018 and was inducted into the United States Hockey Hall of Fame in 2019 for his contributions to the sport.

Thanks to Fort Dupont and Henderson, Abercrombie learned to play the sport and progressed in his hockey life. But he was subjected to doubters and detractors, mostly confused at a Black man playing in a white-dominated sport. Abercrombie walked the hallways at school, dressed in his hockey gear, only for classmates to tell him to take off his gear in favor of wearing football pads.

Black people don't play hockey.

Despite those naysayers, Abercrombie more than proved he belonged in the sport.

Abercrombie helped his high school team—Gonzaga College High School—win its first-ever league championship in his final year of high school. When Abercrombie studied business administration at Hampton, a Virginia-based HBCU, he walked the halls with a hockey stick and ball. Abercrombie would also pass the time stickhandling in the school's student center. When costs were too expensive for Abercrombie to play for a local team, the Hampton Roads Junior Whalers, he instead took an assistant coaching job at his old high school. But the dream of being at the pro level persisted.

When Abercrombie learned one of his former high school teammates got an invite to a Washington Capitals development camp and skated alongside Evgeny Kuznetsov, that gave Abercrombie all the motivation he needed to pursue opportunities to play pro.

"I have to least try and give it a shot," Abercrombie said. "Because I have teammates that played [Division I], teammates that are now turning pro. I need to make a run at this. I didn't know anything about training. I didn't know anything about working out. I didn't even know anything about ways to get into professional hockey. I just knew that this was something that I wanted to attempt."

Abercrombie eventually got a tryout with the ECHL's Toledo Walleye after graduating from Hampton in 2008. According to the *Tennessean*, Abercrombie was cut three times by the Walleye before a coach told him to seek opportunities overseas for more experience. And that is what led to Abercrombie joining the West Auckland Admirals in New Zealand, of all places, ahead of the 2011–12 season. If a team manager wasn't driving Abercrombie to games, a superfan of the team was offering Abercrombie a ride to the arena.

"You talk about rugby culture on ice, that's exactly what it is," Abercrombie said. "They love physicality, they love the fights. They love the booze before, during, and after. It is about as perfect of a hockey community as you could ever want. And they don't know anything about the sport."

Abercrombie sought other pro opportunities and tryouts after his lone season in New Zealand. But he knew he needed more training, which led him to stay in Whitby and ultimately to his chance encounter with Graeme Townshend and the coaching gigs that followed.

Even before joining Tennessee State, Abercrombie made significant strides in coaching. A limited number of Black people have emerged as hockey coaches at various levels.

Dirk Graham was the first Black head coach in NHL history when he coached in Chicago during the 1998–99 season. Paul Jerrard spent time as an assistant for three NHL teams while bouncing other minor league spots across the hockey landscape. Mike Grier worked his way up from scout in Chicago to assistant coach in New Jersey. Grier eventually became the NHL's first Black general manager in July 2022. Joel Ward, a longtime NHLer, is behind the bench for the Vegas Golden Knights as an assistant. And some wonder how much longer until he gets a head-coaching opportunity.

"Honestly, he has that it factor," reporter Tarik El-Bashir said. "People will listen to him. He could be a head coach."

Names like Jason Payne and Joel Martin can be found at the ECHL level while Kelsey Koelzer is the first Black female head coach in NCAA hockey history. John Paris Jr. got a professional coaching job four years before Dirk Graham did, becoming the first Black coach in pro hockey. When his team, the Atlanta Knights, won a championship in 1994, he was the first Black coach to win a title as coach of a pro team. One more for good measure: Fred Brathwaite works with goalies as part of the AHL's Henderson Silver Knights. Previously, he spent time with the New York Islanders, Hockey Canada and in Germany with a pro team.

When TCU begins play in 2026, Abercrombie can say he's part of a coaching fraternity. Abercrombie can say he is responsible for building an entire HBCU Division I men's hockey program from scratch. Abercrombie spent months sifting through a list of nearly 280 players, recruiting dozens of potential skaters in the hopes of building a squad. When Abercrombie was interviewed for this book in Summer 2024, he didn't even have a coaching staff in place.

Abercrombie first heard about the men's program when it was unveiled in June 2023. He didn't initially show interest in the gig because the team wanted to be recognized as a club for the 2024–25 campaign with intentions of jumping to Division I hockey in 2026, according to the *Tennessean*. But when the school reached out in December 2023 to ask if he'd be interested in applying for their vacant head coach position, Abercrombie let the school know that they should playing Division I hockey much sooner than their original timeline demanded.

By April 2024, Tennessee State had made up their mind and hired Abercrombie.

"Duante' Abercrombie's appointment as TSU's head coach of hockey is a testament to our dedication to breaking barriers," TSU president Glenda Glover said in a press release announcing Abercrombie's hiring. "We recognize the profound significance of bringing hockey to an HBCU and providing our students with unparalleled opportunities that will enrich their college experience. This bold move builds upon the TSU legacy that we had envisioned for the institution as a comprehensive university offering a wide range of academic and extracurricular programs, with a continued commitment to excellence."

While Abercrombie is committed to TSU, his coaching aspirations go beyond the NCAA. And his supporters know it. Townshend believes that Abercrombie will win a Stanley Cup and own an NHL franchise one day. But even those aspirations seem small to Abercrombie's own desires.

"I want four Cups in four different ways," Abercrombie said. "I want four Cups as a head coach; I want four Cups as a GM. I want four Cups as a president, and I want four Cups as an owner. I've never thought about that until I went to Toronto and I got a chance to experience a successful head coach, a successful GM, a successful president, and a successful owner all in their own ways all operating successfully in their individual position. Four just happens to be my favorite number, and who's to say it happens or it doesn't.

"But can you imagine the type of work, the type of relationships, the type of community engagement and the type of life that I have to live to be able to achieve something like that? Whether I get there or not, that's what I want to be known [for]. That type of legacy is what I want to leave."

15

Kelsey Koelzer

On a June day in 2016, Kelsey Koelzer was ready for vacation. The plan was to drive to the Jersey Shore with her mom and enjoy some time off. Koelzer had just finished her junior year at Princeton University and was months away from her senior year with the women's hockey team.

As she sat in her car, her phone buzzed repeatedly. Texts and notifications galore. Relatives and friends were desperately trying to reach her. Koelzer eventually connected with her uncle.

Why didn't you tell us?

Koelzer was confused. But after her uncle told her what they had seen, she immediately checked social media. She figured she'd be drafted into the National Women's Hockey League after conversations with one of their franchises, the New York Riveters. Koelzer had an excellent junior year with Princeton. She was named a first-team All-American—the first-ever in her university women's hockey program's history. Koelzer was a top-10 Patty Kazmaier Award finalist, was named the best defender in the Eastern College Athletic Conference, and was a finalist for ECAC Player of the Year. If that wasn't impressive enough, Koelzer was also named the Ivy League Player of the Year and a first-team Ivy Leaguer and helped her team win the Ivy League Championship.

Despite an impressive junior season, Koelzer was surprised to be taken first overall in the 2016 NWHL Draft. As a result, she became the first Black hockey player in any North American–based professional hockey league to be chosen first overall in an entry draft.

"I didn't even know that I was the first Black player to be drafted first overall. Nobody had even mentioned that at the time," Koelzer said.

That is how she made history the first time around.

Nearly a decade after her NWHL success, Koelzer is the head coach of Arcadia University in Cheltenham Township, Pennsylvania, a 14-minute drive from her hometown of Horsham. It is a program that Koelzer has seen from the ground up since she was 24 years old in 2019. The team has been on the ice since 2021. In 2023–24, Arcadia University hosted a playoff game for the first time. The following season, Koelzer guided the school to a Middle Atlantic Conference final appearance. When Koelzer took over in 2019, she accomplished something that had never been done before: she became the first Black woman to be a head coach of an NCAA hockey program.

"She knows the game really well," Princeton University women's head coach Cara Gardner Morey told William Douglas of NHL.com in 2021. "She knows what it takes to win, and I think she knows what it's like to have a winning culture. She has a strong voice, she's confident in what she knows but she's also humble. She's one of the best of all-time and to see her giving back to the game this way is awesome."

"It is something that, at the beginning of my career, I definitely think there was some nervousness and maybe some like trepidation on my end about being so young and being responsible for young women that are not that much younger than me to be honest," Koelzer said. "It was an adjustment. It was a learning curve. But now I think, at this point, it just feels so natural for me. Taking that natural step out of playing and applying everything that I've dedicated the rest of my life to so far."

KOELZER REMEMBERS BEING EXPOSED to hockey from as early as five or six months old. She remembers watching her cousins play hockey and going to their games and tournaments. Koelzer started skating when she was around three or four years old and within months was already playing on a house league team as a defender. Koelzer spent most of her youth career on all-boys teams. Her aunt made jerseys for her and her teammates.

Koelzer's mom, Kristine, worked two jobs. She was an office manager for a company that focused on packaging products and worked the snack bar at the local rink, the Face Off Circle. It was Kelsey's second home "through and through." When her mom worked the bar on Saturdays, Kelsey would skate on her own for two hours.

Finally, as a Pennsylvania child, she grew up a fan of the Philadelphia Flyers, watching stars like Jeff Carter, Claude Giroux, and Mike Richards. She also loved watching players like Jarome Iginla and Joe Sakic.

"I really have loved it every single day," Koelzer said.

Koelzer eventually played on girls' teams just as she was about to enter high school. On those girls' teams, Koelzer switched from defense to forward. She played for, and became captain of, two all-girls teams: the U19 AA Lady Patriots and the New Jersey Jr. Rockets. Koelzer also played for her high school boys' team at Hatboro-Horsham High School. Unfortunately for Koelzer, that's where she experienced an on-ice racist incident.

As she remembers, an opposing player tried to hit Koelzer. But she evaded the hit. However, as the player came back toward Koelzer, he called her "nigger." According to the *New York Times*, Koelzer responded by attacking the player "across the head."

"It was one of those rage moments where you just kind of have an out of body experience," Koelzer said. "I wound up going after him and retaliating a bit. I wound up getting a penalty for it, whereas he didn't. I mean, obviously, the refs had no knowledge at the time of what had happened. It was just one of those really surreal moments where I was like, really? I've made it this far and you're going to say that? I'm sure people have said things behind my back that I didn't hear previously, per se. But this was the first one that, to my face making eye-to-eye contact, that someone had ever used the term like that toward me. So, you know, that was definitely a pretty eye-opening moment. My teammates, luckily, had my back."

Koelzer rose above the moment and continued her youth hockey career, eventually being recruited for Princeton. Despite suffering from a torn meniscus and ACL during her junior year of high school, Koelzer was healthy in time for her debut season at Princeton. Koelzer was recruited as a forward, but she experienced growing pains in her first year as she only scored six goals and 10 points in 31 games.

Her goals and point totals improved in her sophomore season, where she made the positional switch from forward to defense. The spring before the season, Koelzer was asked about switching back to defense because the Tigers would be short a player at the back end. The move paid off as she was named a second team all-conference player in addition to first-team Ivy Leaguer and named to the All-Academic team for the second straight year.

"I was able to just really thrive in that position and really kind of find my game, find my stride," Koelzer said. "It was just such a drastic difference from my freshman year, where I just struggled. I struggled to make an impact in games. I struggled to get ice time. I struggled to find my place."

And then came Koelzer's banner junior season, which put her on the New York Riveters' radar.

THE RIVETERS WERE A franchise in the National Women's Hockey League. By 2016, the league was entering its second season with the Riveters, the Boston Pride, the Connecticut Whale, and the Buffalo Beauts.

Chad Wiseman, a former NHLer, was the Riveters' head coach. The Riveters were the league's worst team in 2015–16 and they were granted the first overall pick for the 2016 NWHL Entry Draft. But it wouldn't be easy for the Riveters to scout talent. Wiseman and the Riveters spent time searching for video and studied Koelzer's statistics carefully. Once they learned she would be willing to join the team, thanks in part to her living close to New York, they felt comfortable drafting Koelzer and having her skill set on their team.

"She's an elite skater, a great shot defenseman," Wiseman said. "She played with an edge. She played with tenacity. She had a skill set. She could shoot the puck as hard or harder than most women in that time. Elite offensive mindset. [There were] a lot of positive attributes to love about her as an athlete. So she was a great fit for us."

Koelzer signed with the Riveters in March 2017 and joined the team in their semi-final series against the Buffalo Beauts. She made her regular season debut later that fall—the Riveters changed their name to the Metropolitan Riveters to reflect the fact they were playing in New Jersey—and made an instant impact. Fourteen points in 15 games with the Riveters. An All-Star Game appearance and an All-Star Game MVP. And a playoff berth in her first full season. The Riveters were the league's best after ending the regular season with a 13–3-0 record.

Meanwhile, Koelzer juggled her hockey schedule with her workdays as a corporate recruiter. She began her days with workouts before commuting to work. Koelzer would eat dinner during her 90-minute drive to the Riveters' home rink, the Prudential Center in New Jersey.

"It was really, really challenging," Koelzer said.

Fortunately, a successful playoff run made it worth Koelzer's while. The Riveters were once the worst team in the NWHL in their inaugural season. By 2018, they reached the NWHL final against the reigning champion Buffalo Beauts. Those same Beauts eliminated the Riveters from the playoffs in 2017. The Riveters scored once in their championship final against the Beauts. It was all they needed. Forward Alexa Gruschow scored the lone goal in the first period and the Riveters hung on to win the 2018 Isobel Cup.

The Riveters' turnaround from worst to first was complete.

"It went through the defender's legs and I just saw it on the other side and somehow, I was able to lift it up high that close," Gruschow said, according to The Victory Press. "I think I fell over the girl's stick and flipped all around and celebrated on my butt, and it made it even better."

"It was like one of those crazy nailbiter games against the Beauts, which was our rival that season," Koelzer said.

Koelzer had her moment with the trophy, a sweet moment for the young defender who hadn't won too many championships at that point in her career.

"The teams I was on weren't necessarily winning a ton of tournaments," Koelzer said. "Junior year, when we won the Ivy League Championship, that was just an awesome first experience to have. That trophy kind of moment. But there was obviously something so different and special doing it at the professional level where you have a bunch of fans that aren't moms and dads from the team. With where we were at, the whole team went out in New York City that night to celebrate."

For those counting at home: Koelzer ended her 2018 with an Isobel Cup, an All-Star Game appearance, and MVP honors. Anyone would be riding high after a successful season on the ice despite whatever challenges they faced. That moment would only last for so long, however.

It was a different story through the 2018–19 campaign. Koelzer's juggling of work and hockey proved to be too tough to overcome. It became a "brutal" season.

The Riveters also had a new head coach in 2018–19. Wiseman stepped down at the end of their championship season and took a job in his home city, as head coach of the Burlington Cougars of the Ontario Junior Hockey League back in Canada. Another former NHLer, Randy Velischek, was hired as Wiseman's replacement.

Koelzer registered zero points in 14 games during her second NWHL season, battling a broken foot and a dislocated left shoulder that needed surgery. The Riveters ended their season with a loss in the semi-finals against the Minnesota Whitecaps.

A tough season gave Koelzer plenty to consider. Did she want to do another season, hustling through work and hockey, all the while battling injuries in an environment completely different from her first season? Then, on a summer day in 2019, Koelzer took a call from her aunt who worked in the English department at Arcadia University. Her aunt had spoken with the university's athletic director about an opportunity that surfaced.

Arcadia is starting a women's ice hockey team, an NCAA team. I really think you should apply.

Koelzer went home that night and worked on her résumé and later submitted. By September, Arcadia unveiled Koelzer as their new head coach. The first Black woman to be at the head of an NCAA hockey program. All at the age of 24.

"I did a lot of soul-searching," Koelzer said. "A lot of questioning of whether I was old enough to do something like this. But ultimately, everybody around me was like, don't doubt yourself. If they didn't think you could do it, they wouldn't have offered you the job."

Sure enough, Koelzer built her program. Once the puck dropped on the 2021 season, a roster was assembled. All but one player on the team were freshmen.

"It was just after COVID," Koelzer said. "We started in October of 2021. So, the players that really kind of took a risk on me. They were so excited to even have an opportunity that maybe they thought they didn't [or] they weren't going to have just because of circumstance and situation. [To] have the opportunity to start something new and make history themselves was obviously something that was really exciting for them."

The Knights began the season losing their first six games of the season and ended the year with a 10–15–1 record. Since then, Koelzer's team has improved year-by-year. The program improved to 13 wins in Koelzer's second year as a coach and then 15 wins during the 2023–24 campaign. Arcadia's win total jumped to 20 following the 2024–25 season after starting the season with eight consecutive wins.

As the team improves, so does Koelzer's profile. The head coach has used her profile in the name of helping the sport's culture for marginalized communities.

Koelzer was a founding member of the NHL & NHLPA Female Hockey Advisory Committee in 2019 and continues to be a member. The committee was founded in the hopes of "accelerating the growth of female hockey in North America while also ensuring more women and girls have the opportunity to experience the benefits that hockey offers", according to the NHL. The committee also features women's hockey superstars Angela James and AJ Mleczko.

Koelzer and fellow Princeton graduate Melissa Parnagian also lobbied the United States' Congress for Boston Bruins legend Willie O'Ree to be awarded the Congressional Gold Medal. Parnagian worked for the NHL's Office of Social Impact, Growth & Legislative Affairs at the time and now operates as a manager of Player Programs and Culture Initiatives. United States president Joe Biden signed a bill to award O'Ree the honor into law February 2022, making O'Ree the first hockey player to receive the medal.

"I've been able to speak at NCAA headquarters multiple times," Koelzer said. "I was featured on *Good Morning America*. All of these really awesome opportunities that presented themselves to a 24-, 25-year-old. If I were to sit back and think about that now, obviously it does sound kind of crazy. But for me, at the time, I was so excited to get started and be able to prove myself. So, yeah, I'm very fortunate that Arcadia took a chance on me, really. I had not much coaching experience prior to that, so they definitely took a risk. But I would hope they'd say it paid off at this point."

16

Tony McKegney

Tony McKegney and his Quebec Nordiques teammates were bummed out and badly bruised as they cleaned out their dressing rooms. It was impossible not to be considering the series they'd just played.

McKegney and the Nordiques should've had the edge over the Montreal Canadiens in their 1984 second-round Stanley Cup playoff series. They had in the regular season, winning five of their eight matchups. Instead, it was the Nordiques whose season ended early after dishing, and taking, repeated punches to the face.

The day before their locker-room cleanout, the Nordiques were eliminated in the sixth game of their second-round series against the Canadiens, played at the legendary Montreal Forum. Game 6 of that series has a name: the Good Friday Massacre. It's the most physical, charged, animosity-filled chapter in the Battle of Quebec saga that raged from the Nordiques' entering the NHL until their move to Colorado in 1995. Geography makes Quebec and Montreal natural rivals in the context of the NHL. But the fans and players fully embraced their contentious nature.

What should have just been a usual scrum after the whistle between two opposing players slowly turned into a growing dogpile at the end of the second period. At the far left of the developing melee, Canadiens forward Chris "Knuckles" Nilan cocked his left arm back and connected with Nordiques defenseman Randy Moller. If you were on the ice and you didn't have a dance partner then, you definitely had one after that.

"I remember Dale Hunter was just sort of hanging on to his brother Mark Hunter, so there's two brothers involved in one of the pair offs," McKegney said.

Legendary play-by-play man Bob Cole provided the soundtrack on the broadcast.

This is a brawl to end all brawls!

McKegney remembers being paired with Canadiens legend Bob Gainey during the dust-up. But McKegney wasn't thinking about throwing elbows with the multiple–Selke Trophy winner.

"I just wanted to get it over with," McKegney said. "Because I just wanted to win the game. That's what I was thinking about for just winning that game."

In one corner of the ice, Nordiques forward Louis Sleigher grappled with Canadiens defenseman Jean Hamel. Sleigher eventually unleashed a rocking punch of his own.

"Louis Sleighter sucker punched Jean Hamel and knocked him out cold," McKegney remembered. "And for some reason, it ended that."

Until the third period as both teams returned to the ice. More bad blood spilled, more punches, more scrums. McKegney tried his best to hold back Hall of Fame defenseman Larry Robinson from another developing dogpile. And no punch would go unpunished by the referees.

"It seemed like we were the ones that lost one of our better players. Each ejected," McKegney said.

According to Sportsnet, 11 players were ejected between both sides. More than 200 penalty minutes were accumulated. Ten ejections were given, five of them to Nordiques players: Sleigher, Peter

Šťastný, Wally Weir, goaltender Clint Malarchuk, and Dale Hunter. Their nights were over.

"After the game I hope not too many children in the province of Quebec were watching that hockey game tonight. It's very disappointing. It's disgusting," then Nordiques head coach Michel Bergeron said.

The Nordiques, however, still held a 1–0 lead once the madness ended. They had even added a second goal two minutes into the third period. One win away from a Game 7 that would've elevated the Battle of Quebec to another level with a deciding game. The Canadiens wanted no part of that. They promptly scored five unanswered goals to take the lead and put it out of their provincial rival's reach. Quebec added a third goal late in the period, but it wasn't enough. The Canadiens dusted the Nordiques from view with a 5–3 victory, forever made memorable by the pugilism on display.

That explains why McKegney and his teammates were so dejected at their stalls, eating pizza and drinking beer to wash their sorrows away.

And not far from McKegney was Alex Van Halen—yes, from the band Van Halen—polishing his fifth beer while sitting in the Nordiques' dressing room. Van Halen would tip the beer onto his lips, lean his head back and drain every drop. Alex then grabbed a sixth beer and kept drinking.

"They had to go for soundcheck or something," McKegney remembered. "And Eddie [Van Halen] came in and said, 'Look, don't let my brother drink any more beer. We got a show to do.'"

Van Halen had played in Montreal the night before Game 6 and was set to play in Quebec City the day after the Nordiques' loss. The band was on tour for their album *1984*, released in January of that year. The album features some of the band's greatest hits like "Panama," "Hot for Teacher," and the iconic "Jump."

The band huddled together at a Quebec City hotel bar and watched Game 6. They couldn't believe what they were seeing. Grown men throwing fists at each other, delaying the game for minutes on end.

"They were just mesmerized from what they saw the night before with the brawl. They'd never seen anything like it," McKegney told Sportsnet. "They're sitting around with the road crew as this game heightened and it drew everybody to it. I remember them asking us, 'How do you guys do this? Is this what you do every game?' We're sitting there with black eyes. They thought we were crazy."

McKegney has reminisced about the Good Friday Massacre many times before. It's one of many enduring moments across his lengthy and eventful hockey life.

BEFORE THE BLACK GOAL scorers who made names for themselves in the late 1990s and the beginning of the 21st century onward, whether they be Jarome Iginla, Anthony Duclair, Evander Kane, Anson Carter, or others, there was Tony McKegney. He was one of the first Black players to enter the NHL. But unlike contemporaries like Mike Marson or Bill Riley, McKegney wasn't a fighter—which explains why he didn't get caught up in any of the Good Friday Massacre madness.

"He wasn't like a flashy player by any means. And I don't even remember him being a fighter," *Hockey Night in Canada* executive producer Joel Darling, son of Sabres broadcasting legend Ted Darling, said. "When you think of some other Black players around that time, they probably had to earn their stripes through fighting.

"[Tony was] a really solid player that you know was a goal scorer. A guy who wasn't really flashy or anything like that. But just a hard-working player who got the job done."

McKegney was a great source of inspiration for players like Iginla, who could always point to him whenever detractors mentioned the lack of Black players in the NHL.

"It gave me ammunition, and confidence, to be able to look at guys and find them," Iginla said. "Sometimes it would be like, 'Grant Fuhr. Ah, well he's a goalie.' So, I'd have to find forwards. I'd have Tony McKegney. Look, he's scored 40 goals."

"I got to meet [Iginla] at an All-Star game in Atlanta," McKegney said. "It was just a nice compliment to say that when he was growing up in a schoolyard where he was the only Black person playing ball hockey, and when anybody gave him any problems, he could point to me as being a Black hockey player."

McKegney was originally born in Montreal to a white mother and a Black Nigerian father. But he was soon put up for adoption. A white family based in Sarnia, Ontario, adopted McKegney when he was 13 months old. McKegney was the youngest of five, with three older brothers and one older sister. One of his older brothers was Ian McKegney, a pro hockey player who played three NHL games with Chicago during the 1976–77 season. From a young age, Tony took to hockey. His adopted father, an engineer, built a hockey rink in their backyard with nets, boards and even lights.

"I had a hockey rink from December, typically before Christmas time until March," McKegney said. "Every minute beyond studying for school and eating meals, I was on a hockey rink. The advantage of doing that was that when I got to play in regular leagues, I was so much better than everybody else because I had my own hockey rink. It was playing against people that were four years older than I was, which is my older brothers. That was their friends. So I was dominating people. When I was six years old, I was better than 10-year-olds."

Once McKegney became a teenager, he joined the local Junior B team, as had his older brother years earlier. When Ian played, they were known as the Legionnaires. When Tony joined, they were the Sarnia Bees. At 14 and 15, McKegney played alongside much older teammates, some as old as 21.

Following his time in Sarnia, Tony joined the Kingston Canadians of the Ontario Major Junior Hockey League and firmly established himself as a goal scorer. In his third season with the team, McKegney scored 58 goals and 135 points in 66 games. McKegney left little doubt that he'd end up as a pro player thanks to his junior success. The next stop for him after four junior seasons was the World Hockey Association, where he'd join the Birmingham Bulls and former junior teammate and future NHLer Ken Linseman.

But before McKegney even stepped foot in Alabama, his contract was shredded. When Bulls fans heard that a Black player would be added to their roster, they boycotted. In response, the Bulls decided not to have McKegney on their team.

"It was the first time in my life I saw my mother cry when she read about it in the newspaper," McKegney said.

McKegney wanted to join the WHA to avoid being stuck in the minors if he wasn't going to get regular NHL time. Instead of the Bulls, McKegney signed a contract with the NHL's Buffalo Sabres. Despite playing a handful of games with the American Hockey League's Hershey Bears during his rookie season in 1978–79, McKegney spent most of the season with the Sabres. The forward scored eight goals and 22 points in 52 games in his debut year with the Sabres.

McKegney remembers learning from teammates and 50-goal scorers like Richard Martin and Danny Gare about how to score goals at the NHL level.

"We used to stay on after practice and we'd shoot 100 pucks after every practice," McKegney said. "No goalie, but we just concentrated on not missing the net. To me, it was the key. Even during games, we just wanted to hit the net. Because if it didn't score, there was a rebound there. And that was the whole mindset of not missing the net."

McKegney took that insight to heart. His goal totals jumped from eight to 23 in his sophomore season. In his third year, McKegney's goal total reached 37 and he established himself as a goalscorer.

As McKegney progressed through his career, he'd occasionally encounter Black players whether on his team or on opposing teams. Val James, the first Black American player to play NHL games, played with McKegney during the latter's fourth NHL season. But even if his time in the big leagues was short, his reputation preceded him. McKegney and his teammates had heard stories of James "annihilating people" in the minor leagues.

McKegney remembers James' NHL debut, a Sabres game against the Philadelphia Flyers during the 1981–82 season. James sat for most of the game but he made his presence felt in the third period.

"Honest to God," McKegney said. "The puck went into the corner, and he was first guy in the corner, and it was like the parting of the Red Sea. Nobody went near him."

Three of James' seven NHL games played that year were against the Boston Bruins. In his third encounter, James went toe-to-toe with one of the NHL's premier enforcers.

"He beats the s—t out of Terry O'Reilly twice in the same game," McKegney said. "Annihilated him."

James had battered O'Reilly to the point it was seared in a few Bruins fans' minds. When the Sabres visited Boston the following season, a Zamboni driver approached McKegney to tell him about their last encounter.

Hey, you played pretty good here last year.

"I thought he knew me as a goal scorer, and he thought I was Val James," McKegney said. "He looked me up and down and he thought I was the guy that beat the s—t out of O'Reilly in Boston at the Garden."

That incident occurred in McKegney's fifth and final season with the Sabres. It was McKegney's best season pointswise as a Sabre, with 36 goals and 73 points in 78 games. The following offseason, McKegney was moved to Quebec City, the first trade of many in his career and the first of two stints with the Nordiques. His first time in Quebec City was short: 105 games, 36 goals, 72 points and a front row seat to one of the biggest brawls in NHL history.

McKegney bounced around a few stops through the remainder of his career, spending time with the Minnesota North Stars and the New York Rangers. Those tenures preceded his time in St. Louis, beginning in 1987. McKegney joined forces with Bernie Federko and Doug Gilmour, the team leaders in scoring that year, and even had a 30-goal scorer in Mark Hunter. A young Brett Hull was on the Blues having just come from thc Calgary Flames. Hull scored six goals and 14 points in 13 games with St. Louis that year.

By season's end, however, McKegney led all his teammates in goals, notching his first-ever 40 goal season. Until Jarome Iginla surpassed the mark during the 2001–02 season, McKegney's 40-goal season stood as the most goals scored by a Black player in a season. McKegney's milestone goal came in the final game of the Blues' season with 80 seconds to play against the Winnipeg Jets. It tied the game at four goals apiece.

"It was a shot from the point which I tipped in," McKegney said. "It was one of those slow [ones], we called it a dribbler, that just made its way to the back of the net.

"I was the last person to score more goals than Brett Hull on the same team for a number of years."

After his two-season stay in St. Louis, McKegney split parts of the 1989–90 season with Detroit and Quebec, again. McKegney would stay in Quebec until 1991, when he was traded to Chicago. His NHL career ended after a nine-game stint in Chicago. He concluded his pro career with stops in Italy and San Diego in the International Hockey League before retiring officially after the 1992–93 season.

TONY MCKEGNEY'S SON, DANIEL, just happened to be in Washington, D.C., for a business conference. During a break in his day, he decided to visit the Smithsonian National Museum of African American History and Culture. The museum features a sports portion, showcasing the achievements of the greatest Black athletes across the sports world.

There are valuable and iconic photos, tokens, and memorabilia on display. Among them, a copy of Muhammad Ali on the cover of *Esquire* magazine from April 1968 where the legendary boxer stands with arrows piercing at various parts of his body; a Hank Aaron–autographed Atlanta Braves jersey; a track suit once worn by American Olympian Chandra Cheesebrough, a two-time gold medalist and one-time silver medalist from the 1984 Games in Los Angeles.

When Daniel turned a corner, he found the hockey portion of the museum. The most prominent item featured was a bronze statue of Willie O'Ree—the first Black player to ever play in an NHL game. In a glass case next to the statue, there are other artifacts and heirlooms including a jersey from then-Columbus Blue Jackets defenseman Seth Jones and an autographed stick from former NHLer Joel Ward.

From a distance, Daniel might not have noticed at first glance. But a closer look at the case revealed a row of four hockey cards featuring Black players. O'Ree, Mike Marson, and Bill Riley were featured prominently among those cards. And on the far right was Tony McKegney, in a familiar dark-blue, yellow-striped Buffalo Sabres jersey.

Daniel called his father immediately.

"Did you know you're in the Smithsonian Institute?" Tony remembered his son telling him on the phone. "I probably wouldn't have known if he wouldn't have called me that day, unless I went there physically. I was in that area a couple times, and I never thought to come to Smithsonian not knowing they had a sports area. I didn't know they had that."

While McKegney's legacy isn't the same as other Hall of Famers like Jarome Iginla or media-savvy, flashier players like P.K. Subban, McKegney still has his place in hockey history. Not only does McKegney serve as an inspiration for players who came after him, his goal scoring totals still lead most of the franchises he suited up for among other Black players.

Even McKegney making a name for himself as a goal scorer was bucking a developing trend for Black players who were being used for fighting and physical play more than their goalscoring attributes.

"When I came to NHL, my goal was to be a 50-goal scorer," McKegney said. "And a lot of things have to go right to do that. By scoring 40, it was the next echelon. I've scored some 30s before that: 36, 37, 31. I scored in the 30s, 20s, a bunch of those. But by scoring 40 goals, that's something I can always look back upon, because not a lot of people did that."

Acknowledgments

First, I'd like to thank God. Through him all things are possible, including the writing of this book.

I thank my mom and dad for being supportive of me the entire way as I pursued my career in journalism and media. I hope I've made you proud. I thank my sisters, Kayla and Lauren, who never fail to keep me grounded. It has always been for the best. Thank you to my grandparents for fueling my dreams by teaching and encouraging the importance of reading and writing.

I thank my editor, Michelle Bruton, for being patient and so helpful to me. I thank my agent, Brian Wood, for sending me that email after I wrote that Bill Peters article. I'm sorry I kept you waiting for two days before responding, not fully realizing what the email was about. Thank you, of course, to Triumph Books for taking this project on and allowing me to write these stories.

Thank you to William Douglas, Bernice Carnegie, and Bob Dawson for being incredible guides and resources throughout this process.

A special thank you to everyone who agreed to be interviewed for this book. It is nothing without your voices. To everyone who passed along interviews and books to be used as references, thank you so much. Thank you to all the communications staffers and content coordinators who helped coordinate the interviews and provided photos that helped make this book a reality. Special thanks to Alex Manley, Dan Robson, Jeremy Rutherford, Ryan Pike, and Lisa Weiss for your help on how to write a book. Thank you, Tom Zalatnai, for your proofreading help.

Thank you to my colleagues at The Athletic, the Steve Dangle Podcast Network, and Sportsnet Radio for their support. Thank you to my friends from the *Zone Time* podcast, Omar White, Arun Srinivasan, Samantha Chang, and Avry Lewis-McDougall for their support. *Zone Time* forever.

Finally, thank you, dear reader, for picking up this book. I hope you have an understanding of how important Black people have been throughout the history of the sport and know that they will continue to be.

Sources

Books

Bartsiokas, Tom, and Corey Long. *Angela James: The First Superstar of Women's Hockey*. Burnstown Publishing House, 2021.

Baruchel, Jay. *Born Into It: A Fan's Life*. HarperCollins, 2018.

Carnegie, Bernice and Herb. *A Fly in a Pail of Milk: The Herb Carnegie Story*. ECW Press, 2019.

Fosty, George and Darril. *Black Ice: The Lost History of the Colored Hockey League of the Maritimes 1895–1925*. Nimbus Publishing, 2008.

Fuhr, Grant and Bruce Dowbiggin. *Grant Fuhr: The Story of a Hockey Legend*. Vintage Canada, 2014.

Laraque, Georges and Pierre Thibeault. *Georges Laraque: The Story of the NHL's Unlikeliest Tough Guy*. Penguin Books, 2011.

O'Ree, Willie and Michael McKinley. *Willie: The Game-Changing Story of the NHL's First Black Player*. Viking Canada, 2020.

Pike, Ryan. *On the Clock: Calgary Flames: Behind the Scenes with the Calgary Flames at the NHL Draft*. Triumph Books, 2024.

Russell, Scott. *Ice Time: A Canadian Hockey Journey*. Penguin Books Canada, 2000.

Subban, Karl and Scott Colby. *How We Did It: The Subban Plan for Success in Hockey, School and Life*. Random House, 2017.

Wire Services, Magazines, and Newspapers

Associated Press

Boston Globe

Canadian Press

Cochrane Gazette

Edmonton Sun

Globe and Mail

Hamilton Spectator

Harvard Crimson

Le Droit

Montreal Gazette

National Post

New York Post

New York Times

Peterborough Examiner

Seattle Times

Sports Illustrated

St. Albert Gazette

Sudbury Star

The New Yorker

The Tennessean

Toronto Star

Toronto Sun

Washington City Paper

Washington Post

Websites

albertadugoutstories.com
andscape.com
arcadiaknights.com
atlantichockeyamerica.com
bceagles.com
blackgirlhockeyclubca.org
cardbiz.ca
carnegieinitiative.com
cbc.ca
cbsnews.com
chl.ca
colorofhockey.wordpress.com
ctvnews.ca
cycloneshockey.com
dailyfaceoff.com
defector.com
echl.com
eliteprospects.com
espn.com
espnpressroom.com
fandom.com
fdihc.com
flamesnation.ca
forbes.com
georgeslaraque.com
globalnews.ca
gofundme.com
goodmorningamerica.com
goprincetontigers.com
grantfuhrmkt.com
habseyesontheprize.com

hhof.com
hockeycanada.ca
hockeydb.com
hockeyjournal.com
hockeynovascotia.ca
hockeyreference.com
iihf.com
inflationcalculator.ca
jacksonvilleicemen.com
maritimemuseum.novascotia.ca
mastercardmemorialcup.ca
news.smu.ca
nhl.com
nhlpa.com
nhltradetracker.com
nsshf.com
nytimes.com/athletic
ocaa.com
olympic.ca
olympics.com
ontariosportshalloffame.com
pwhl.pointstreaksites.com
quanthockey.com
sportico.com
sportshall.ca
sportsnet.ca
sports.yahoo.com
theahl.com
thecanadianencyclopedia.ca
theicegarden.com
theplayerstribune.com
tsutigers.com

ushockeyhalloffame.com
vice.com
victorypress.org
youtube.com

Documentaries

Ice Queens. Directed by Kwame Mason. 2023. United States. NHL Original Productions.

Making Coco: The Grant Fuhr Story. Directed by Don Metz. 2018. Score G Production Films Inc.

Willie. Directed by Laurence Mathieu-Leger. 2019. United States. Don Kee Productions.